JOE PATERNO, PENN STATE AND COLLEGE FOOTBALL – WHAT YOU NEVER KNEW

Kenneth W. Werley

University of New Haven Press
West Haven, Connecticut

Library of Congress Cataloging in Publication Data

Werley, Kenneth W.
  Joe Paterno, Penn State and College Football - What you Never Knew
  Kenneth W. Werley

Includes index

  ISBN 0-936-285-228-1 (alk paper)
  1. Anecdotal 2. Football-Penn State 3. Title

Library of Congress Control Number: 2001 135964

University of New Haven Press, West Haven, CT 06516

Printed in the United States of America

To my wife Marie, who never wavered in her conviction that I had an idea worth pursuing, and whose positive attitude provided constant support throughout the six years it took to complete the project.

And in memory of my father, George Werley, Penn State Class of 1924, whose stories of his alma mater were the seeds from which this book sprang.

JOE PATERNO, PENN STATE AND COLLEGE FOOTBALL – WHAT YOU NEVER KNEW

PREFACE

Official sources tell us a Penn State football squad with no head coach bested Bucknell in two football games in November 1887. Because of the scarcity of games, only eleven in the next three years, Penn State did not have a head coach until 1892 and it would be twelve more years before State would have a paid full time coach.

Forming a collegiate football team in the early days of the game meant teaching the rules, objectives and techniques of the game to virtually every player. This could be done only by someone who had played or coached elsewhere. This coach often participated as a player and since the rules of eligibility were not uniform and enforcement was lax, numerous players and player/coaches lettered more than three years and at more than one institution. These football Johnny Appleseeds spread the seeds of collegiate American football wherever they went and as a result all of the one hundred-plus Division I-A football programs in the United States trace their heritage to just a few common sources.

Part one of our book opens in 1967 with a sophomore head coach who, one quarter of the way into the season, had lost more games in his career than he has won. Few observers would guess that the nucleus of this Joe Paterno team would not lose another game under him through the remainder of three full seasons, to eclipse a record that had stood for almost forty-eight years.

Part Two will give us a quick trip through the history of college and Penn State football from the 1900s through 1965; Rip Engle's last year as head coach at Penn State.

Part Three continues the Joe Paterno Era with human interest and behind the scenes stories relating to Paterno and his Penn State football teams.

The legal trespass in which we are about to engage will take us inside the huddle and behind the scenes of college football, where very few gain admission. We will uncover some human interest stories and happenings, many of which took place before any tape or film medium could provide a permanent record. You will therefore be learning of these occurrences for the first time.

Much of the material from the period 1920 to 1924 came to me by word of mouth from my father. Virtually all of the stories my father related to me I have never heard elsewhere. Other Penn State incidents and stores originated with coach and assistant athletic director Sever Toretti, coaches Jim O'Hora and Jerry Sandusky, retired athletic directors Ed Czekaj and Jim Tarman, former players Dennis Onkotz, Dr. Jack Baiorunos, and Keith Olsommer, plus personal conversations with Coach Joe Paterno and statements made by Coach Paterno in the author's presence.

The material in this book contains stories that should be entertaining to everyone. Additionally, a football novice, while enjoying the stories, might absorb some football jargon and knowledge which could prove useful at a later date when the conversation or the TV set is switched to football.

What follows will provide insight into a bygone era of college football and college life, as well as some more recent stories and happenings you might not have heard before.

—Kenneth W. Werley

ACKNOWLEDGMENTS

This book came to be because the author had a story (actually a series of stories) he felt needed to be told, but without the assistance and the encouragement of the following people the story still would be untold:

- First and foremost my wife Marie, who did all the typing, revision after revision, over a period of six years. Without her contribution this book would still be in draft form.

- Chris Furry who critiqued the first draft I showed to anyone outside of the family. Her comments, which she never thought I'd see, made me realize I had a **LONG** way to go if I ever hoped to be an author., Her subsequent coaching, and encouragement were paramount in bringing my dream of a book to fruition.

- My brother Carl who helped edit the manuscript, met with me countless times to offer comments and suggestions and gave me priceless advice.

- My children Kenneth II and Kristine for their well-wishes.

- Margaret DeAngelis for setting me on the right path - grammar and style-wise.

- L. Budd Thalman for his assistance and for his kind words in the Foreword.

- David W. Reager, Esq., for his professional advice and encouragement.

- Dr. Thomas Katsaros, Editor of The University of New Haven Press for giving my book the chance to see the light of day.

- Finally, I wish to dedicate this book to my Father whose stories of Penn State were the seed from which this book sprang and Coach Jim O'Hora (and Betts), Coach "Tor" Toretti and Ruth, Jim Tarman, Dennis Onkotz and Jack Baiorunos all of whom gave generously of their time, their personal records and their memories which were the heart and soul of this book. To all of the above I am forever indebted.

- All of the above made an aspiring writer an author.

FOREWORD

Ken Werley has done a magnificent job of documenting many fascinating facts about Penn State football. His book, obviously a labor of love, is a must- read for any serious Nittany Lion fan. Werley's work is meticulously researched and written in a highly readable style. His anecdotes on legendary coach Joe Paterno capture many of the attributes that make him a celebrated figure in college football.

Werley's affection for all things Blue and White is obvious as he traces the growth of the Nittany Lions' fabled football program through the early twentieth century. From its modest roots Penn State football has grown into a gridiron behemoth; annually drawing sellout crowds to a stadium which has been expanded seven times since it was moved from the center of campus. This fall, with its new capacity of 106,537, Beaver Stadium will entertain its first home crowd of more than 100,000.

From Werley's crisp accounts, you will almost feel like you have pulled on the shoulder pads and the traditional Blue and White uniform and emerged from the south end zone tunnel to the roar of a Nittany Lion sellout crowd.

— L. Budd Thalman

L. Budd Thalman's stellar career has included positions as Vice President for Public Relations with the NFL's Buffalo Bills and Sports Information Director at the U.S. Naval Academy, and, more recently, as Penn State Associate Athletic Director for Communications. Inducted into the College Sports Information Directors of America Hall of Fame in 1998, Thalman is the Author of "Quotable Joe: Words of Wisdom by and About Joe Paterno."

CONTENTS

I
It Was a Very Good Three Years

II
Fifty Years, Only Six Head Coaches

III
The Paterno Era - Thirty-Six Years and Counting

I

IT WAS A VERY GOOD THREE YEARS

CHAPTER 1

The Eve of a Pass or Fail Test

November 10, 1967, Friday P.M., State College, Pennsylvania

This week, in the classroom, had been mid-term exam time for most of the Penn State football players, an opportunity for a player to raise his G.P.A. To-morrow afternoon on the gridiron, the team would be tested as a whole and there would be only two possible grades - pass or fail!

It was only Friday afternoon but already this had the making of a weekend that would be long remembered, if only for the profusion of red and white colors and the Southern drawls that seemed to be in front, behind and alongside every Penn Stater on College Avenue. These undefeated North Carolina State invaders with wins over North Carolina, Houston, Florida State, Maryland and Duke and ranked number three in the country were in State College in force and they weren't a bit hesitant about letting the local people know which State team would be leaving the field to-morrow on the short end of the score and which State team would be taking a lion skin back to Raleigh to put in their trophy case. Weren't the experts and the odds-makers picking the Wolfpack by a double digit margin over the Lions and hadn't the Lions lost two of the seven games they had played?

That evening in his customary Friday night meeting with the Press a second year head coach, a month shy of forty-one, would hold court. The main subject being the game the next day, which would mark the re-start of a nineteen game series between these two State Universities, that so far consisted of four games played in 1920-1925 and a single game contested in 1956. Also there would be talk of Joe's young team and the progress it had made dating back to the second game of the season.

But there was another item of huge interest and that was the much anticipated head-to- head meeting involving Earle Edwards, the Penn State alumnus now coaching North Carolina State and the ex-Ivy League player who now held the head coaching position Edwards had so dearly coveted, felt he certainly deserved, and until the announcement was made, thought was his.

The N. C. State coach, Earle Edwards, was a Penn State grad, Class of 1931 and an assistant coach there from 1936-1948, leaving just one year before Rip and Joe arrived. In fact the two happenings were the result of one occurrence. When Bob Higgins stepped down as head coach of the Penn State football team at the end of the 1948 season it was the overwhelming opinion of Penn Staters, including Bob Higgins, that the job was going to Earle Edwards. However, history shows that Joe Bedenk became Penn State's twelfth head coach which drove Edwards to leave Penn State and join "Biggie" Munn's staff at Michigan State. When Joe Bedenk left Penn State after just one year, the Lions hired Rip Engle who brought a young quarterback coach, Joe Paterno, along with him. Now, the Penn State head coach was this former Brown University, Ivy League quarterback while the N.C. State coach was the former Penn State player and assistant coach who came to N. C. State by-way-of Michigan State.

These Friday night sit-downs, which had begun only recently, were already eagerly anticipated by the sports reporters who were invited and by their host who had proven right from the start to be a quick-thinker. Joe gloried in this give and take with the press and his friends, because he always gave better than he took. Self-assured, with glass in hand, Joe now moved about the room acknowledging everyone there. One did not have to be a fortune teller to predict that there were good times ahead for Penn State and its very confident head coach, "Just call me, Joe." Interestingly, not even the most optimistic Penn Stater realized how soon the good times would begin, in fact they had already started. And no one could have predicted that this forty-ish bachelor with tinted glasses and the quite evident Brooklyn, Italian accent would achieve the success he did at bucolic Penn State.

Paterno's influence over the years has ranged far afield from Centre County, Pennsylvania to the extent that he is presently the best known, most widely recognized figure in collegiate football. But following the next day's game, Joe, in an off-handed comment, would fire the opening shot in his campaign against college football players who were in college just to play football. Paterno and Penn State would become more outspoken about recruiting only football players who were capable of doing college work and graduating with a meaningful degree. This one man, one school crusade alienated many schools including those who already were trying to "raise the bar" and others who felt Paterno was a hypocrite or given time would be just like the rest. And this "Grand Experiment" as Joe so proudly labeled it came across as a holier than thou stance and hurt Penn State in the AP and UPI polls in the years that followed. But, 322 wins over the next thirty-five years (1966-2000) and a mellowing in his demeanor would crown Joe as the most revered and respected coach in Division I football and the winningest coach at one university in the annals of college football – if his team could pass their test tomorrow.

CHAPTER 2

Saturday Morning Mid-Terms, Afternoon Finals

November 11, 1967 Saturday morning   Stone Valley Engineering Camp

While most of the Penn State student body and the Penn State fans in their hotel rooms continued to slumber, there was com motion in the Stone Valley Lodge and in the proximity of the Lodge entrance.

Defensive coordinator and line coach Jim O'Hora, and linebacker coach Dan Radakovich talked near the entrance door while a dozen neatly dressed players were milling about, preparing to board a university shuttle bus which stood there with its engine and windshield wipers running. It wasn't raining but the cool, foggy air was depositing a fine mist on all the glass surfaces reducing visibility from either side.

The bus was there to transport those students who had Saturday classes, back to campus in time for their "eight or nine o'clocks." Some players were facing blue books, for others this was just a normal Saturday class – although a pop quiz was always a possibility.

Players had the option of rescheduling a Saturday class, on a home game day just as they would do if it were an away game, but that would mean four classroom hours in that subject the following week and the players who took Paterno seriously when he said, "Academics come first," preferred to stay as current as possible. Since next week might involve an away game and unexpected occurrences have a way of appearing when least expected, it's not difficult for a player, who has so little free time during the season, to fall behind in his classwork. A player who is academically ineligible, or merely in danger of becoming ineligible, will be benched by Paterno just as quickly as if he were playing poorly.

One of the first players to board the bus was linebacker Dennis Onkotz. Onkotz preferred to pick out his row and then put his jacket or some books on the seat next to him to indicate he wasn't looking for a seatmate. Onkotz wasn't anti-social, in fact when time permitted he was affable and smiled easily. But his approach when faced with a test in the classroom or on the gridiron was to gather himself within and shut out all external stimuli.

In State College last night on the eve of this pivotal game, there was no talk about the fact that some players at that time were cramming for Saturday morning exams or even the fact that Saturday morning some of these players would be arising at 6 A.M. in order to be back on campus for eight o'clock classes. Why was there no concern being manifested? Was it because all Penn State fans in 1967 believed that football players were enrolled at Penn State to get an education and luckily they just happened to be good football players? Or was it because the fans were 100% behind Paterno when he said, "Academics come first and football is second." The answers to the last two questions are both, "No." The answer to the first question is very simple, no one was concerned because the subject had never been an issue before.

The subject, Saturday classes would be a widely discussed topic when Paterno divulged after the game that his sophomore linebacker Dennis Onkotz had taken an important exam just hours before playing the best game of his young career against N. C. State.

CHAPTER 3

Young Lions Must Mature Quickly

Saturday afternoon 1:30 P.M. Beaver Stadium

This would be the sixth start of sophomore Denny Onkotz's first varsity season. Most people who followed Penn State football knew that Denny and his other sophomore teammates (John Ebersole, Steve Smear, Jim Kates, Neal Smith and the unrelated Johnson boys, Pete and Paul) were all starting on defense for Paterno. Although the season was almost three-quarters completed, the media continued to emphasize the youth aspect whenever they wrote or spoke about State's defense, using terms such as, "State's sensational sophomores" or "Penn State's Nittany Lion Cubs."

In the late sixties a college football player's career comprised thirty-three games. Thus after seven of those thirty-three games had been played, more than twenty percent of a player's career was behind him. But Onkotz and his cohorts showed a maturity on and off the field that far exceeded seven games or one-fifth of a career. In fact, their head coach characterized them as "one of the most mature teams I ever coached." He lauded them further when he proclaimed, "I learned a lot from them."

Offensively Joe had some dependable seniors such as quarterback Tom Sherman, center Bill Lenkaitis, split-end Jack Curry and tackle Rich Buzin complemented by junior stand-outs Ted Kwalick, Bob Campbell, and offensive linemen John Kulka and Dave Bradley.

The fact that so many underclassmen (sophomores specifically) were starting on defense and making significant contributions testified to the change that had already occurred in Joe's second season as head coach. Joe and his assistant coach and confidant Jim O'Hora had really stepped out of Rip Engle's shadow and they weren't looking back. Veteran sports-writers covering Penn State football knew that there was indeed a new head coach at State by merely looking at the depth charts.

In fact, a statement attributed to Rip Engle when he was the head coach, highlights the difference in philosphy most succinctly. A few years ago a reporter noticing some outstanding players on State's freshman team attempted to speak Rip's mind for him when he said, "You must be eagerly looking forward to these kids playing on the varsity next year when they're sophomores." Rip's reply was, "There's just one thing about sophomore football players; they generally don't help you very much until they're juniors or seniors." There's an abundance of truth in that statement which seems to parallel a statement attributed to Yogi Berra. When an out-of-town friend, asked Yogi's opinion about dining at a certain well-known restaurant, Yogi replied, "Nobody goes there anymore, it's too crowded."

Here in the first half of the game Onkotz was living proof that a football player can attend Saturday morning classes and still perform at a high level that afternoon. In fact if Denny did as well in his morning command performance as he was doing in his Saturday matinee role he must have gotten rave reviews. So far, the Lion "Backer" had played a steady, at times sensational game, being in the right place at the right time, reading his keys and doing some ad-libbing from his position; since certain defenses allowed him to free lance and "fly to the ball." Denny thrived on those situations where he might break-up a pass, tackle a ball carrier for a loss, or in some other way disrupt the opposing team's offense.

The past week's seemingly endless repetitions against the scout team had already borne fruit. From his "Backer" position Onkotz recognized a particular N.C. State offensive-set and anticipated they would run a play where the quarterback tries to hit his tailback on a pass route across the middle. The N.C. State brain trust and quarterback Jim Donnan chose to call this play now because they correctly expected Penn State to be in a defensive alignment where Jim Kates, the "Mike" linebacker, would be responsible for covering the tailback on a pass play. They were correct in their play call and as Barchuk, the tailback came across the middle he already had more than a step on Kates who was more adept as a run defender than a pass defender. Everything was going just as it should from N.C. State's perspective when quarterback Donnan's arm came forward and he released the ball.

In most instances the receiver would pull the ball in and begin a sprint toward the opponent's goal line. But on this particular play there was one *little* thing that N.C. State hadn't anticipated. Penn State was in a defense where Onkotz after quickly identifying the formation and checking one key was "freed up." Moving across the field the opportunistic linebacker cut right in front of the intended receiver to intercept quarterback Donnan's pass and before any N.C. State player could recover Onkotz was on his way to the N.C. State end zone putting six important points on the scoreboard for the young Nittany Lions.

Having been burned once by Onkotz, the N.C. State offensive coordinator began a series of plays on their next possession which he hoped would put a few first downs together and more importantly, set Onkotz up for a counter play designed to take advantage of an aggressive linebacker. The misdirection play they were building toward was expected to be good for twenty-five yards or even a touchdown, which would provide six needed points and a huge swing in the momentum of the game. The trap was being baited carefully with a recurring sequence of plays: pass or run on first and second down, run on third. The third down running play was up the middle if N.C. State needed less than two and a half yards and for two and a half to five yards it was a sweep with pulling guards.

It was now third down. N.C. State was on their own 44 yard line with five yards to go for the first down. The stage was set! The 'Pack now substituted two players. Number 84, a tight end, was one substitution. With two tight ends in the game a running play was likely. Removing the wide receiver also suggested the next play was not going to be a pass. Might the next play be the sweep with the pulling guards? The second substitution came on the field as Onkotz was calling the defense. His arrival, however, did not go unnoticed. Out of the corner of his eye, Denny saw that #25 had joined the Wolfpack huddle.

The N.C. State offense was at the line of scrimmage in what looked to be a run formation. If the play was to be a sweep Onkotz's key would be the "near triangle" consisting of the tailback, fullback, and the nearer of the two guards. In the variation N.C. State would run off this base play, the near triangle is the cheese bait. With the snap of the ball the bait moves to the *offense's right*. The tailback (with the ball?) the fullback and the pulling guard all go to the right and all the other offensive players seem to be headed in that direction. With this preponderance of movement to his left, a cooperative prey (a linebacker just reacting to his keys) will take a *step to his left* and be leaning toward more movement in that direction and SNAP! THE TRAP SHUTS! The center and the near tackle on a double-team seal off the obliging linebacker who took the bait. Now, right back through the hole vacated by the near guard comes #25 with the ball which has been given to him on a counter play and #25 runs until somebody in the secondary brings him down or until he's in the end zone.

Onkotz, the Lion linebacker being baited, may have been born at night but it wasn't last night. He knew from experience to be wary of the overly obvious. As soon as Onkotz saw player #25 he remembered something he had seen several times in practice this past week. When the play started and his key, the near triangle, pulled and took off to his left Onkotz didn't succumb to the obvious nor did he laboriously ponder, "Let's see, this might be a misdirection play. If it is, I shouldn't follow the bait I should stay home and if I'm right, the play will come to me. Or I could move just a step or two, then again…" No, Onkotz shot right through the hole vacated by the pulling guard, as he had done all week in practice when the scout team ran this play, and the instant #25 got the ball from the quarterback the ball-carrier ran into a concrete (pardon me Konkrete) wall, #35, Dennis Onkotz. And right then and there this N.C. State drive died. Denny later confided, to me, "If I had been a half step faster I would have taken the hand-off from the quarterback myself and I'd have had my second touchdown of the game."

This play not only didn't result in a momentum change in N.C. State's favor but it gave further confidence to the young Lions. It was a confidence builder they could use later when the game was on the line.

CHAPTER 4

Behind Locker Room Doors

A ccording to Onkotz, Paterno's pre-game and halftime locker room talks varied but they were always good theater. Sometimes they were motivational or encouraging, if that's what Joe felt was needed. Other times he might challenge the team's resolve or unfavorably compare them to previous squads. If the team was not focused, Joe would criticize them even if they were winning. On the other hand, if they were losing but playing as well as they could, Joe would give them the verbal equivalent of a pat on the back.

Today Joe's halftime talk, before they re-took the field, was limited to just a few sentences indicating that he probably felt they were playing hard and intelligently.

Fans imagine that while the bands entertain at half-time the offensive coaches and the defensive coaches have their squads grouped around them while they diagram new plays and formations on the blackboard, as well as unveiling plays they withheld in the first half. Or they visualize the head coach launching into a Knute Rockne "Win One for the Gipper" speech. In reality, the players come in, take some liquids, then sit on the floor, chairs, tables, whatever is available while their coaches point out what went well, what didn't and what adjustments need to be made. The assistant coaches, will make some small changes which can have important effects. Recall N.C. State's trick play which sought only to influence Onkotz to take a step to his left and be leaning in that direction to enable the two offensive linemen to easily take him out of the play. When an offensive blocker meets a defensive player straight-on it will take his best technique to control that defensive player since he's not sure where the defensive player intends to go. However, if the defensive player has already taken a step to the offensive blocker's right and is leaning that way, a simple push by the offensive player can open a large hole straight ahead or to the left. Thus the half time adjustments instituted by the coaches are generally small such as, "Smear (Steve Smear) when we're in "Eagle" and they show "two tight" (two tight ends) you line up on his outside shoulder instead of on his nose and Ebersole (John Ebersole) you widen a step so the guy blocking you can't reach you with his drive block." Just a minor movement, changes the angle of the offensive player's block and affects which way he can take his man.

Not wanting to clutter their minds and take away their aggressiveness, Coach Radakovich ended by repeating one of his tenets to his linebackers, "Remember, when you act, do it 100%, don't vacillate. None of this stop, go, stop, yo-yo action. You do no good getting caught in no-man's-land – that just takes you out of the play. You know I won't come down on you if you make a wrong read as long as you go 100% - even if you are wrong your unexpected action can cause havoc."

Joe was probably pleased, even satisfied, with his team's first half effort and performance, consequently his remarks were limited to reminding the squad how hard they had worked as a team starting back in August, and the fact that there was still half a game left to play. With that, he and the other coaches and trainers left the room, to give the players and captains five minutes to themselves.

As the scoreboard clock wound down the Bowl representatives who had come to see N.C. State, were becoming increasingly aware there were two very good football teams battling it out on the field below. It did not appear to the scouts that N.C. State was overrated at their number three ranking. Rather, it appeared that Penn State this day was playing like a Top Five Team. In fact no one in the press box doubted this back and forth game would have made a great TV Game-of-the-Week. Had a Game-of-the-Week TV crew been doing a telecast of this contest, their commentary late in the fourth quarter might have gone something like this:

Play by Play Announcer: "Well, sports fans we have been treated to a magnificent game here today - a game that has not as yet been decided. Penn State has looked very strong, with their All-American candidate Ted Kwalick scoring the only offensive touchdown of the game up to this time. Meanwhile their defense has held number three N.C. State to just two field goals, thanks to their linebacker Denny Onkotz who has played like an All-American himself. How do you see it Cal?"

Color Man: "I'll tell you Pat, coming into this game I was intrigued by everything I had heard about this young Onkotz and all I can say is he's even better than I expected. I don't know of another linebacker in the country who returns punts. And he's not just a stopgap return man, he could return punts for 99% of the teams in the country. Besides that, he is such a heady, instinctive player you completely forget he's only a sophomore. Like that pass interception he returned 67 yards for a touchdown. He just came out of nowhere and plucked the ball out of the air. I'm sure the N.C. State quarterback Donnan never expected him to be free and then break on the ball like he did."

Pat: "Cal, plays like that have made this as interesting a game as I've seen in a long time. Penn State has led in this game since they scored their touchdown but every time it's looked like Penn State would widen their lead, N.C. State rose to the occasion. Then when it seemed as though

N.C. State was taking control of the game the Penn State defense stepped up and kept them out of the endzone. The two teams seem *so* evenly matched. It's a shame that either team has to lose. Of course it *could* end up in a tie."

Cal: "That brings up an interesting point. What is N.C. State's strategy? They have been moving down the field very methodically. Do you get the impression that they decided at the beginning of the drive they wouldn't turn down a big play but rather than going into a helter skelter two-minute offense they are going to use up all the clock they can, so that Penn State won't have time to retaliate after they score."

Pat: "That's the way I see it too, but I wonder if they've made up their mind about going for the tie or gambling all or nothing on the win?"

Cal: "You know, public opinion and the media may not be very kind to N.C. State either way. If N.C. State should manage a 14-13 win, the media and the pollsters, who didn't see how well Penn State played, will probably downgrade them since they managed only a one point win over an unranked team. But these young Lions *should* be ranked, based on the way they played today."

Pat: "That's another interesting point that I want to touch on when we come back after this station break."

****

Pat: "As I was saying, when you assign a ranking to this Penn State team you must consider this is *NOT* the team that started the season. On defense they have seven sophomores starting and three more on offense. You can't pin the Navy loss on them because very few of them played any meaningful minutes in that game. Joe just began working these younger players in, one or two at a time in the Miami game, which they won, and since then they seem to be getting stronger and more confident every game."

`Pat: "Strange as it may sound when I say it —I think N.C. State could live with the loss better than Penn State. Everybody knows that on an occasion you run into an opponent that's just too hot to handle that day. N.C. State wouldn't have to feel like they blew the game - they just ran into a buzz saw of a defense. On the other hand should Penn State lose, the loss will stay with them longer because they'll know they should have won the game. Being such a young team they need this win badly, otherwise all next week they'll be thinking, 'you know we should have won that game, we had it right in our hands and we let it get away.'"

Cal: "Yes Pat, this is the time in a game when a winning tradition can come to the forefront and help a team. But building a winning tradition takes time. Some fans consider teams like the New York Yankees, the Boston Celtics or Notre Dame to be lucky, however these teams never wait for a lucky break. They're always optimistic, they think positively, and they're too proud not to hustle to the very end and often something favorable does happen.

Pat: "N.C. State started this drive with four minutes remaining. They were deep in their own territory and they have been using up the clock with a time-consuming take-no-chances drive. It's obviously going to be this one drive and go for one or two points and done."

Cal: "Yes, I agree. I wonder if the coaching staff, actually Earle Edwards, because this is the kind of decision the head coach must ultimately make, has decided whether they will go for one or two. Kicking the PAT would be surer and they'd still be undefeated. Going for the tie might cost them a spot or two in the polls, but it's a possibility."

Pat: "Right Cal, but first they've got to get the ball into the end zone and I don't expect this Penn State team to roll over and play dead for them."

Coach Joe Paterno circa 1967

14

CHAPTER 5

"The Stop" Started It

A minute and 28 seconds remained in the game and the football was resting on the Penn State two yard line. At this moment the 46,487 fans in the stands and surrounding the field, the fourth largest home crowd ever and the biggest home crowd to see a Joe Paterno team play, were all eerily quiet. The cyclonic noise which abated just seconds ago was absent as though the eye of a hurricane was passing through; but all present knew the noise and fury would re-appear momentarily and suck up everything and everyone in its path.

NCSU had used their next to last time out to discuss this fourth down play and barring a penalty, the whole ball game, the entire 58 minutes and 32 seconds of rock'em, sock'em, controlled mayhem now appeared to hinge on just *one play* – the next one. Quarterback Jim Donnan was at the west sideline in the cool, bordering on cold, shadow of the press box talking with head coach Earle Edwards, assistant Al Michaels and the other coaches in the press box who were trying to zero in on that one play that would bring the chest-swelling inhalation of sweet victory or the longest ride home this team had ever experienced. During time-outs such as this, definite, confident, and prompt decisions are of the essence. This is no time for diagramming plays in the dirt. The sideline coaches and people in the press box must all be on the same page. Therefore the coaches have a laundry list of plays, from which to choose based on down and distance needed for a first down, a touchdown or to get close enough to attempt a field goal. In the present situation as the offensive coordinator and the head coach look over their play list they rule out a quarterback sneak because two yards is too far for a guaranteed successful quarterback sneak. A short pass, swing pass or pitch play – are all dismissed when quarterback Jim Donnan confirms that it is much darker at the south goal where the ball is, than here at mid-field. The field has no lights and a pitch or a pass that isn't well up in the air so it can be seen against the brighter sky background could easily be misjudged or not seen. After all it was 4:17 P.M. Eastern Standard Time on a November afternoon in State College and Mother Nature seemed to be adding to the drama by dimming the stage lights.

For N.C. State everything began to point toward a simple straightforward play (ISO 40) with their best ball-carrier, tailback Tony Barchuk, carrying the mail. An isolation play (ISO pronounced eye-so) expects to *iso*late the blocking fullback on the linebacker and thereby clear the way for the #4 back plunging directly over center (the zero hole). Thus ISO four zero is ISO forty. The staff consensus was that State would go with their four-four since this was their most balanced defense and gave them the broadest coverage. Of course, had they asked, any military strategist could have told them that the commander who tries to defend against everything ends up defending nothing.

During this same time period, on the east side of the field there was a tightly knit circle of three coaches, two of whom were talking to Onkotz who was nodding his head Yes, Yes, Yes, and a student manager with a clip board next to quarterback Tom Sherman and a few offensive team members who were silently standing near-by, praying they would be going onto the field after the next play. Fifty yards away ten Penn State defenders standing together in the shadow of their own goal line appeared isolated and alone. The ever-increasing gloom seemed more ominous to the fortunes of the home team than to the visitors because the visitors white uniforms made them stand out and look larger than life while the Penn State blue uniforms seemed to blend into the equivalent of a celestial black hole where gravity is so strong even light rays can't escape.

Dan Radakovich up in the press box had already said to Coach O'Hora, " 'O' it's dark down there, they might go with a misdirection play, tell Onkotz to alert Ebersole and Johnson they must *NOT* get suckered in." Coach O'Hora now thinking out loud said, "I can't see them going with a straight drop back pass, or any pass, considering the light, except maybe a fade/corner pattern. They'll probably go "two tight" (two tight ends). If our outside backer or the end on that side can hold up the tight end, just a count, we have very little field to cover." Paterno stood by, as Coach O'Hora said to Onkotz, "O. K. Denny get back in there," all the while he maintained a tight grip on Onkotz's #35 jersey so that Onkotz wasn't going anywhere until he released him - "Tell Ebersole and Johnson to penetrate and "break down," no getting suckered in, they are to "stay home," look for counter-action. Now, no penalties we don't want to give them an extra shot at the end zone." Still holding the jersey and taking a few steps with Onkotz he said, "Line-up four-four, go Eagle" and started Onkotz into his jog back to the huddle with a kindly push. The referee was preparing to mark the ball ready for play, and now the hurricane was returning; the roar, increasing and expanding, seemed to suck people up out of their seats, the "eye" was past and the full fury of the storm was once again upon one and all in Beaver Stadium.

Jim Donnan was gathering his teammates in the Wolfpack huddle while #35 the only Penn State player with his back to the Wolfpack players, was giving his calls a bit louder and more measured than usual, however with no sense of panic—"Line up four-four, go Eagle on "Shift." It would have made great theater drama if the "Caller" (Onkotz) had been the dramatic type. Someone who would either have encouraged his teammates with a brief rallying call such as "Let's go get'em," "Let's show them what we're made of", or something similar. Onkotz however would never say anything of that nature since he himself wouldn't respond to such blatant rah–rah stuff. As we saw previously in the bus ride from Stone Valley to campus, he resolved everything internally even opining to the author that he never really understood why, prior to the game, some players would thump each other on the shoulder pads, hit each other on the helmet or even bang helmets. (He remarked with a grin that he once saw an NFL film clip where two players banged helmets but the one player forgot he didn't have his helmet on and he suffered a nasty gash.). To Onkotz this was just a waste of energy and adrenaline which a player might need at the end of the game, just as he and his teammates would now.

The Lions broke their huddle lining up in their balanced four-four look with inside backers Jim Kates #55 and #35 Onkotz about where the offensive guards were going to position themselves as the 'Pack came up to the line of scrimmage. This was it! The game, the season, a bowl game, TV exposure, recruiting advantages "the whole ball of wax." Quarterback Donnan gave a preliminary look at the defense and got ready to call the signals for the center to snap the ball and set the play into motion. Right then Onkotz barked out "Shift," and instantly Penn State went from their "even front," an even number of down linemen, four in this case, to an "odd front," five down linemen. Responding to the "Shift" call, linebacker Kates, thirty pounds heavier than Onkotz, jumped in among the defensive down-linemen and nose to nose with the N.C. State center. This was a defensive move that didn't bode well for Donnan and the 'Pack, considering that the play that had been called was planned to go straight "up the gut". And where there was supposed to be nothing but end zone ahead, Jim Kates had plugged the hole with his 235 pound body and poised directly behind him like a cat, or more appropriately a Nittany (Mountain) Lion was #35, Onkotz.

The game wasn't lost and the play wasn't doomed; superior effort could still pull N.C. State through. Also Donnan was aware he had one time out left. He could call "time" go back to the sideline and come back with a different play. Calling time out would normally be the percentage play, however here at the south goal with all the student noise and the minimal lighting Donnan feared, and rightfully so, that at this time of high tension and with all the noise present, one of his teammates not being able to hear or see clearly might move or jump offsides if he deviated from his usual snap count rhythm. Should someone move resulting in a procedure penalty, the ensuing five yard penalty would have been catastrophic. Getting two yards on one play has a good chance of success. Getting seven yards on fourth and goal is as likely as "holing" a forty-foot side hill putt.

The play clock was now down to seven seconds; for Donnan it was time to play the hand he was dealt or fold. Onkotz's eyes narrowed in anticipation as he recognized this offensive set, having seen it a number of times in practice this past week.

The center snapped the ball and twenty-two players went into action but the action of ten players in a rectangular area nine feet wide by eighteen to twenty feet in depth was all that mattered. At the snap #55 Kates came up and under the center driving him back into the QB's face. This impeded the forward thrust of the fullback trying to lead the tailback into the "zero" hole and into the end zone. With a pile-up right where tailback Barchuk wanted to run he had only one possible chance - the jump play; where the ball carrier goes airborne up and over his teammates and into the end zone.

When a player with Onkotz's intelligence, ability and experience sees the offensive play unfold before him, he *doesn't* reach back into his Herculean bag of tricks and on his own individual effort make the Play of the Year. What he does is recognize, react and repulse the way he has been coached and prepared for just such a situation. Onkotz said as his career progressed at Penn State he was never confronted, in a game, with a play or a situation for which he wasn't prepared. Onkotz knew where to expect the play and when Kates effectively "submarined" the play, there was only one place the tailback could go and that was "up and over". The fans in the stands now saw a Penn State #35 leave the ground and meet N.C. State's #35 on a solid sure tackle, above the players sprawled on the ground. For a moment the two of them seemed frozen in mid-air and then straight backward went the ball carrier Barchuck, and as he hit the turf with a thud, N.C. State's hopes for an unbeaten season crashed to earth with him. And to this day, Penn State fans need say only two words "The Stop" and anyone who was there knows exactly what the words mean, and when and where it happened.

Now one minute and twenty-one seconds of game time remained before this victory could be officially entered into the Penn State win column.

CHAPTER 6

What's Better Than Three Runs and a Punt?

While ten of the eleven Penn State offensive players returned to the field and huddled down in their end zone, Paterno was standing on the east sidelines next to the eleventh one, his senior quarterback. With one hand on Sherman's shoulder and looking right at him, Paterno reiterated to him what the first two plays would be. If Sherman were a few inches taller and had a stronger arm he might be playing in the NFL a year from now, but right now Paterno was happy with the qualities that Tom *had* and the two things he lacked were inconsequential because throwing a pass on one of the next three downs wasn't even an option as far as Paterno was concerned. Their one-sided conversation concluded, Tom trotted toward his teammates and the referee made the circular motion ending in a kind of karate chop that started the play-clock running.

For any reader who doesn't already know, there are two types of clocks used in college football games. One is the game clock which tells the viewer how much time is left in that particular quarter. The game clock starts when a play begins (on a kick-off it begins when the ball is touched AFTER the kicker kicks the ball), and runs until the quarter ends or until one of the following occurs:

1.   There is an incomplete pass.
2.   The ball or the ball-carrier goes out-of-bounds.
3.   A team time-out is taken.
4.   The referee invokes an official time-out which he may do at his discretion, to measure for a first down, to confer with his officiating crew, to discuss or mark off a penalty, to correct a possible error (for example the scoreboard or a sideline marker showing the incorrect down or one of the clocks, game or play, showing the wrong time), for an injury on the field, etc.
5.   There is a score by either team.
6.   A punt goes into or through the end zone.
7.   A first down is made and until the sideline chain crew gets the first down markers repositioned.
8.   There is a change of possession.
9.   There is a TV time-out.

10.   The game clock does NOT stop with two minutes remaining in the second and fourth quarters as it does in the NFL.

The other clock is the play clock. This clock is a digital clock which starts at 25 seconds and runs down to 00 seconds. After a play ends, the referee waits until the football is spotted and the umpire backs away from the ball he then indicates (the motion mentioned previously) that the play clocks (there is one at each end of the stadium) shall begin their count down from twenty-five seconds to zero; the offensive team must snap the ball to start their next play before the clock reaches zero or they will be assessed a five yard penalty for "delay of game."

Paterno was happy with his center-quarterback tandem so he was as comfortable as he ever is during a game, even when he's leading! Actually it's possible that he's even more uncomfortable when he has the lead than when he is behind. Consider. When you're ahead you have to be prepared for everything the other team can do to take the lead away from you. Whereas when you're behind you need only concentrate on what you want to do to gain (or regain) the lead. Typically Paterno was already thinking beyond the outcome of the two plays he had given Sherman. He was playing out scenarios in his mind considering what he would do if they fumbled and N.C. State recovered or should the first down play go for six or more yards, trying to anticipate anything that might happen. But for now the mantle of power had been shifted from Paterno's shoulders to the shoulders of Tom Sherman and his teammates, and all he could do was watch and trust.

With a clap of twenty-two hands in unison the Lions break the huddle and come up to the line of scrimmage. Senior center Bill Lenkaitis positions himself over the football adjusting the ball in his right hand to be sure he has a good grip and that the ball feels comfortable - not wet or slippery. Being careful not to lift the ball he will check that his distance from the ball gives him just the right angle of elbow- bend and the right amount of knee-flex which will enable him to deliver the football into Sherman's waiting hands swiftly and precisely while he fires off of the ball.

When he snaps the ball, Lenkaitis in one smooth fluid motion of his hand will take the ball which was resting with its long axis pointed north and south (goal line to goal line -most football fields are laid out this way) and in one deft motion, as quick as the strike of a rattlesnake, he will rotate the long axis of the ball so that by the time it's between the QB's outstretched palms the long axis is now pointed east and west (from sideline to sideline). In this position the laces of the football will meet the fingers of Sherman's right hand precisely; thus negating the necessity for the quarterback to regrip the ball, regardless of whether he intends to pass or hand-off.

The offensive five interior linemen (two tackles, two guards and the center,) who are so important, get very little favorable recognition. Occasionally on a "sweep" the announcer or "color man" may point out a tackle who made a "seal" block or maybe a pulling guard with a "kick-out" block, but rarely does a center get noticed unless he botches a snap, is involved in an illegal procedure penalty or misses a block. However, the center is the nerve center of the offense because no play starts (legally) until the center snaps the ball. If the center is nervous and fidgety ("a nervous Nellie" in the Paterno Football Dictionary) this will affect the quarterback and the entire interior line and will diminish the likelihood of a successful play.

The center's duties vary according to the head coach's preference. Some coaches have the center identify whether the defense is in an "odd" or an "even" front, for the most part at Penn State the quarterback does it. Possibly this is because Paterno was a quarterback and as the quarterback he preferred to be in control.

The center (while keeping the snap count foremost in his mind) will call out the blocking scheme. This affects all the linemen because it is *not* true that each offensive lineman automatically blocks the man "on his nose" (the man across from him). Sometimes the center will combine with one of the guards to double-team a defensive tackle or he may be responsible for a linebacker. Along with these duties he must never forget the snap count because that guarantees a "blown play." (Should another lineman forget the snap count he can "go" on ball movement and possibly get away with it but not the center-quarterback combo.)

And if all of the above were not enough, we come to the one quality a Penn State center must have to the point of excess and that is POISE, a Bill Lenkaitis attribute. When the game is on the line and all the linemen are trembling with an overdose of adrenaline and making threats or defaming your mother and while 90,000 fans are screaming at the top of their lungs, the center must make the snap just like he has done on every "rep" on every practice day, just as he does when his team is up by 40 points or down by the same amount. He must not snap it too soon, nor must he be late; either way the success of the play that was called may be compromised or doomed. Yet, he must know his quarterback and take into account what happened on the previous plays. Was the quarterback "sacked" on the last play before he was able to set-up? If so will this quarterback pull out a split-second early on this snap etc.? (It is interesting that another center Paterno praised for his poise and calmness under fire also had a Lithuanian last name and also went on to become a dentist. He was one of the author's all-time favorites and was featured in *Boy's Life* as a Boy Scout -of-the-Year honoree, Dr. Jack Baiorunos.)

At this juncture of the game it doesn't matter how smart Paterno, his sideline coaches, and those in the press box are, or the level of Joe's anticipatory powers. Only two things matter now, how well the players have been prepared and how well they will execute. At stake is the team record, BIG dollars in bowl pay-outs, future alumni-giving (because winning and alumni-giving are directly proportional) and the effect on those blue-chip football recruits who might be seriously considering your school, players who can push your program to a higher level. Also there is the manner in which the various media will report the game, thus influencing how readers and viewers will perceive this team, because when viewing a team, on TV or reading an account of the game, perception is reality. All of these things hang in the balance. At the onset of this next play as well as all the plays in this and every game, the fate of both teams is in the hands of twenty-two players, who, on average, are twenty years of age. This age factor is something fans should never lost sight of.

The play which quarterback Sherman called in the huddle along with the snap count, "Thirty I BAM on two" was, much like N.C. State's last call, a running play right up the middle. However this play varies from ISO forty in several ways. Firstly, it is a quicker hitting play because the ball carrier is the "3" back (the fullback) and since he lines up in front of the tail back, (the "4" back in the "I" (formation) the fullback gets to the line of scrimmage quicker. The ISO play asks the fullback (the primary blocker for the tailback) to isolate the middle linebacker and block him. In Thirty I BAM (pronounced thirty-eye-bam) the fullback is the ball carrier (not the blocker) and since the tailback lines up behind the fullback he can't return the favor and block for the fullback so he generally carries out a fake. In the huddle Sherman had made several orderly and measured admonitions, after making the play call, "No check-off - go strictly on the count, on two. Backs protect the ball everybody be alert for a 'fire call'; on two, break!"

Sherman checks the play clock at the north end of the stadium, it shows eight seconds, no problem since he's not going to audible. Without a trace of urgency Sherman taps Lenkaitis on the right hip as he sets his linemen down. Now getting under center he barks out, "Three thirty-nine, three thirty-nine" then, "Hut One, Hut Two 'on Hut Two center Lenkaitis gives Sherman a perfect snap and he in turn gives the fullback Tom Cherry a flawless hand-off and Cherry slams into the line. The N.C. State defenders showed their poise by not jumping off sides even though they had to be all fired-up. There was very little offensive line push since N.C. State was stacked against the run with eight-men on or *very* close to the line of scrimmage. Penn State had only seven men on the line of scrimmage and only five of them, at most, were involved in trying to block and wedge out the interior half dozen defenders. (The QB doesn't block, the ends and wide-outs are too far away from the action thus it is just the interior five linemen who have the responsibility of getting some forward "push".) Cherry gained about two yards, while hanging onto the football with both hands, as N.C. defenders clawed at the ball. While Cherry was still under the pile an N.C. State player called "time" and the game clock stopped at 1:18.

On second down Sherman gets another perfect hand-up from Lenkaitis and gives the ball to Charlie Pittman who tries to get through the line over right tackle. But N.C. State continues to play tough against the run, ignoring any threat of a pass play. Pittman gains less than two yards, partly because he is more willing to go down then to struggle for extra yardage and take a chance of being stripped of the ball. N.C. State has no more time-outs left and the clock will soon go under one minute to play.

Sherman is now joined in the huddle by fullback Don Abbey who replaces Cherry at that position. Abbey brings the third down play, "Keeper automatic, but just to the line of scrimmage even if it's not covered."

Sherman then gives the team the play, "Quarterback Keeper on "down." Sherman makes sure he catches Lenkaitis' eye and mouths "Automatic" and Lenkaitis acknowledges the call. At the line of scrimmage Sherman taps Lenkaitis' flank a certain way. Before the opposition, or their teammates can move "Len" snaps the ball to Sherman and unloads on the nosetackle. Sherman gives a pretty good impression of someone slipping on ice and goes down at the line of scrimmage before anyone touches him. No Gain. It is now fourth down and Tom Cherry returns to the huddle. Earlier in the season Cherry had taken over the punting chores when Bob Campbell went down with a shoulder injury and soon it will be apparent why Paterno substituted for Cherry for just one play.

With fourth down and 6 yards to go for a first down, Penn State "has" to punt and considering their field position and the way the last three plays went, things are definitely not looking up for the young Lions. This next play will be crucial. It could be disastrous. But Paterno had been thinking one play ahead. On third down he had brought Tom Cherry the punter, *not* Tom Cherry the fullback over to the sideline so that he could be sure there would be no mix-up on the play he wanted executed on fourth down.

The team breaks the huddle and lines up in punt formation with Cherry the punter standing just inside the back line of the end zone. The protector, the other player in the backfield who is stationed approximately half way between the center and the punter and a few steps to the side of a direct line from center to punter, now gives the signal to the center to hike the ball *when* the center is ready. The center pass to the punter is so critical that the center does it when he feels just right, *not* on the command of the protector or the punter. The center is the one who pulls the trigger! On this occasion the center snap is perfect and Cherry catches the ball cleanly and goes into his three-step punt routine. (Penn State punters now use a two step routine.) BUT HE DOESN'T PUNT THE BALL! He veers left then runs at a sharp angle toward the southwest corner of the end zone and as the first N.C. State defender gets close he runs out of the back of the end zone with just eight seconds showing on the clock. N.C. State has recorded a safety and the score is now 13-8. A touchdown for N.C. State on the ensuing free kick will win the game for the 'Pack without the need to kick the point-after-touchdown.

Let's review what transpired on the previous four plays, from the Wolfpack's point of view. N.C. State had kept Penn State from making a first down. Priority #1 accomplished. They had even kept the Lions from advancing the ball as far as the 10-yard line. This meant the Lions would have to go to maximum protection on their fourth down punt. Priority #2 accomplished. It's not possible to have maximum protection AND maximum coverage so you choose one or the other if you can't use normal protection and normal coverage. Forcing Penn State to go to maximum protection augured well for the 'Pack since a better than average punt return would be the most likely result. On fourth down the N.C. State coaching staff made a wise decision. Rather than go for a block they opted to put on a return since they had correctly guessed that Joe would go for maximum protection. Furthermore the N.C. State brain trust realized a blocked punt *could* go out of the end zone for a safety which wouldn't help them. So priority #3 wasn't to "block that kick" as many N.C. State fans were urging their players to do but to set-up a return which would get the maximum amount of yardage in the minimum amount of time on the punt return. There was to be no dancing around or evasive running by the punt returner. He was to get down field on a straight line hopefully inside the 20-25 yard line. If there was no hope of getting to the twenty five yard line or better, the runner was instructed to get out-of-bounds and stop the clock. But either way the runner was told explicitly, "Don't run out the clock unless you're absolutely sure you're going to score." Getting tackled at the one yard line as the clock runs out does the team no good. The punt returner must leave the offense time for at least one play, if he can't score.

The coaching staffs on both sides had hit the nail on the head. N.C.

State, while they wanted to score certainly didn't want to cause a safety. On the other hand Penn State had thought ahead and realized a safety can't possibly hurt us UNLESS we also give up a touchdown on the ensuing "free kick" or the one remaining play NCSU might get off. A TD on the free kick or on the one play from scrimmage could beat the Lions without the safety but a touchdown following a "free kick" was much less likely than on the return of a punt from short or tight punt formation. Thus taking the intentional safety had a HUGE up side and a small downside as far as Penn State was concerned.

In sum total what did each side get out of the intentional safety?

N.C. State got two points they really didn't need. Had N.C. State been able to give the two points back and make the Lions punt the ball from scrimmage they would have done it without a second's hesitation.

In exchange for the two points, Penn State got some very nice perks. What exactly did the safety do for the Lions?

1. It prevented a blocked punt. The rules state that a team after giving up a safety "shall put the ball in play via a free kick from its own 20-yard line." A free kick means the other team must stay ten yards away until the ball is kicked, thus they may not, and cannot, block the kick.

2. It gave Penn State far better punt coverage, since no players needed to stay back to protect the punter, before running up field to tackle the punt returner.

3. The punter was allowed to punt from the 20 yard line instead of the end zone which should cause the punt return man to catch the ball at least twenty-five yards farther from the Penn State goal line.

4. It virtually assured a longer, higher punt since the punter wasn't hurried in any way.

5. Since there was no snap the kicking team was assured there would not be a bad or a mishandled snap which could result in a recovery by the defensive team, in or near the end zone. Only the punter would handle the ball.

Suffice it to say punter Tom Cherry did get off a nice high kick and the punt return man was downed after an insignificant gain. The game clock showed just seconds remaining and it was stopped on the change of possession. There was time left for one play. Jim Donnan led his offensive mates up over the ball for one last gallant effort to win the game.

The way the game actually ended would seem too contrived if Hollywood had written the script. But the records show that quarterback

Donnan dropped back quickly and deeply like he was going to throw a "Hail Mary Pass" into the end zone. A very logical call. However the play call actually was for a screen pass to the left which could have surprised some defenses. But it didn't surprise Penn State's defense. The 'Pack's best ball carrier #35 Tony Barchuk had slipped out of the backfield and after falling in behind his blockers he hauled-in the screen pass and turned to follow his blockers down field for the winning score. But in a true ending, not one written in Hollywood, Penn State's Onkotz shot in behind the blockers and on a sure clean solo tackle brought the ball-carrier Barchuk to the ground to end the game as the Penn State bench erupted on to the field followed by a huge contingent of Penn State fans. In total Denny Onkotz intercepted a pass and ran it in for a TD, made the stop on the goal line to help preserve the win and on the very last play of the game he stopped N.C. State's last gasp effort with a solo tackle. For all these heroics Denny was named Associated Press Defensive Player of the Week. When questioned later about the goal line call, Coach Edwards said simply, "We went with our best player and our best play, your player just beat our best play."

On the strength of this major victory Pennsylvania, and in fact Eastern football, had their new "King of the Hill." A King that would finish in the Top Ten nationally, nineteen out of the next thirty years. In the East over the same thirty years Pitt, Syracuse and West Virginia outranked State four, three and two times respectively while State was top dog twenty-one times. As stated back in Chapter One "there were good times ahead for Penn State and its very confident new head coach, 'Just call me, Joe.'"

No sportswriter wrote in his account of this momentous game, "Mark my words, in years to come people will look back and say on Saturday November 11, 1967 Penn State football came of age." Even the most optimistic Penn State fan upon reading the account of the N.C. State game didn't say out loud, "that UCLA loss was the last one we'll have until 1970." Only hindsight can pin-point such occurrences, witness the following dialogue from a French TV skit;

A weary French obstetrician returns to his home at 3 A.M., after being at the hospital for a delivery which took an inordinate amount of time. As he undresses to go to bed his wife awakes, she asks if he is "all right" and what time it is. The doctor replies, "I'm fine, but really tired and it is ten after three." The wife is sympathetic and asks, "Did the delivery take that long?" The doctor replies, "Yes it did, but it was worth it. Guess who was born this morning?...Charles DeGaulle."

CHAPTER 7

The Pitt–PSU Rivalry and Joe's First Bowl

Following Penn State's defeat of third-ranked N. C. State many of the TV, radio, newspaper and periodical media were giving some credence to rumors that a pride of lions (Nittany Lions) were on the rampage up there in Centre County, Pennsylvania. And suddenly there were "big game scouts," pardon me, "bowl game scouts" interested in Joe Paterno's young Lions as an attractive opponent for some Southern team in a post-season game. Penn State still had two games left on their 1967 schedule - a home game against the Ohio University Bobcats, a game that Penn State should be able to win handily and then it would be time for Pitt to visit State College for only the second time since 1955. The prospect of Pitt playing in Beaver Stadium had the fans, the team and the student body buzzing in anticipation.

But first there was the obligatory game with Ohio University. In the first period, State's big fullback Don Abbey scored at the four and a half minute mark. Defensive back Bobby Capretto then ran an interception back fifty yards for a TD. And three minutes later punt returner/backer/caller Dennis Onkotz hauled in a punt and returned it fifty-six yards for a touchdown. In the fourth period Frank (Spaz) Spaziani blocked a punt and took it in for a score. The good looking Spaziani played numerous positions at State ranging from quarterback to tight end and defensive end, all of which probably stood him in good stead when he became an assistant coach after graduation. Spaziani was also the subject of a mock confrontation between Paterno and some media or fans, at which time he was asked whether Spaziani was such a versatile athlete that he could play a number of positions better than the next man on the depth chart at each position or was he being afforded favored treatment because of his name. When Paterno was asked whether he was playing "Spaz" because Spaziani was Italian, Joe shot right back, "Absolutely not! I'm not playing him because he's Italian - I'm playing him because *I'm* Italian".

When he was running for President, John Kennedy similarly deflected criticism regarding his enormous wealth, and rumors he was trying to buy the Presidency. Whenever this criticism was raised on the campaign trail, he would reach into his pocket and pull out what looked to be a crumpled, dog-eared telegram supposedly sent to him by his father. John would "read" the telegram thusly, "Dear Jack, "Buy only as many votes as you need to win. I'll be dammed if I'll pay for a landslide."

After dispatching the Ohio U. Bobcats by a score of 35-14 Penn State could now turn all of its attention to their traditional season- ending opponent Pittsburgh.

When Paterno came to Penn State with Rip Engle, the Pitt-Penn State rivalry was more of a massacre than a rivalry. Of the last thirty games played Penn State had managed a meager five wins and two ties (and the two ties occurred back in the 1920 and 1921). If one were to view this rivalry as a boxing match the referee would have stepped in and halted the bout somewhere between World War I and World War II.

From a boxing match perspective we will review the entire history of these grudge matches from the first in 1893 to the last in 2000. We will consider each game played between Pitt and Penn State as a round in an old time boxing match between "The Penn State Kid" managed 1918 – 1949 by Hugo Bezdek, Bob Higgins and Joe Bedenk and "The Steel City Slugger " who had in his corner Glenn Scobey "Pop" Warner, Dr. John B. "Jock" Sutherland, Charles Bowser, Clark Shaughnessy, Wes Fesler and Walter Milligan in that order 1918 – 1949. (In early boxing matches a knock-down constituted a round. Today a round is three minutes.)

Rounds 1-6 "The Penn State Kid" came out of his corner "throwing leather" and won the first six rounds (1883, 1896 and 1900 - 1903). Interestingly, the 1900 and 1901 games were played in Bellefonte and the other four were held in State College. Thus, in rounds, The Penn State Kid was blanking his opponent six to zero.

Rounds 7-15 Of the next nine rounds "The Kid" won six while "The Steel City Slugger" shrugged off his lethargic start and took three rounds from "The Kid." Still it looked like an easy victory or even an early knockout; with "The Kid" far ahead twelve rounds to three.

Rounds 16-24 Possibly "The Kid" punched himself out in the first twelve rounds, as "The Slugger" rallied to win six of the next nine rounds, while the best "The Kid" could manage was to win one round and salvage draws in two others.

Rounds 25-39 Starting in 1922 "The Slugger" won thirteen of the next fifteen rounds. There were no games in 1932-1934 which would indicate that our mythical bout was such a mismatch that it was temporarily halted. However the contest was resumed and at the end of the thirties (1939) "The Slugger" was now ahead twenty-three rounds to fourteen with two rounds even.

Rounds 40-49 Rounds forty through forty-nine saw "The Slug-ger" stretch his lead to twenty-nine to eighteen over "The Kid".

With "The Steel City Slugger" ahead of "The Penn State Kid" by eleven rounds and with the gap growing ever-larger, the "Penn State Kid" made a change in his corner. Leaving the cozy confines of Centre County "The Kid's" backers went far afield to bring in "Mr. Nice Guy" (Rip Engle) to take "The Kid" into the Fifties. (The "Steel City Slugger" also made a change in his corner replacing W. S. Milligan with a Casanova – Leonard J. Casanova.)

Rounds 50-65 The corner changes seemed to benefit "The Kid" more, than "The Slugger" as he took nine of the next sixteen rounds, with one round ending in a draw. The fight now stood at twenty-seven rounds for "The Kid" and thirty-five for "The Slugger."

Rounds 66-94 Both fighters now made "corner" changes which would have far-reaching repercussions. "The Slugger" would replace John Michelosen, who had an overall winning percentage of .531, with Dave Hart, an unfortunate choice, while "The Kid's" choice of "The Brooklyn Brawler" (Joe Paterno) would prove to be a life-saver. Of the next thirteen rounds the "Penn State Kid" won twelve, putting "the Kid" in the lead thirty-nine to thirty-six. And with eleven rounds won, and six lost and one draw in the next eighteen rounds (1979 – 2000) the "Penn State Kid" now leads 50-42 with four rounds even. (Since Penn State's eleven game schedule must now include eight Big Ten games each season, it appears that the September 16, 2000 game will probably be the last one in the Penn State – Pittsburgh series for a number of years.)

Beginning with the 1903 game EVERY game had been played in Pittsburgh through the 1965 season except for 1931, '39, '42, '55 and '64. As one of his first acts "The Brooklyn Brawler" went jaw to jaw with the powers-to-be when he insisted the series must be on a home-and-home basis. He didn't back down even though he drew flak from both corners. If he hadn't stood his ground, where might Penn State football be today? If State had continued to play 11 of every 12 games in Pittsburgh would Penn State be in the Big Ten? No way. What kind of student body support would Penn State football have if the last game each year were played in Pittsburgh and the PSU students had to travel to Pittsburgh each year? Consider the economic impact on State College and the University. What would be the reactions of Penn State season ticket holders from New York, New Jersey, Eastern Pennsylvania, etc., if every year they had to drive to Pittsburgh to see the Pitt game.

So the Pitt game, this frigid November day in 1967, was more than just another round in a long bout between two rivals, it was a breakthrough of major psychological importance. Pitt now knew they were no longer calling all the shots. There were also the tangible changes - Pitt had to travel to State College, play on State's home field, their fans had to sit in the visitor's section, their team had to use the visitor's locker room, and wear the visiting team uniform. Pitt's fans and teams now had to go "on the road" as often as State's fans and teams had to. This meant they now had to take that LONG trip home after a defeat (and it seems ten times longer when you lose). And to the delight of Penn Staters, Pitt *won only four* games at Penn State from 1966 through 2000.

Like his counterpart, Joe Paterno at Penn State, here in 1967, Dave Hart was in his second year as Pitt's head coach, however he and Paterno were traveling in opposite directions. Unless his Panthers could take the measure of the Lions on their home field, Hart would post his second consecutive one win and nine loss season, which would push him to the brink of the cliff as far as his job was concerned.

Last year coming into the Pitt game Joe needed a win, otherwise Penn State's twenty-seven consecutive year non-losing season streak would end on Joe Paterno's "watch." This year instead of playing to avoid a losing season Joe's young Lions were charged-up to go out and win a bowl berth for themselves.

It now looked as though State would win eight of ten regular season games a feat no one would have predicted after the season-opening loss at Navy coupled with the season-ending injury to Mike Reid. And while Joe always thinks positively even he might not have foreseen the events that were suddenly propelling him and his young Lions, ready or not, toward a Top Ten finish and a post season bowl game. The Top Ten finish would be only State's fourth such finish in the Associated Press rating which started in 1936. The 1947 team finished 4th, the 1962 team ended up 9th and the 1963 team 10th.

November 25, 1967 Saturday Beaver Stadium

The day of the Pitt at Penn State game dawned C O L D ! With snow flurries. It was one of those days that thirty years later a Penn State linebacker, Brandon Short, would epitomize as exactly the kind of day that brought him to Penn State to play FOOTBALL, some Penn State Football! A day when you could see your breath, your nose was dripping, blood was on your football pants and on your forearm pads and with the wind blowing snow into your face while you scratched at the partially frozen turf trying to get a foothold for the next play. Let's face it, you don't get this effect when you play football indoors and you definitely don't get it on a humid, hot day with a broiling sun overhead. In heat and high humidity no one says, "Wow, what a great day to play football." And no one will ever say what Ernie Banks the Chicago Cubs Hall of Fame shortstop would say on a beautiful, hot, double header day during the baseball season, "Let's play three to-day."

The author attended the above Penn State - Pitt game and it was so-o-o cold. How cold was it? It was so cold that despite keeping our Olds 98 toasty warm the hard-boiled eggs in the trunk were frozen solid when we got out to tailgate. This never happened before and hasn't happened since. It also brings to mind another one time occurrence which the author witnessed at this same game.

On this frigid day Pitt took the field (the north end) first. While they tried to warm-up wearing leotards/long sleeved sweatshirts and stockings, holding their arms folded in front of themselves, jumping up and down, it was painfully clear they were minding the cold. Five minutes later State's football team came out of the opening in the stands at the northwest corner running onto the field next to and/or through part of the Pitt squad. The team was led by that tough, hard-hitting safety Tim Montgomery from Kane, Pennsylvania, the give-no-quarter, ask-no-quarter kind of player who seemed to be a tough-as-nails smaller edition of John Ebersole, Mike Reid, Denny Onkotz, Bill Lenkaitis etc. As the Pitt squad's attention was drawn to the Lion players, at first just a few seemed to take notice, but soon most of the Panthers stopped their drills and just stood motionless watching Tim and his fellow starters come on to the field with no jackets, no hooded capes to ward off the snow and wearing most amazingly of all - short sleeves, bare-armed from biceps to fingertips (no gloves)! The posture, the body language and reactions of the Pitt players seemed to say, "These guys are Supermen - we don't have a prayer!" The game itself was notable mainly because it was being played in State College. Pitt was 1 and 8 coming into the game and wasn't expected to beat State or even give them a run for their money. Form held true and PSU scored 14 points in each of the first three-quarters to lead 42-0 before Pitt got six points to make the final score 42-6.

Hart *was* dismissed after the *1968* season when he recorded yet another one and nine season. Hart's three year record of three wins and twenty-seven losses was remarkably consistent in terms of wins and losses but in his third year the margin of loss (the difference between the victors score and Pitt's) skied to all-time proportions. The opponents outscored Pitt 393 to 99 with Pitt losing to UCLA, Syracuse, Miami, Notre Dame and Penn State by fifty-six, thirty-three, forty-eight, forty-nine and fifty-six points respectively.

Penn State in recognition of their miraculous turnabout, from 1-2 to 8-2, was offered and accepted an invitation to play Florida State in the 1967 Gator Bowl Classic. This was Penn State's third Gator Bowl game in the sixties. Under Rip Engle, Penn State took the measure of George Tech and lost to Florida in 1961 and '62.

In a game that Penn State would almost certainly have won had the Gator Bowl been in Pennsylvania not Florida, one questionable officiating call and the weather sent the Lions home with a bad-tasting 17-17 tie. The Lions scored first on a 27 yard field goal by quarterback Tom Sherman. The "Tom Sherman Show" continued with Sherman hitting Jack Curry and Ted Kwalick on ten and twelve yard scoring plays and the Lions led 17-0 at halftime.

Florida State got on the board in the third period to make the score 17-7, then Charlie Pittman fumbled the ensuing kick-off leading to another Seminole touchdown. Later, on fourth and inches on their own 15 yard line in an effort to keep possession of the ball and run-down the clock, Penn State tried a quarterback sneak which failed to get the first down. The failure of this play in 1967 probably cost Penn State a National Championship on January 1, 1979 because of Joe's unwavering prejudice against the quarterback sneak after the 1967 sneak that backfired. Everyone of us has tried something on one occasion, been burned and never tried it again. Losing on our first trip to the race track has been a blessing in disguise for many of us and has kept us from becoming inveterate gamblers like the "pony player" on his way to the track who implored The Lord above, "Please God let me break even today, I really need the money."

From Paterno's viewpoint he was like the little old lady who had a bad experience on her first-ever airplane ride. When someone asked how she liked her first ride she replied," Actually that was two rides - my first and my last." So too was this Joe's first and last quarterback sneak for many years at a pivotal time. Back in 1967 in Florida, Tom Sherman swore that he had the ball *well* beyond the yard marker but was pulled back by his belt and when the ball was marked there, Penn State lost the ball on downs. Penn State led 17-14 with 15 seconds left in the game but FSU kicked a field goal and the game ended in a 17-17 tie.

Penn State just plain ran out of gas and was running on tired, rubbery legs almost the entire second half. The "tired legs" were due partly to the weather. Mostly however, Paterno in his desire to have his team as sharp as possible and ready for FSU's high-powered offense, in the opinion of at least one player, had worked the team too hard. Now, he is always looking for signs that his team might be having tired legs coming out of the August pre-season work-outs and as the season wears on. The fine-tuning at the beginning of the season has to be decided each year based on temperature, humidity, etc. Paterno does tend to work the team *much harder* if the opening day opponent is on the *weak side* and he goes *easier* on the squad if the opening opponent is *more formidable*.

On the airplane trip back to Pennsylvania after the Gator Bowl game and the 17-17 tie, split-end Jack Curry came forward to the first class section where the coaches were ensconced and said, "Joe, the guys back there took a vote and they wanted you to know that it was unanimous - we all think…you blew it." Whereupon Curry wheeled and returned to the coach section (which ironically is where the players were, not coaches). Obviously the messenger was a senior, and someone who would not be going through another spring practice or pre-season with Paterno as his coach.

There has been a lack of unanimity over the years regarding the way tie games should figure into a coach's or team's winning percentage. The author, and others, disagree with those who just disregard ties. The following example will show the inequality of so doing. Coach A wins nineteen games over two years and ties five, losing none. His winning percentage if the ties are thrown out is 1.000. Coach B wins twenty-three games and loses one, this gives him a .958 winning percentage which trails Coach A's 1.000 percentage, but we all know who is the more successful of the two coaches, based on wins, losses and ties. The approach we will use in assessing winning percentages will count a tie as half a win and half a loss. Now if we re-figure Coach A's and Coach B's winning percentages, Coach A's percentage re-figures to .896 percent while Coach B's remains at .958 a much more realistic appraisal of the success of the two coaches. We will consistently use this approach throughout the book.

November 1970 Beaver Statium Pictorial Showing Beaver Stadium
(capacity 48,344).

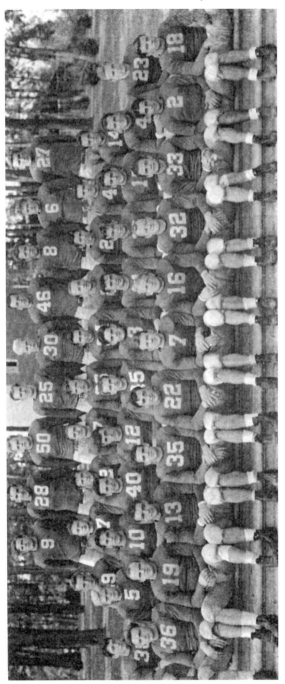

Front Row: Ellwood, Hanley, Peel, Gianantonio, Toretti, Harrison, Metro, Wuenschel, J.G. Patrick, Gentilman Barantovich.
Second Row: Woodward, Peters, Kniaz, Mori, Platt, Patton, Barcalow, Nemeth, Ickes, Alter, Washabaugh, Ewalt.
Third Row: Horn Nonemaker, Duras, Cicak, Gajecki, Radcliff, Rollins, Lucas, Ciocca, Conte.
Back Row: Kopach, Stravinski, Parsons, Briggs, Kinnard, Crowell, J.R. Patrick, White, Vargo.

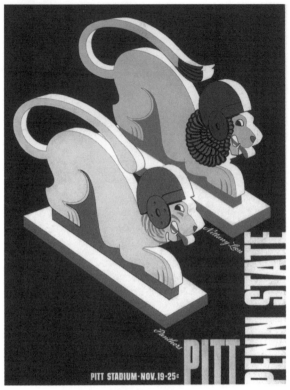

1938 Pitt - Penn State game day program.

Pin from the 1970s, which was popular
among Penn State rooters during the
height of the PSU-Pitt rivalry.

CHAPTER 8

Where "The Stop" Started

Approximately seven miles north of Allentown, Pennsylvania and 65 miles north of Philadelphia lies the town of Northampton and for those familiar with the area it quickly brings to mind two things – its cement/concrete industry and its talented and tough football teams. Thus, it's understandable that N.H.S.'s male athletic teams are known as the "Konkrete Kids".

When the author was a student at Palmerton High School, the "Blue Bombers" along with Northampton and six other teams made-up the Lehigh Valley League and Northampton was the undisputed football "King of the Hill." It was Palmerton's bad fortune each year, to play Northampton the last week of October. With Halloween so close to the date of the game, even in our own home town, Palmerton's Blue and White colors were out-numbered by Orange and Black decorations which happened to be Northampton's school colors.

In the towns of Palmerton, Slatington and Stroudsburg, kids could be seen playing basketball or baseball all-year-round; only in Northampton would you see high school kids and twenty year-olds passing a football around in the heat of the summer months. During one eleven year period Northampton captured the Lehigh Valley League football title eight times and had three second place finishes. To accomplish such a feat at the college or high school level you must have an adequate supply of athletes, some pride and tradition as well as good coaching.

Penn State linebacker, Dennis Onkotz, played his high school football for Al Erdosy and he felt his coach was every bit as good a high school coach as Joe Paterno was a college coach, and Erdosy had the record to validate Onkotz's assessment. Erdosy turned out a plethora of talented football players, thus one might wonder why Penn State didn't recruit more "Konkrete Kids." The answer in brief was Syracuse, and Ben Schwartzwalder.

In the late 1940s Ben Schwartzwalder,the ex-paratrooper from West Virginia, was the head football coach at Muhlenberg College in Allentown before moving on to Syracuse University. Understandably with Northampton High School turning out excellent football players right under his nose, Ben tapped that source repeatedly at Muhlenberg and later at Syracuse. Meanwhile over a period of twenty years 1948-1967

Penn State was able to recruit just two Konkrete Kids, Onkotz and Gerry Farkas. Possibly Northampton players felt more comfortable with the Orangemen of Syracuse, as we mentioned previously Northampton's colors are orange and black. Oddly enough in 1965 when Onkotz had reduced the list of colleges he was considering to just two, it came down to Penn State and Princeton. And what might Princeton's colors be? Orange and Black.

Denny Onkotz began playing football for Coach Erdosy in his sophomore year at Northampton High School and #48 (that was his uniform number in high school) had a lot going for him namely the following:

1. Once you've broken the code, Onkotz's uniform number tells you he was big. At Northampton High, in the 1960s, football uniform numbers were related to your coat, or suit size. Thus Number 48 was probably the biggest back on the team.
2. Onkotz played basketball, where he impressed Penn State assistant coach George Welsh with his speed up and down the court and his rebounding determination and aggressiveness.
3. Onkotz was intelligent and applied himself in school. Thus when it came time to choose a college he was able to go wherever he wished.
4. He never smoked, drank or tried drugs.
5. He had good eye-hand coordination.

Playing both ways in high school as a sophomore, Onkotz began to build a reputation as a hard hitter on defense and a top–notch running back. Because of an injury he suffered in a scrimmage with Easton High School in his junior year, Erdosy used him only on defense until the final game that year. In his senior year his knee was sound and he again played offense and defense.

Entering his senior year at Northampton High School it was expected that Onkotz would be the featured running back (the number 7 back according to Coach Erdosy's numbering of his short punt formation). This back gets the most carries, the most glory and the majority of the touchdowns. But Al Erdosy had a problem. He did not have a good #8 back, the *most important* back in the short punt formation. The #8 back doesn't carry the ball very often, but he handles the ball on virtually every play. It is his ball handling, faking, blocking etc., which makes the short punt formation such a potent offense and the timing of every play depends on him. Evaluating his players like a teacher, Coach Erdosy had two players who would grade-out at B+ or A as the #7 back but they merited only a C as the #8 back. Onkotz could do an A job at either spot, thus for the good of the team he became the #8 back.

A good #8 back must have natural eye-hand coordination and then he must do countless repetitions to fine-tune this quality. The #8 back takes the snap from the center and he must do this without looking at the ball. It is helpful that the snap is short, but it must be done flawlessly and repeatedly. Thus the majority of every offensive practice session was spent snapping, catching, faking, handing off, until Onkotz could catch the ball while reading the defense and maybe even change the play AFTER the ball was snapped. This taught him to catch the ball with his hands. In Onkotz's opinion too many football players try to catch the ball against their chest /shoulder pads and since these pads are so unyielding – the pass, punt or pitch tends to bounce off. His daily catching practice made Onkotz sure-handed on defense, where he turned many a pass into a Penn State touchdown, and as we shall see made him a unique linebacker—one who returned punts.

When the recruiting in-fighting began, Onkotz was considering several schools. However one by one he turned down all but Princeton and Penn State. Regarding the other schools, Onkotz said, "I knew they weren't being truthful with me when they promised I would start at running back my sophomore year. I asked several of the recruiters the names of all the running backs they had in their present freshmen, sophomore and junior classes. Then I asked "Am I better than all of them?" I also asked, am I the only running back you're recruiting? Their promises just didn't ring true. Penn State promised me nothing."

When it finally came down to just Princeton and Penn State, Princeton was pushing harder for Onkotz than Penn State for one very good reason. Princeton needed him more than Penn State did.

A 1965 survey of the high school football teams in Pennsylvania, or across the county would have revealed that a minimum of 70% of the teams operated out of the "T" or "I" formation. Probably 90% to 99% of the Division I college football teams did likewise. Penn State was in that 90% to 99% but Princeton at that time was in the roughly 5% using the single wing formation. In the "T" and "I" formations the center hands the ball up to the quarterback, in a direct exchange. In the single wing and the short punt formation the center "hikes" the ball to a back who is positioned one or more steps farther removed from the center than the conventional "T" or "I" formation quarterback. In the single wing or short punt formation, the ball, once hiked, is in free flight, for a period of time, until it reaches one of the backs. Letter of intent day wouldn't arrive until February but the Princeton Tigers were hoping to receive a

Christmas present by that date in the shape of a big, smart, tough, athletic football player who could score 1200 plus on his SATs and had played three years of high-caliber prep football as a single wing/short punt formation back. There were precious few high school seniors in the country who would meet those specifications.

But in the end Princeton lost out. Onkotz said he would not have gone wrong at either school, but Penn State was an all-around more comfortable fit. Joe had made his parents feel comfortable during his official visit, during the time George Welsh who recruited him, and his upperclassman guide showed him around. Looking back Dennis told me he never had reason to second-guess his decision.

When he arrived at Penn State the coaching staff was looking at Onkotz as a running back. While demonstrating plays as a back on the foreign team, reports were that he and Mike Reid (who had come to State the year before Onkotz) had some helmet–rattling collisions, but as Onkotz said, "I certainly wasn't going to back down to him."

Going into his sophomore year at Penn State the 1967 depth chart showed Onkotz behind Bill Rettig at the Hero position. This is a rather typical scenario for an offensive back you recruited who doesn't fit into your offensive plans. A quarterback or halfback who can't play in the offensive backfield or as a receiver will have to move to the defensive side of the ball. Most halfbacks and quarterbacks are not physical enough or lack the size to play anywhere except defensive halfback, free safety or strong safety. The combination linebacker/defensive halfback strong safety is called the Hero in the State four-four defense. In a 3-4, 4-3 or 5-2 defense he is called the strong safety. Some players such as Shelley Hammond and Kim Herring would have been great tailbacks but they either chose to play safety, defensive-back or Hero, thinking ahead toward a "Pro" career and knowing they were too light to play tailback in the NFL or they were needed more on defense than on offense. Onkotz went from Hero to Backer, despite weighing only 205 pounds, when the position change to linebacker envisioned for Mike Reid never materialized.

Just three games into the 1967 season State lost its punter and punt returner Bob Campbell to an injury. Tom Cherry took over the punting chores but the punt returner position was in turmoil. Several players proved unequal to the task and every fumbled or mishandled punt caused Paterno acute agony. One day in practice after two or three fumbled punts JoePa lost his Italian temper and stopped practice yelling at the punt return man, "Get outta there! Can't anybody catch the football! Get somebody back there who can." At a time like this nobody is going to volunteer – in fact a player just wants to be as far from Joe as possible. Paterno yelled again, "Well, who is it going to be? We don't have all day, let's go!" One of the assistant coaches yelled out, "Onkotz, get out there!" Onkotz trotted out there and proceeded to field three punts flawlessly and suddenly he had another job. After practice Coach Patrick had Onkotz catch some more punts and with "Pat's" coaching and Onkotz's ability honed on the practice field at N.H.S. Onkotz became a unique commodity, a middle linebacker at a major football power who returned punts for his three year varsity career.

Going into his junior year the *Penn State Media Guide* had this to say about Onkotz: "Onkotz was probably the most spectacular member of PSU's outstanding sophomore crew." Even Paterno was quoted as saying, "Onkotz could become one of the greatest linebackers we have ever had." In 1967 he was the only sophomore selected to the First Team All-East squad and was honorable mention on the UPI All-American team. Onkotz was in on 118 tackles 74 of which were solo tackles. He also had six interceptions for 179 yards (an amazing "stat") and two touchdowns and returned one punt for a touchdown.

What kind of running back Onkotz would have been cannot be said with certainty but a John Cappelletti type is very plausible. However, inside linebacker was his best position and to the coaching staff's credit they moved him there early in his sophomore year and he stayed there the rest of his career.

Speaking of Cappelletti, his story was the mirror image of Onkotz's. "Cappy" was recruited as a linebacker and even in his sophomore year he was still being used as a defensive back (and a punt returner). Cappelletti did not become a tailback until his junior year. As a consequence of being a tailback for only two years John ended up sixth on the career rushing list even though he holds all the rushing records for number of 200 yard games in a season, in a career and for consecutive 200 yard rushing games. Through 1996 he was tied for most 100 yard games in a season with Lydell Mitchell and Blair Thomas at eight. The five players ahead of "Cappy" in the career rushing yards category are Curt Warner, Blair Thomas, Matt Suhey and D.J. Dozier, all of whom competed for four years, and Lydell Mitchell who played three years. As previously stated Cappy was an offensive back for two years only.

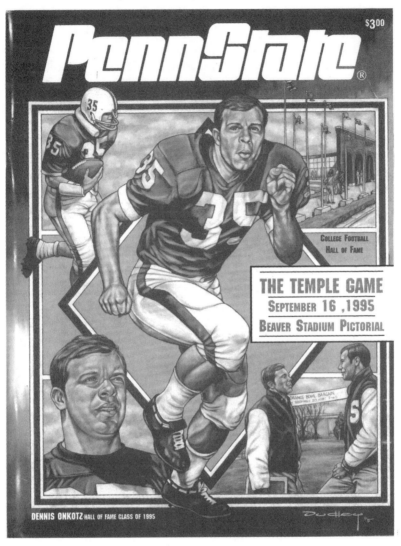

Dennis Onkotz, Hall of Fame Class of 1995, with fellow, two-time All-American, Ted Kwalick (Lower Right corner)

CHAPTER 9

Get Me Some Good Players to Play With

Entering into the 1968 season the Penn State defense became even stronger when Mike Reid was pronounced 100% fit and ready to return to action. Playing it safe the coaching staff decided to reverse their proposed move of Reid to linebacker and return him to defensive tackle. The change was made for two reasons. Firstly, to protect his injured knee, an injury which caused him to miss the 1967 season. Blockers don't come at a defensive tackle's knees from as many different angles as is the case with a linebacker. Also opposing linemen don't get the running start at a lineman's knees that tight ends, fullbacks, and wideouts do when blocking or cutting a linebacker.

The second reason was in case Reid had lost a half step, in his new position it wouldn't be as apparent. If his speed now might be just above average for a linebacker, that would make him one of the fastest defensive tackles in the country. This presented opponents with the proverbial rock and a hard place conundrum. The coaching tenet is that "you run *away* from strength and you run *at* speed." With Reid's speed, conventional wisdom would say "run at him." However as ferocious a warrior as Reid was, running at him only seemed wise when you saw him move laterally on game films or if you weren't the blocker or ball carrier who was told to "attack him…go right at him".

In the late '50s, Penn State had signed a "blue chipper," in Dave Robinson, but it was six years before the Lions hit the football recruiting jackpot again, this time with Altoona linebacker/fullback Mike Reid. Early in the recruiting process, Reid told "Tor" Toretti, State's chief recruiter, that he was coming to Penn State which raised the spirits of Penn Staters everywhere. As the recruiting season shifted into high gear on its way to the finish line the only question Tor was asked oftener than the perfunctory, "How's it going?" or "How're you doin'?" was, "What's the word with Reid, is he still coming? or "What do you hear from Reid?" During this period of less than 100% certainty, Engle and Paterno were trying not to nag "Tor," but they really wanted Mike Reid. First of all he was right in their backyard and he was probably the number one high school linebacker prospect in the country. He was on every college's wish list, and if someone, somehow, stole him right out from underneath Penn State's nose it would hurt Penn State's image and the credibility of its football program. Reid belonged at State, he wanted State, and State wanted him. If somehow they lost Reid it wouldn't be a pretty picture. Besides being a very special football player he was a very special person. How special?

Mike Reid as we said before was one of the top football players in the country. If we parlay that with a young man who was an excellent student, an accomplished pianist, a budding actor and composer we have a unique individual. Matter of fact, name, if you can, another All-American football player in the last thirty years who was a music major in college, and while there performed as a concert pianist and starred in an on-campus production of a Broadway musical such as "Guys and Dolls." Reid was also a PIAA heavyweight wrestling champion and had a reputation as an anti-hippie student. This philosophy of Reid's resulted in an uncorroborated confrontation between him and some persons who wished to tear down the American Flag in front of Old Main. The flag didn't come down.

On a memorable day in the 1964-1965 recruiting season Toretti stopped by to check on Reid. Reid opened the conversation asking, "How's recruiting going?" Torretti replied, "Mike it's looking good. We have one of the best backs we've had since Lenny Moore coming, a super tight end, some lineman who look very good, it's looking like a very good year and we're sure counting on you." Reid leaned forward and flatly stated, "Coach I'm telling you as sure as we're sitting here I am committed to Penn State. It's where I've always wanted to go, then, and now. If anybody gives you any flak about me, tell him what I've just told you and that I told you to stop wasting your time contacting me. Instead put that time to better use and get me some good football players to play with."

Tor got up, shook hands with Mike and said "O.K. Mike we understand each other. It'll be some weeks until I call you, on the other hand you can call me anytime. I'm out on the road quite a bit but you know Cheryl Norman don't you?" Reid nodded yes. "Well you can get a message to me anytime. She knows where I am every day." As Tor went out the front door and down the walk Reid spoke out, "Good hunting." "Tor" acknowledged the sentiment with a wave and a smile as he fairly bounced to his car door, feeling as though a 225 pound weight had just been lifted off of his shoulders. If they lost Reid now there could be only two reasons. One, someone behind Tor's back, kept contacting him and drove him away, or they never had him in the first place. Nothing that Rip, Joe, Ernie McCoy, the Penn State athletic director, or anyone else could say now, would make him contact Reid oftener than he felt was appropriate.

The "legend" of Linebacker U probably reflects back to Dave Robinson, although Robinson became a linebacker in the NFL after playing mostly as a defensive end at State. The next blue chip recruit with some linebacker lineage was Mike Reid who played that position and fullback in high school and was projected to be the starting inside linebacker in 1968. But, as explained previously, Reid played as a defensive tackle at State and in the NFL. Reid performed "on Sunday" five years before leaving the Pros and moving on to his true love composing and performing music.

The rapid succession of All-American linebackers beginning with Dennis Onkotz gave credence to the appellation Linebacker U. Onkotz who was an All-American in 1968 and 1969 trail-blazed a path for a procession of Penn State All-American linebackers continuing with Jack Ham (1970), Charlie Zapiec (1971), John Skorupan (1972), Ed O'Neil (1973) and Greg Buttle (1975). From 1976 through 1997 there were only two more, Shane Conlan (1985 and 1986) and Andre Collins (1989), and Penn State became known more as Tailback U. than Linebacker U.

Interestingly three Penn Staters in the 1960-1992 era played linebacker for twelve years each in the NFL, Dave Robinson, Jack Ham and Matt Millen. Only Ham played linebacker at State. Millen came to State as a linebacker, as did Bruce Clark, but the two teammates, who became best friends, both ended up as defensive tackles and I doubt any college team ever, had two better defensive tackles on the field at the same time. *No* team could handle Clark or Millen one-on-one. Mike Reid was an equally dominating tackle, so Nittany Lion fans have seen some of the best.

Tor' Toretti with son Mike blocking, run up against All-American and All - Pro, End/Linebacker, Dave Robinson. (Photo courtesy of Penn State Sports Information Department)

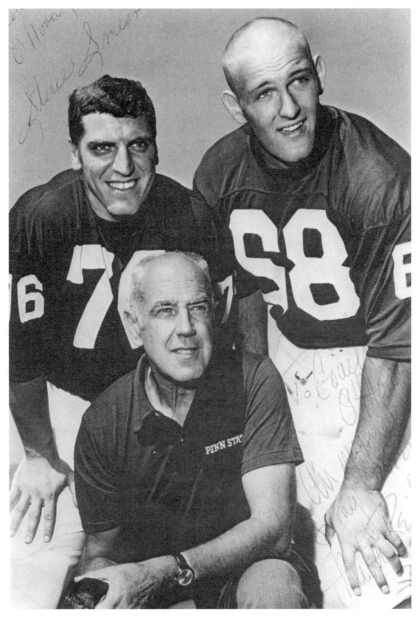

Defensive Coach O'Hora with two of his stalwarts (left to right) Steve Smear and Mike Reid. (Photo courtesy of Coach Jim O'Hora)

CHAPTER 10

How Much Does a Good Player Weigh?

In sports where an individual posts a number, such as a golfer's or bowler's score or a runner's time the number is a direct indicator of that participant's skill and ability when measured against any fellow competitor on the same golf course, lanes or track under similar conditions. However the use of numbers such as weight, height, biceps size, weight-lifting ability, speed in the forty yard dash will not infallibly predict the better of two or the best of a group of boxers, wrestlers, football or basketball players. And any attempt to use just those numbers to qualify or disqualify an athlete being recruited is a risky approach, as the following story will point out.

On a State College January day, defensive tackle Steve Smear came bounding up the concrete steps to the second level of "Rec" Hall. Here, Smear hoped to see chief recruiter "Tor" Toretti on behalf of a certain prep school football player. Smear passed the main football office, designated simply as Room 234, without slowing and continued down the hall to Toretti's office. A quick look revealed no one inside, so Smear "did a one-eighty" and headed back to 234. The football office actually consisted of a series of rooms around the perimeter of an open area where numerous football trophies were on exhibit and large pictures of All-Americans from by-gone days hung on the walls.

Just inside the room was the gatekeeper, Joe's personal secretary, now Administrative Assistant, the professional and affable, Cheryl Norman. Smear saw that "Tor" and Coach O'Hora were engaged in conversation which gave him the opportunity to make some small talk with Cheryl and kid her about her one-traffic-light hometown of Port Matilda, which is a bit like the pot calling the kettle black when you hail from Johnstown, Smear's native city. Smear did have Johnstown on his mind, and specifically Bishop McCort High School where he went to school. And now as Toretti left the assistant coaches' room and walked toward the door, Smear intercepted him, and came right to the point.

"Tor, I just talked with Jack and he still doesn't have an offer from anybody bigger than Marshall, Richmond or Virginia Tech. Somebody said you're holding one grant that you want to use and I doubt there's anyone out there you can get who's better – he's a heck of a player".

Tor replied, "Steve we have a card on him but Joe won't give a grant to a six foot, 190 lb. linebacker - he might not let a kid that size walk-on."

Smear answered, "Tor, I know he can play for us he's really quick and he's tough… he's tougher than I am".

Tor replied, "Now come on, Smear I doubt he's tougher than you are. You wouldn't back down to him, would you…huh?"

Smear said "No, but he wouldn't back down to me or Reid either. He's tough enough to play here and have you seen him lately? You know he went to some prep school in Virginia, Massanut… something and he's bulked up a bit and he'll get bigger. But you'll love his speed. He'd be a great Fritz, he's six foot two inches, and probably pushing 210 (pounds)."

Tor raised his eyebrows and then motioned for Smear to follow him as he walked down the hall to his office. Upon entering his office Toretti turned his back on Smear, saying "Let me see here," he went to his file cabinet and pulled out a file folder and some 3 X 5 cards.

Tor consulted his material then he questioned Smear, "You say 210?, we have him at 196 and 6 foot plus. You're saying six-two?"

Smear said, "Close to six-two and over 205."

At this point Jim O'Hora entered the room just in time to hear the tail end of the conversation, which he recognized, so he asked, "Is this about the kid from McCort? Didn't we come to the conclusion he wasn't big enough?"

Toretti replied, "Yeh, but Smear is saying he's put on some pounds at prep school and he's really trying to sell me on how quick and tough he is."

Smear quickly said, "He's home now. If you don't want to go to Johnstown, he could come here maybe play some pick-up basketball. You could see what a good athlete he is, how quick and he can jump too!"

Tor said, "O.K. get him here day after tomorrow. If he's "six-two and 210" we'll go to bat for him and twist Joe's arm to give him that scholarship, but only if he meets the criteria." Now he's O.K. academically, you're sure?"

Smear, beaming ear to ear, said, "No problem there and he'll be here."

Sure enough our mystery player showed up as scheduled, probably wearing at least four pairs of sox since they would measure his height in his stocking feet. With a locker lock and keys in his gym shorts for hidden added weight, they put him on the scales and applied the measuring tape. Maybe Toretti, or whoever did the measuring, "gave" a pound or two, and/or a half-inch or an inch, but Toretti said on many occasions afterward, "Can you imagine if we had turned him down because he was a half inch too short or a pound light, we never would have gotten Jack Ham, one of the best linebackers Penn State and the NFL ever had!"

Ham was an immediate contributor in his sophomore year making the starting line-up in 1968 and playing extremely well. He blocked three punts in his first season, a feat equaled only by Andre Collins in 1989. Jack starred for the Lions all three years 1968, '69 and '70 (was an All-American in 1970) and was drafted by Pittsburgh in the second round of the NFL draft. He played for twelve years, all of them with the Pittsburgh Steelers. He was on four Super Bowl title teams and was voted to the All-Pro team *nine consecutive years.* Ham was a unanimous choice on the NFL Team-of-The-Decade for the '70s, was voted NFL Defensive Player of the Year in 1975 and is one of four Penn Staters enshrined in the Professional Football Hall of Fame.

Following his retirement after the 1999 season, linebacker coach Jerry Sandusky, who coached Onkotz, Ham, John Skorupan, Ed O'Neil, Greg Buttle, Shane Conlan, Andre Collins, Lance Mehl, Chet Parlavecchio, Trey Bauer, Brandon Short and LaVar Arrington, said he thought Ham was the best linebacker of them all (and Arrington was the best athlete ever to play defense at Penn State). According to Sandusky once Paterno got a good look at Ham on the practice field they decided he was one player they should not try to change in any way.

And some people thought he might be too small!

Pro Hall of Famer Jack Ham with presenter, Joe Paterno. (Picture courtesy of William Simco)

CHAPTER 11

So You'd Like to be a Head Coach?

During the first thirty years of one-platoon football a varsity football squad consisted of possibly fifteen players. Since freshmen were not allowed to play on the varsity, the eleven starters might typically consist of five seniors, four juniors and two sophomores. However, an occasional team might have seven seniors. Following their graduation, which would rob the team of 63% of its starters, a team would go through one, or even two seasons, described as "rebuilding years."

In today's two-platoon football, a team consists of twenty-two starters. Since freshmen are eligible, it is possible that a major football power might at the end of a season graduate just eight starters. This would affect only 36% of the starting team. And since teams such as Nebraska, Florida State and Penn State are two or more deep at various positions, the media might say, "They don't rebuild, they just reload."

If you would like to measure your football acumen against Joe Paterno, a young head coach back in 1968, you can do so beginning with spring practice.

Coming into the 1968 spring practice sessions, Paterno was solid defensively, but graduation had stripped much of the firepower from his offense. Gone were quarterback Tom Sherman, his favorite receiver, Jack Curry, co-captain, center Bill Lenkaitis and tackle Rick Buzin who was playing his best football at the end of last season. The passing attack would need to be rebuilt, from the ground up and a two-man team like Sherman and Curry isn't put together in one spring practice, or even in one season. Their pitch and catch style offense used short and medium "out-patterns" to attack the defense. This possession type offense, doesn't attempt long passes often, in fact, Curry caught only three touchdown passes in two full years 1966 and 1967. But they did keep "moving the sticks".

Paterno's quarterback in 1968 wouldn't come close to matching Sherman's numbers. Kwalick would still be there as a receiver but a team can't throw to its tight end as often in a game as Sherman did to Curry. For his running game Paterno's backfield consisted of two threats, the brilliant but oft-injured 190 pound Bob Campbell, a slashing type runner, and the 190 pound Charlie Pittman, more of a finesse ball carrier. Neither was a power runner.

Spring practice brought forth very few answers, which left Paterno genuinely concerned. Fullback Don Abbey had knee surgery and Frank Spaziani wasn't playing football, not because he was Italian and not because Paterno was Italian but because he was playing baseball. And the two back-up sophomore halfbacks counted on for depth, Gary Deuel and Fran Ganter, were both sidelined with injuries as spring practice came to a close.

So entering into pre-season, drills with a September 21st opening game, what is your strategy? What is an aspiring young coach, like Paterno (or you) to do? Listening to him, over the years, you probably remember most or all of the little cliches he uses such as – special teams are very important, we need a good kicking game and we have to hold penalties and turnovers to a minimum. He'll also stress field position, not giving the opponent a short field to work with, making some big plays, playing a sound defensive game and controlling the pace of the game.

Paterno never says, "We have to throw for at least three touchdowns this game, or we 'll need two hundred yards from our tailback, or if we don't get three hundred yards passing and at least fifteen first downs we can't win."

Let us analyze Paterno's philosophy and what he does want, *not* what he doesn't.

He always wants a solid running game for at least two reasons. Reason number one; Paterno wants a physical team, one that can wear down the opposition. In pass blocking you stand-up, back up and try to hold your man away from your quarterback. For this you need size and linemen with good feet but there 's no premium on toughness or aggressiveness. In run blocking you must pull and lead or explode off of the line of scrimmage. Here size can help but agility, quickness, strength, toughness and explosiveness are most coveted. This physical style of play is the trademark of Penn State football. Reason number two is to control the pace of the game. It's never Paterno's objective to win a game 40-38. It may happen, but he didn't plan it that way. With a superior opponent, Paterno likes to hold the score in the 16-10 or 20-14 range late in the game, then his team, if it plays smart, can come away with a 17-16 or 21-20 win. Paterno puts a premium on good special teams and a good kicking game. Special teams are utilized most often when you, or the other team, punt and when you, or the other team, kick-off. Goal line defense, field goal and point-after-touchdown attempts also are considered to be special team situations but we'll concentrate on just punting and kicking off, and returning punts and kick-offs.

If you can consistently manage to return the football within thirty yards of the prior line of scrimmage, you'll be in the driver's seat. In contrast if your opponent must start every drive on or inside his twenty yard line you'll discover something very quickly. An opponent who can regularly and repeatedly drive the ball eighty to eighty-five yards to score multiple touchdowns is probably better than you. If, however, you are competitive you will discover that somewhere in your opponent's eighty-plus yard drive, he will have a big penalty or there might be a fumble, a busted play, a dropped pass, a sack, a large loss on a running play, or an interception. The occurrence of any of these can turn the ball over to you or cause the offense to punt, thwarting their drive. Good special teams burden your opponent with poor field position making him feel like the field is tilted and he is continually driving uphill, while your team is rewarded with good field position making your team feel like it is running downhill; a big psychological difference.

Consider a basic fact when talking offense versus defense. On offense if a certain aspect of your offensive package is weak you avoid that area. If you can't run wide, you run up the middle or pass. If you can't pass protect, you run screens, quarterback draws, roll your quarterback out, run the ball more, use shovel-passes, etc. You delete any weak aspect from your offensive package.

If you have a problem on defense your opponent will exploit it and you can't force him to attack elsewhere unless you bolster this area by weakening some other area. Now you have two areas of relative weakness and a smart quarterback will audible at the line of scrimmage to take whichever one you are giving him on that particular play. If your defensive front four is sub par and can't put pressure on the opposing quarterback you either have to let him throw unhurried, in which case he will pick your defense apart, or you will have to gamble and blitz more frequently than you normally would.

If you are blitzing to cover up a weakness you might gain an advantage on one or several plays. This might cause one or more of the opponent's running plays to blow-up in his face but you will also give up some big plays because you blitzed with the wrong defender or at the wrong place or time. The loss you inflict on a running play might be as much as a seven-yard loss. The big plays you give up by gambling will likely go for ten yards or more, with the ultimate being a touchdown.

Blitzing on a passing play might get your team a sack, pinning a five to fifteen yard loss on the offense, but before you tackle the quarterback for a big loss he might throw the ball away. If he can't do that, once he has lost 20 yards, he's going to quit retreating. He is NOT going to lose 70 yards, but if you get beat on a blitz on a passing play the offense might get 70 yards, or more.

A blitz might be "picked up," by a back who sees what is coming and leaves his area and assignment to block the "blitzer." Or the quarterback might anticipate the blitz and alert one of his eligible receivers with a "hot call" to break - off (shorten) his route and be alert for a quick pass. If this is done quickly enough the quarterback will be able to get rid of the ball before the blitzer can get to him. If either of these counter - strategies of the offense works, the offense will likely gain from five yards to a touchdown. Thus your successful blitzes depend to some extent on luck to do moderate harm, but when your luck runs out you suffer major damage. A defense that blitzs once too often recalls the old truism, "he who lives by the blitz, dies by the blitz."

However, if you are blitzing because you have superior talent and size, or because the offensive line is inexperienced or lacks cohesiveness, then your blitzing will wreck havoc. This is why in any football all-star game there are very definite limitations placed on the defense as far as blitzing. If an offensive line has not had sufficient time to work together to become a cohesive unit they will be unable to cope with all the stunts, loops, zone blitzes etc a defense can throw at an offense. So blitzing can be quite successful if it is part of your complete defensive package. It is *very* successful if the opponent's line is inexperienced, lacks cohesion or if your defensive rush is overpowering. Mixed in with your other schemes you can employ it when it isn't expected which increases the likelihood of a favorable result.

But above all else remember, if you have a weakness on defense the opposition will hammer away at it and exploit it to the maximum. If you have a weakness on offense you can choose to stay away from it - a choice (staying away from a defensive weakness) you can't force on your opponent.

So what did Paterno do in 1968 with a very limited passing game and no ball-control power-running game? He chose to play a smothering, aggressive defense, going for blocked punts, interceptions, playing field position and intelligent football. How did his strategy fare?

Let us review the objective facts. During the 1966 and 1967 seasons the Lions were led at quarterback by Tom Sherman. Sherman had two quality receivers both years. In 1966 in just seven games, he threw six touchdown passes, four to Ted Kwalick and one to Jack Curry. Sherman threw for approximately nine hundred and fifty yards with Curry getting five hundred and eighty of those yards and Kwalick three hundred and seventy yards. In 1967 Sherman threw thirteen touchdowns, two to Curry, four to Kwalick and Sherman notched sixteen hundred and sixteen yards with Curry and Kwalick garnering twelve hundred and fifty of those yards. Unfortunately Sherman threw as many interceptions as touchdown passes which would barely earn him a passing grade in that category. But his twenty-five hundred yards passing and nineteen touchdowns passes in less than two full seasons puts him among the Top Fifteen Penn State quarterbacks.

Chuck Burkhart was the quarterback in 1968 and 1969 and in his first season, he threw for eleven hundred and seventy yards and six touchdowns. In 1969, his senior year, Burkhart threw for barely eight hundred yards and *one touchdown*. In his career Chuck threw for just over two thousand yards, this included seven touchdowns and *sixteen* interceptions – *more* than two interceptions for each touchdown, emphatically a failing grade.

Now let us summarize and compare below, the aforementioned statistics for the two quarterbacks along with three team statistics which should mean more to you the aspiring head coach, and Joe Paterno, than all the individual statistics.

Tom Sherman Starting quarterback 1966 and 1967	Chuck Burkhart Starting quarterback 1968 and 1969
2588 yards in completions	2076 yards in completions
19 touchdown passes	7 touchdown passes
19 interceptions	16 interceptions
Team Record 1966, 1967	Team Record 1968, 1969
13 wins	22 wins
7 losses	0 losses
1 tie	0 ties

I hope you did what your mentor did – put your money on your defense. Even before the '68 season started, Paterno knew he had a defense that could not only keep their opponents *off* of the scoreboard but with a little luck it could actually put points *on* the board or at least set up the offense in good scoring position. On paper, it appeared the Lions had lost five defensive players who were of any import (identified by + marks in the table on page 60) but defensive coach Jim O'Hora knew he actually had eight returning starters plus John Ebersole a back-up player with talent and experience and the newcomer Jack Ham. In reality O'Hora had ten frontline players just waiting to be turned loose on their 1968 opponents.

1967 Line up		Defense	1968 Line up	
Spaziani**	Jr.	DE	Spaziani***	Sr.
+ Litterelle**	Sr.	DE	Lippincott*	Sr.
Pringle**	Sr.	DE	Stofko**	Jr.
Smear*	So.	DT	Smear**	Jr.
+ McBath***	Sr.	DT	Reid**	Jr.
Ebersole*	So.	DT	Ebersole**	Jr.
Onkotz*	So.	ILB	Onkotz**	Jr.
Kates*	So.	ILB	Kates**	Jr.
Johnson, Pete*	So.	OLB	Johnson, Pete**	Jr.
+ McCormick**	Sr.	OLB	Ham*	So.
Johnson, Paul*	So.	DHB	Smith, Mike*	So.
+ Capretto**	Sr.	DHB		
Smith, Neal*	So.	DHB		
+ Montgomery**	Sr.	Safety	Smith, Neal**	Jr.

* Indicates number of letters won by the end of the season

Before the '68 season began there were two significant position changes. Actually there was just one change. The other change involved a change that wasn't made.

In 1967 Mike Reid sat out the year and Jim Kates and Denny Onkotz were the inside linebackers. For the 1968 season Kates was supposed to move to defensive tackle and Reid was projected to be an inside linebacker. For reasons explained earlier, this change which had been penciled in, didn't occur. The change that did take place involved Neal Smith and it proved to be a winning move.

Neal Smith was moved to safety, a more natural position for him, and this 150 pound high school football player, who walked on at Penn State, intercepted eight passes to tie a single season school record. While carrying a heavy academic load as a civil engineering major, Smith still found time to put his leadership qualities to good use another place, with the Naval ROTC. In 1969 Smith would intercept ten more passes and be selected as an All-American.

A fellow NROTC member Lincoln Lippincott did a yeoman's job at defensive end on the 1968 squad and later found himself a shipmate on the *USS Saratoga* with his defensive coach's son, James R. O'Hora.

And as the 1968 season played out, the only question mark position, Neal Smith's old defenisve halfback spot, was capably filled by a committee comprising George Landis, Mike Smith and Terry Stump.

Ham in his first year blocked three punts, two of them helped to beat UCLA and Miami, and was in on sixty-five tackles, thirty-nine of them solos, recovered three fumbles and intercepted a pass.

Lincoln Lippincott III (Left) and James R. O'Hora (right) aboard *USS Saratoga* during 'Desert Storm.' (Photo courtesy of James O'Hora Sr.)

CHAPTER 12

The Triple Threat Tailback
He Can Run, Kick and Pass, but Sometimes He Shouldn't

Penn State started the 1968 season against service academy rival, Navy and it was readily apparent to the fans and Paterno, that Jim O'Hora's defense could be downright *offensive*. The Lion defense came up with four fumbles, five interceptions and a fifty-two yard punt return by Paul Johnson who cut in front of a surprised Denny Onkotz to field the punt and take it all the way for six points, as part of a 31-6 Penn State win.

The next week the defense held Kansas State to just twenty-eight yards rushing and sacked the K-State quarterbacks for minus twenty-five yards as the Lions beat the Wildcats 25-9. Campbell (one hundred and twelve yards in eighteen carries) and Pittman (one hundred and six yards on twenty-five carries) combined for two hundred and eighteen yards rushing. However, Campbell left the game with a shoulder separation and the team doctors predicted he'd be lost for two months.

After two home games the Lions went on the road to Morgantown, West Virginia where it took an Onkotz pass interception (his tenth in thirteen games) to make the final score 31-20. Besides Onkotz's big play the defense recovered a fumble and intercepted another pass.

The fourth game was a trip to the West Coast to meet the last team to beat this Nittany Lion squad. Last year the Golden Bruins beat State by virtue of a blocked punt and this year Jack Ham returned the favor with Jim Kates scooping up the ball and going thirty-six yards for a touchdown. The defense intercepted two passes, recovered a fumble, sacked UCLA quarterbacks for twenty-six yards in losses, along with the blocked punt for a rather easy 21-6 victory.

The next two outings showcased Ted Kwalick. At Boston College he caught five passes, including a diving thirty-one yarder for a touchdown in a 29-0 rout in which the Lion defense garnered four interceptions, recovered a fumble and again blocked a punt.

The next Saturday found the U.S. Military Academy visiting Penn State for only the fourth time in seventeen games between "The Black Knights of the Hudson" and the Nittany Lions. In this series Penn State won the first game in 1899, 6-0. Starting in 1955 the rivalry became an annual affair, still the Lions didn't win a second game until 1959 by this time Army had won six and tied two of the ten games played. The fourth quarter of the 1968 game saw Army poised to take the lead, if they could successfully execute an onside kick, as the Cadets had narrowed the score to 22-17. The onside kick was well executed and since Army had more players involved in the melee at mid-field than State, there was a better than 50-50 chance that the West Pointers would come out of the "scrum" with the ball. Seconds passed, which seemed like half minutes, as the vast majority of the spectators waited for the officials to unpile the players and determine who had the ball. On the east side of the stadium a fraction of the total crowd saw the ball exit the pile and then like an unraveling mystery story Ted Kwalick drew the attention of more and more spectators as he raced to the north end zone and when he reached the ten yard line everyone realized Ted Kwalick had the football and it was a Penn State touchdown. Army scored again but the final score was 28-24 in favor of State.

On November 9, 1968 Miami returned the Lion's visit to the Sunshine State last year, the game wherein all those sensational sophomores received their baptism under fire. Those defensive neophytes in 1967, were now battle-tested upperclassmen and they sent Miami packing in a come-from-behind 22-7 victory in which the defense intercepted three passes, recovered two fumbles, blocked a punt and limited the Hurricanes to thirty-two yards rushing. The Lions were now 7-0; 15-2-1 over the last eighteen games and an unbeaten 14-0-1 in the last fifteen.

Penn State next traveled to College Park, Maryland where the offense outdid their defensive compatriots by amassing four hundred and seventy five yards of total offense in a 57-13 triumph over the Terrapins. Kwalick grabbed five passes for fifty-six yards. The defense again intercepted two passes, snatched up two fumbles and blocked a punt. Bobby Campbell, who returned to action in the Army game, along with Charlie Pittman Gary Deuel, Joel Ramich, Don Abbey and Steve Smear (on an interception) all scored touchdowns. It was the most points yielded by a Maryland team since 1917.

The maturation of the Penn State offense continued as the Lions scored sixty-five points against Pitt, a total exceeded by only three opponents going back to 1890, when Pitt was known as WUP, the Western University of Pittsburgh. The Lions scored the *first ten times* they had the ball with Charlie Pittman doing the honors three times as State rolled up six hundred and eighteen yards in total offense while they held the Panthers to minus seventeen yards rushing. Ted Kwalick corralled five passes for one hundred and twenty-one yards, then early in the third period Paterno removed all the starters as Penn State registered a lop-sided 65-9 win.

December 7, 1968 Saturday afternoon Beaver Stadium

Originally this meeting between Syracuse's Saltine Warriors and State's Nittany Lions was scheduled for the third Saturday in October. In Central Pennsylvania, October days feature crisp mornings and moderate afternoon highs significantly cooler than September's 70° to 90° highs. These four or five Saturdays generally represent Pennsylvania's ideal football weather. To avid Penn State fans moving an October game to the first Saturday in December seemed almost sacrilegious, as well as risky from a weather standpoint.

Historically late season *November* football games at University Park can be uncomfortably cold. Sleet and snow are not unusual during this month which *precedes* December. Awareness of the above weather facts would explain why this was Penn State's first home game in December since State began playing football. Furthermore this game and the 1979 game against Pitt would be the only December games played in State College in a span of more than 110 years (1887 to the present).

When dawn "broke" on October 19, 1968 (the original game-day) there was no big orange ball in the east. In fact it was raining. The precipitation continued throughout the day ending only after 5 P.M. Contrastingly dawn arrived on December 7th clear, sunny and cold, but with no precipitation. Sitting on metal stadium benches with the temperatures around freezing doesn't bring to mind the adjective toasty. Nonetheless spectators can dress for the cold weather and be relatively comfortable. Rain on the other hand, if it falls with sufficient intensity, will circumvent virtually all spectator defenses. Thankfully, umbrellas are prohibited in Beaver Stadium. Umbrellas in use in the stands at a football game do two things: First they deflect the large majority of the falling precipitation away from the umbrella holder and onto the people in front, behind and to either side of the holder. Furthermore if everyone brings an umbrella and uses it, whose umbrella goes on top? Secondly umbrellas block the view of the fans behind the umbrella-holder. Persons who put up an umbrella when seated in the stands at a sporting event show no concern for the people around them.

As we arrived at Beaver Stadium this cold December Saturday, the author, his wife Marie and their guests, two Camp Hill football players prepared to leave the warmth of the car for the bitter cold outside. Once out of the car it was immediately apparent that we had one article too few of the requisite cold weather gear. Marie now realized that what she thought was her navy blue heavy coat was my black Borgana coat. The two young football players with their short jackets were inadequately dressed for the cold weather despite my advice given earlier in the week, thus they couldn't help. I volunteered to lend my coat to Marie and put the one blanket we had around myself. Marie vetoed any such move saying she would stay in the car and listen to the game on the radio, since it was her oversight.

When the three of us approached our seats, the Halls, Thomases and Galleys, people with whom we had been sitting for years, promptly asked if Marie was at home sick. When I explained what happened, there was an immediate George Bush-like response that " this shall not stand." A quick foray into the parking lot with our friends produced an assortment of ski jackets, blankets, even a fanny bag. A slight detour to our car where we rescued a tearful Marie who was listening to the pregame show and a prompt return to our seats where Marie was greeted by the applause of our game day neighbors, enabled us to sit down just before arising for the Star Spangled Banner. During the game well intentioned persons continued to pass items down to Marie until she was so warm she feared she would faint. Surreptitiously we re-routed some of the items to our two guests seated next to me, which they didn't refuse, and Marie got to see a December game where she said she was hotter than any September Penn State game she ever attended.

As for the game itself, this last game of the regular season was pitting a 9 and 0 Penn State team, ranked third in the country, against an unranked Syracuse team of invaders from the north (the mirror image of the N.C. State game the previous year when the third ranked Southern-based Wolfpack invaded State College.)

Syracuse had lost but three games this season, all of them on the road. There was a close 14-10 loss to Michigan State; however the other two losses were double-digit spankings by California 43-0 and West Virginia 23-6. Nonetheless a win over Penn State would give the Orange their tenth season, in the last eleven, with seven or more victories. From 1958 through 1967 the Lions and the Orangemen had met ten times and the New Yorkers had prevailed in seven of the ten games. Thus it might seem on a cursory glance that Ben Schwartzwalder had Penn State's number. But Ben was just one and one against JoePa and this Penn State squad had not tasted defeat since the third game of their 1967 season.

The Lions were led by two players who would receive All-American recognition at the end of this year (Onkotz and Kwalick). Mike Reid, Charlie Pittman, Neal Smith and Onkotz would be first team All -Americans in 1969 and Jack Ham would be similarly honored in 1970. Some very good football players like John Ebersole, Steve Smear and Jim Kates were never anointed as All-Americans. In a bit of irony Ebersole's eight year pro career equaled the total "Pro" careers of Reid (5 years), Pittman (2 years) Onkotz (1 year) and Smith (zero) combined.

Another player, Bob Campbell, was certainly gifted enough to have made someone's All-American team if injuries had not curtailed his playing time. Few players in Division I football are their team's "go to guy" at halfback, the team's punter (and a good one) and the team's punt return man. It was Bob Campbell's injury and the lack of success in replacing him as a return man that thrust Denny Onkotz into the punt returner role which Onkotz never relinquished until he graduated.

Apalachian, New York's, Bob Campbell was an on-again, off-again favorite of Paterno's. Campbell could elicit great praise from Paterno, "Bob compares favorably with Lenny Moore and Roger Kochman the two best running backs I've seen at Penn State, but Bob can do more things than either of them." Campbell however could also do some negative things, which he must have known would put him on the express elevator from the penthouse to the basement. The studious looking Campbell however seemed unable to keep from doing those things.

In his final home game at Penn State, New York native Bob Campbell (#23) was fittingly or ironically pitted against PSU's New York State archrival Syracuse University. Before the game was very old, Campbell had opposing coach Ben Schwartzwalder kicking the ground, throwing his hat and trying to stomp it as Ben watched Penn State shred his #2 ranked defense to the tune of 422 yards of total offense by game's end. Campbell set a PSU record with an 87 yard touchdown run from scrimmage in the second quarter. And *by halftime* he had 207 yards on just 14 carries, a record that stands to this day. Campbell scored again in the third quarter on a 19 yard touchdown run to give him a total of 239 yards gained rushing (plus 3 catches for 20 yards). Unfortunately that touchdown run put Campbell in Paterno's dog house Big Time! A place from which he would not emerge for almost a month and this punishment deprived him of the all-time Penn State single game rushing record. A record which he most certainly would have set had he not been "benched" with more than a quarter yet to play in the Syracuse game. While Paterno is genuinely concerned about running up the score on a defeated foe, if the press box, where the official statistics are kept, notices that a Penn State player is approaching a record they will alert the coaches upstairs who will in turn notify the coaches on the sideline of the situation and Paterno will often let the player return for a play or more to break the record then remove him for the rest of the game.

Campbell, on this sensational day would certainly have broken "Shorty" Miller's record of 250 yards gained in a single game set in 1912. Since the final score of the PSU-Syracuse game was only 30-12. Campbell might have gotten several carries as late as the fourth quarter. To find out how #23 ended up in the doghouse after he seemed to be headed for the record book penthouse let's go back to a replay of that touchdown run of

Campbell's.

The ball is sitting on the Syracuse 19 yard line at the north end of the stadium. The football is on the hash mark closer to the Syracuse bench and Coach Schwartzwalder is creeping up the sideline for a better view. Quarterback Chuck Burkhart takes the center snap and drops back as though to pass but during his retreat he slips the football to Campbell on Penn State's draw play and Campbell bursts through the drawn-in linemen and linebackers and once past them, #23 shifts into overdrive and glides into the Syracuse endzone. Touchdown Penn State, six points and 239 yards rushing for #23, punter and runner par excellence. Express elevator to the Penthouse Suite going up! But now our triple threat tailback reveals his other weapon, his passing arm. With decent form Bob heaves a nice spiral ¾ of the way up into the northwest corner of the stands. Express elevator to the basement going down! Exiled to the bench where the injured players and those who will not be playing sit, Campbell's yardage odometer rested on 239 yards rushing for the game, never more to move.

Paterno has never condoned excessive post-touchdown or quarterback-sack celebrations and throwing a football into the stands definitely falls under the heading of excessive celebration. The penalty for this crime is exile (to the bench). According to some reports Paterno also told Campbell he owed the university $33.00 for the football.

January 1, 1969 10:30 P.M. The Orange Bowl, Miami Florida

With the ball situated on the 50 yard line and 1:16 left in this Orange Bowl game, Kansas is leading Penn State 14-7. In the huddle Chuck Burkhart calls a pass play where tailback Bob Campbell recently returned to Paterno's good graces, is moved up into the slot or on the wing to get him into the defensive backfield as quickly as possible. Just before the huddle breaks, money-player Campbell says to quarterback Burkhart, "… just throw it as far as you can – I'll be there." Well, Chuckie did, and Bobby was. Penn State now had a first down on the Kansas 3 yard line, a 47 yard gain! There could be time for just three or, at most, four more plays. On first down Tom Cherry (FB) plunges into the line for one yard. Second down, Tom Cherry (FB) again goes into the line no gain. Third down still two yards to go. Joe sends the play in, a hand-off to Charlie Pittman off right tackle. The ball is snapped to quarterback Burkhart, Chuck gives the ball to Pittman who hits up into the line on the right side. But there's no give in the Kansas line, and suddenly a panic-stricken Pittman realizes he doesn't have the ball. How, he has no idea, he must have fumbled. Simultaneously there's a tremendous roar emanating from the Penn State side of the end-zone, something good has happened for

Penn State.

Without the knowledge of the PSU coaching staff or the other ten players on the Penn State team and completely unexpected by the Kansas team and their coaching staff, Chuck Burkhart has ad-libbed. Instead of giving the ball to the tailback Charlie Pittman going right, Burkhart put the ball on his hip and ran left into the end zone on what is called a "naked reverse," or "naked keeper," so called because the ball carrier probably feels naked having no one running interference for him.

The score is now Kansas 14, Penn State 13, and the moment of truth has arrived. Should Penn State go for the tie to keep their non-losing streak intact or go all out for two points and the win? A two point PAT is only successful about 1 in 3 times, while a one point kicked PAT is successful over 90% of the time. So kicking the PAT would have been the percentage "call" but gambling like he did last year in the Gator Bowl game against Florida, Paterno sends in the two point play. The call is a passing play, a fade pattern to Ted Kwalick, State's All-American tight-end in the right rear portion of the end zone. However from the snap it is obvious there are Kansas defenders everywhere. There is no room for Campbell and Kwalick, (who both ended up in the same corner of the end zone) to maneuver and Burkhart's throw is over their heads and out of the end zone. Spontaneously the Kansas players and fans begin their post-game celebration. But seconds later, what at first appeared to be some insignificant white debris in the end zone is identified as the white penalty handkerchief of Back Judge Foster Grosz, who informs the referee that Kansas had 12 men on the field. Penn State is now afforded a second try from the one yard line. This time Penn State goes to its money player again and Bob Campbell slices off left tackle and into the end zone to close out his collegiate career posting the two-point conversion, which gave State a 15-14, win.

Postscript – In the aftermath of the victory Joe supposedly asked the coaches in the press box why they didn't see the twelfth defender, what they were doing? Their responses according to one of Joe's banquet lines was "We were all cheering or praying just like everybody else."

CHAPTER 13

It Happened in the Fifth Quarter

Coming into the 1969 season the defense again was the stronger of the two platoons losing only one starter, defensive end, Frank Spaziani. In spring practice Paterno had tried some position changes along the offensive line in an attempt to plug three very large holes created by the graduation of Ted Kwalick (TE), Dave Bradley (OT) and Co-Captain John Kulka (OT), he even went to the defensive side of the ball to steal linebacker Pete Johnson for a trial at tight end.

Much to his discomfort, starters Mike Reid, Mike Smith and George Landis had permission to skip spring practice. Reid was on the track team while Landis and Smith were playing baseball. The absence of these three players plus the fact that nobody could seriously threaten Jack Ham and seniors Ebersole, Smear, Onkotz, Kates, Paul Johnson and Neal Smith's starting jobs, resulted in an uninspiring performance by the defense as a whole. Paterno and all the players knew that they would be a far superior and more cohesive unit come the fall. Thus the defensive players sensed there wasn't a lot of purpose in getting the spring practice first team defense meshing like a finely tuned engine when everyone knew a different unit would be starting when the season opened. But Paterno, as head coach, couldn't fall prey to this kind of thinking. Consequently he was frustrated with the lethargic play of the defense in the spring practices, though fully knowing what was going on. He was therefore quicker to yell at the defense and more than willing to be quoted in the media about his dissatisfaction with practice.

On offense besides the loss of Kwalick at tight end and tackles Dave Bradley and John Kulka, there were other shoes to fill such as spark plug Bobby Campbell and steady Tom Cherry. The return of Charlie Pittman (HB) and Don Abbey (FB) was a start and the rapid development of sophomores Lydell Mitchell and Franco Harris helped to fill the shoes of Bob Campbell and Tom Cherry. Mitchell adopted Campbell's uniform jersey so State again had a #23 outstanding tailback and Franco Harris would be the first of many Penn State fullbacks over the years who would be both big *and* quick.

Penn State opened the 1969 season with two easy wins 45-22 over Navy and 27-3 over Colorado. At Navy the groundskeeping crew, in an effort to counter State's team speed, has left the grass so high that even from the elevated stands fans could hardly see the tops of the player's shoes. Navy could not match State speed-wise, so the ground crew allowed the grass on the field to go uncut for the better part of two weeks to produce a "slow field." Against Navy, in spite of the high grass, Harris and Mitchell scored the first touchdowns of their three-year careers.

On September 27, 1969, Colorado came to town, for the first meeting ever between these schools, led by the Buffalo's much heralded quarterback, All-American candidate Bob Anderson. Anderson was held to four yards rushing in the game and the next week Coach Eddie Crowder moved Anderson to halfback. Following the conclusion of the Colorado game Coach Crowder kept Bob Anderson and a few other players at his side. Then, in the north end zone he put the remaining players through some drills and a work-out much to the amazement of the fans in the stands. Some thirty-eight years previously in 1931, a nearly opposite scenario was played out on New Beaver Field and while it was opposite to the Colorado scenario it had its similarities.

For Penn State's 1931 Homecoming Day, Pitt made its only football appearance in State College between 1902 and 1939, and Coach Jock Sutherland had been less than thrilled about the excursion into the hinterlands, beginning when the game was first scheduled as an away game. Pitt was at its high water mark from 1925 through 1938 while Penn State was at its nadir from the late 1920s to the 1940s due to the administration's decision to go "Simon Pure" (give no athletic scholarships). From 1925-1938 Pitt won 106 out of 134 games and their teams were invited to the Rose Bowl four times. However their lone success in four trips to the West Coast following their 1927, 1929, 1932 and 1936 seasons was a 21-0 triumph over Washington on January 1, 1937. During this period the Panthers had twenty-four All-Americans, including Joe Skladany, Bill Daddio and Marshall Goldberg who were selected twice.

The week before the Penn State game, Pitt played Notre Dame in the second game of an eight game series. And for the second year in a row Notre Dame beat the Panthers by the score of 35-19. Coach Sutherland felt some of his players had let down in the Notre Dame game and Jock didn't like losing even to the big teams on their schedule like Army, Nebraska, Carnegie Tech, Ohio State and Notre Dame so he decided to make a statement. In one shrewd maneuver Jock sent a very strong message to his starters and he definitely thumbed his nose at Penn State's football program and anyone who had had anything to do with scheduling this road game. Jock sensed that some of the stars on his team were looking ahead, even before the Notre Dame game, to showing off at Penn State, running up a big score and showing those hicks what a real football team looked like. They would show those farmer boys a real team, one different from the visiting teams Penn State fans had grown accustomed to seeing, such as Lebanon Valley, Marshall, Bucknell, Waynesburg, etc. In 1931 State lost to Waynesburg 7-0 while in 1929 and 1930 Pitt beat Waynesburg 53-0 and 52-0.

Jock's clever maneuver followed this script. He started an all second-string team. As they wore down the Penn State team, which had no more than a handful of players who could have been significant contributors on the Pitt team, he substituted the third string and then cleared the bench, except for the first string who did not play a down, in the 41-6 win.

But that's not the end of the story. After the game was over, Coach Sutherland brought his first team (remember this was one platoon football) out on the field or behind the stands, accounts vary. Here they went through signal drills showing off their high-stepping synchronized backfield to the "countrified" spectators.

The reader needs to understand two things to fully appreciate the situation. In 1931 teams did not always go into a huddle to call their plays. They sometimes lined up with seven men on the line of scrimmage and four players in the backfield. From this alignment the quarterback called the play. He called a series of numbers in order to disguise the play they were going to run. Since the defense could also hear the signals he certainly wasn't going to call signals by saying, "Halfback off tackle on two." Then the quarterback would shout out, "one, two, three, shift." The backfield men would then shift to the formation from which they were going to run the play — single wing, double wing or short punt formation etc.. This shift was designed to keep the defense guessing what the play would be, until the last moment. (For example the double wing was best used for passing and reverses but it was weak up the middle, while the single wing and the short punt formation were strong up the middle and on sweeps.) So hiding the formation to be used, was an advantage for the offense. In fact for a period of time it was legal to snap the football while all four backs were in motion. This proved to be too great an advantage for the offense and later rules led to the offense being restricted, as it is today, to just one man in motion at a time. The player in motion today must run parallel to the line of scrimmage or be angling backward. He may not be moving closer to the line of scrimmage prior to the snap of the ball, as had previously been allowed.

These signal drills were important, as we said, to hide the play to be run from the defense. They were showy, they were also "very cool" and all the backs played a part. In the actual plays the tailback, fullback and wingback got 99% of the carries before the T-formation arrived, but the poor old quarterback, who only blocked (the tailback was the passer), got his chance to shine here, since he called the signals and led the shifts, the others following his cue. In one platoon football when Jock put the offense on the field to run through signal drills he wasn't slighting the defense, the offensive players were the defensive players. After coming on stage and doing their chorus line number the Panthers exited stage right, after which they boarded their buses and returned to the Steel City.

There have been some versions of the above incident which reported that Bob Higgins put *his* team through a scrimmage as a punishment for the poor showing his team made. The author's source who was at the game assured me that the version just relayed to you is the correct version and a different source said that publicly embarrassing his outmatched players didn't sound like something Coach Higgins would do.

CHAPTER 14

What If?

N ow in their senior year, 1967's seven "sensational sophomores" were battle-seasoned, confident veterans and their careers were winding-down like a fairy-tale come true. There were now seven seniors and four juniors who had blended into a sophisticated unit which had more than twenty-five different defenses and coverages to confuse and thwart any opponent.

Now, three years of answering every challenge was drawing to an end. An end that was filled with achievements and honors, seven first-team All Americans, a glorious journey, yet it would prove to end on a bit of a deflating note. An end that would always bring with it a haunting question – what if?

The '69 season began with easy wins over Navy and Colorado, and State was still ranked #2 when they left State College for Manhattan, Kansas for a showdown with Kansas State. The Wildcats, led by quarterback and tailback standouts Lynn Dickey and Mack Herron were trailing PSU 17-0 in the fourth quarter. But Kansas State scored in the final stanza to cut the margin to 17-6 and then after Paterno had fielded a defensive team of reserves Lynn Dickey threw a 63 yard touchdown pass with fifteen seconds left in the game. After what appeared to the pollsters to be a squeaker of a win for PSU, 17-14, the Lions dropped three spots to number five in the polls.

A 20-0 shutout win over West Virginia was followed by a genuine squeaker of a victory at Syracuse. It took two second half touchdowns and in an ending similar to its 15-14 win over Kansas in the Orange Bowl, State converted a two point play for the win when a Syracuse infraction gave the Lions a second chance. Following this close call the Lions dropped to eighth place in the AP Poll.

The Lions then beat Ohio U. 42-3 and put Boston College away 38-16 as #34 Franco Harris scored three touchdowns and #35 Dennis Onkotz returned a punt 48 yards for a touchdown and they rode roughshod over Maryland 48-0 in the third last game of the season. The Lions now occupied the fifth spot in the AP poll.

Pitt provided State with a first half scare as the teams left the field at halftime tied 7-7. The Golden Panthers however did not get a first down in the entire second half as Onkotz set up one of Charlie Pittman's two touchdowns with a 71 yard punt return. Pittman was now nearing Pete

Mauthe's career scoring record of 171 points which had stood since 1912. Quarterback Burkhart was a big factor as he completed 13 of 21 passes for 178 yards, the biggest day of his career and the Lion's won going away 27-7. He, however, had yet to throw a touchdown pass in the 1969 season, a season which in an uncommon fashion didn't end with the Pitt game. State had an appointment with N.C. State set for November 29 on national TV at Raleigh, North Carolina. This would be the first meeting between the 'Pack and the Lions, since "The Stop." This time Penn State was ranked #3 in the country and North Carolina State was unranked.

The Penn State defense had N.C. State's number right from the start as the Lion defense of Reid, Smear, Ebersole, Johnson, Kates, Onkotz, Ham, Landis, Hull and the two Smiths held the Wolfpack to 21 yards before leaving the game in the fourth quarter. The final score was 33-8 as Chuck Burkhart hit Charlie Pittman for his first and only touchdown pass of the regular season when Charlie wrestled the ball away from a 'Pack defender.

The fantastic Penn State Nittany Lions had burst onto the national scene winning twenty-one consecutive games in two short years, and a season that had begun at the very end of August was now down to one last game. One last chance to wear the "home" blue jerseys and those distinctive white helmets which in 1969 featured the traditional single blue stripe and the blue number on each side matching the player's uniform number (the helmet numbers disappeared in the mid-1970's).

But, for all their playing success, something that happened off the playing field would haunt Penn Staters for fourteen years, continually raising the question, "What if?"

1969 Defensive Team (left to right, top to bottom) Paul Johnson, Neal Smith, Tim Horst, (standing in for George Landis), Jack Ham, Dennis Onkotz, Jim Kates, Mike Smith, Gary Hull, Steve Smear, Mike Reid, John Ebersole."(Photo courtesy of Dennis Onkotz)

CHAPTER 15

How Long? Forever!

The 1969 seniors had provided the leadership for two or more seasons, some letting their deeds speak louder than words, like Denny Onkotz, others mixing words and action. Sometimes a captain provided a wake-up call for a player who wasn't concentrating or putting forth the effort that was necessary, other times a pat on the back was needed. Just to cover all the bases, occasionally one captain got in the player's face regarding his perceived lack of effort, with the other captain later providing some positive words.

The seniors wanted to set the standard high for all the Nittany Lion teams to follow, and so far their game plan was on target. A loss in this last game, which would be on national television, was not an option, not even being carried from the battlefield on your shield in defeat would be acceptable. This was a very mature group of seniors taking a very mature approach to this last test. "Probably the most mature squad I have ever had," Paterno said at some point.

Some individuals, and some groups of individuals, like the seniors on this team, know inside how good they are and they don't need a lot of adulation and hoopla from outside sources to reassure them, but it's always nice to receive recognition. This Penn State team didn't get the national recognition it would have gotten in later years after Penn State football had a better track record.

State's 1969 team had started the year ranked second in the country probably because they finished in second place at the end of last year and the returning squad was virtually the same as the '68 team. However once the season started, the narrow three point 17-14 win over #20 Kansas State definitely "underwhelmed" (to borrow a word from legendary sportswriter "Red" Smith) the pollsters and State was replaced in the #2 spot by Texas.

However the jockeying for the #2, #3 etc., spots seemed to be of little import as last year's National Champion Ohio State was looking more and more like a repeat titleist in a landslide. The Buckeyes opened the year with two big intersectional wins, a 62-0 stomping of Texas Christian and a 41-14 win at Washington. There followed six consecutive wins over Michigan State, Minnesota, Illinois, Northwestern, Wisconsin and Purdue. In those games, in the order played, Ohio State scored 54, 34, 41, 35, 62 and 42 points. It was obviously going to be Ohio State's crown to win or lose. If they beat Michigan, which *Sports Illustrated* assured us was a lock, and then took the measure of their Rose Bowl foe, which almost assuredly would be Southern California, a team Ohio State beat last year 27-16, when USC had O. J. Simpson, they would be #1 in a cake walk.

From where might a challenge come? Penn State had no chance of meeting Ohio State head-on as the Buckeyes were Rose Bowl bound. In fact as was mentioned previously Penn State had stubbed its toe in two games early in it's schedule and Texas had taken advantage of those close wins and had passed State to move into second place.

The Longhorns had opened the 1969 season in fourth place one notch-below their third place standing at the end of 1968. Wins early in 1969 over unranked California 17-0, Texas Tech 49-7, Navy 56-17 and a big win over #8 Oklahoma 27-17, put them in second place and right on Ohio State's heels. What chance did the Longhorns have? One thing they had going for them was the unified voice of the Southwest Conference. If they could win the SWC crown and beat a quality opponent in the Cotton Bowl while Ohio State struggled against USC, maybe the Longhorns could "rope-in" the SWC and the Southeastern Conference votes. Here in 1969, the SEC had no one in their conference who appeared capable of finishing higher than #8 (Georgia, Mississippi and LSU) so there might be some SEC votes to be picked-up if Texas could at least make a run at Ohio State.

As the regular season came down to its final curtain the Nittany Lions were a lonely voice out in the wild and it appeared their fate, as far as being #1 was concerned, was out of their hands. The best they could hope for would be an impressive bowl game win and maybe a USC win over Ohio State in the Rose Bowl, and a Texas loss. Penn State could opt to play Texas in the Cotton Bowl but there were still coaches and ex-players around who hadn't forgotten the bad experience State had in 1947 and things hadn't improved by leaps and bounds in Texas, witness the fact that the Longhorns were still an all-white team in 1966. The assassination of President Kennedy in Dallas in 1963 and newspaper reports of ongoing racial strife also concerned some of the Afro-American players on the squad. From the perspective of these young men in their early twenties, racial strife aside and even if they didn't know that the average temperature in the Austin/Dallas area in January is forty-nine degrees, they did know that Miami, Florida, was beckoning again and chances were nine to one that the temperatures would be conducive to swimming, laying-out, working on the suntan, catching some rays etc. The author was single in 1967 and I know which of the two choices, Dallas or Miami, I would have opted for, in a heartbeat.

Looking at the choice between the Cotton Bowl in Dallas and the

Orange Bowl in Miami based on the weather, and considering the fact that in those days a bowl game was supposed to be a reward for a successful season, the decision would be a "no-brainer." Most of the administration and the well-heeled alumni who would accompany the team on an alumni junket, probably favored Miami. There might have been some who reasoned the team should play out its hand and face Texas in order to finish as high as possible and then **IF** Ohio State should lose, the Lions could claim the Grand Prize. Certainly, the odds against State as an independent, holding the winning lottery stub were staggering but the odds are much worse when you commit the cardinal sin and don't even buy a ticket.

The squad didn't have the luxury of waiting until every team had completed its schedule; a decision had to be made. The choices were fun in the sun or horseback riding and a guided tour of JFK's ill-fated route past the Texas School Book Depository. Meanwhile Orange Bowl representatives were calling the proposed Penn State vs. Missouri pairing, a dream match-up between State's immovable defense and Mizzou's unstoppable offense.

The Missouri Tigers after a 19-17 win over Air Force manhandled virtually every team on their schedule including Big Ten rivals Illinois (37-6), and Michigan at Ann Arbor (40-17). In the Big Eight, Mizzou beat Kansas State 41-38, exactly the same three point margin of victory that Penn State registered, they got by Nebraska 17-7, but were upset by Colorado 31-24 before blowing out Oklahoma 44-10, Iowa State 40-13 and Kansas 69-21 to end up as Big Eight Co-champions, when Nebraska beat Colorado 20-7.

The 69-21 win over Kansas was the setting for one of Kansas head coach Pepper Rodgers' better "one-liners." Thinking that Missouri's coach Dan Devine was running up the score more than was necessary Pepper said, "I thought Dan was piling it on so I flashed him the peace sign from across the field, but Dan only gave me half in return."

The Tigers were led on offense by Quarterback Terry McMillen, who had an absolutely torrid season, running back Joe Moore and wingback/ flanker Jon Staggers. The following rushing and passing records still stood at Missouri going into the 1997 season:

Joe Moore
1. Most carries in one season – 260 (1969)
2. Average yards/carry in a career (for runners with at least 300 carries) 5.2 yards

Terry McMillen

1. Most yards gained per attempt in a season (minimum of 150 attempts), 8.4 yards (1969)
2. Most yards gained per completion in a season, 18.7 yards (1969)
3. Most touchdown passes in a game, 4 (1969), record since tied by three others
4. Most touchdown passes in a season, 18 (1969)
5. Most 300 yard passing games in a season, 3 (1969), record since tied by one other player.
6. Most touchdowns scored and passed for in a game, 6 (1969)
7. Most touchdowns scored and passed for in a season, 25 (1969)
8. Total offense in a season, 2157 yards (1969), third highest.

Right out of the gate if you compared the two head coaches who were going to face each other New Year's Day night you couldn't be criticized if you liked Dan Devine's track record better than Paterno's.

At the age of twenty-eight Dan Devine was the head coach at Arizona State. At the same time, 1955, Joe Paterno was twenty-nine, in his sixth year as a very junior coach on Rip Engle's staff. At the start of the 1958 season Devine had been hired away from ASU, where he had led the Sun Devils to their first undefeated season and a three year 27-3-1 record. Paterno was still an assistant coach at Penn State, years removed from being a head coach.

In 1964 Dan was thirty-seven years of age and had a career won-lost-tied record of 71-18-5 for a winning percentage of .782. He would already be the head coach at Notre Dame except for the fact that Father Joyce, Notre Dame's Vice-President in charge of Athletics wouldn't ask the University of Missouri to release Dan from the contract he had with MU. At the end of the 1963 season Joe was thirty-seven years old and still an assistant coach although he had been approached for a head coaching post at Yale University. Now in 1969 Dan Devine was in his fifteenth year as a head coach and Joe was in his fourth.

However the author recalls some old adage about "staying the course." Paterno became the head coach at Penn State in 1966. In 1976 he was still the head coach, and in 1986, and in 1996, and going into the 1999 season he was still at Penn State and the University's oldest employee in terms of years of service (fifty years).

Devine's stays with the Packers and Notre Dame, his next two head coaching posts, were much more tempestuous than his first two. In his second year at Green Bay, Devine took the Packers to a 10-4 season and a Central Division title, but in his third year when misfortune befell his team he suddenly became very unpopular. And when the Notre Dame head coaching position was offered in his fourth year at Green Bay, he left before the rumors that said he was going to be fired, came true. At Notre Dame, for some reason, Devine never did hit it off with the Notre Dame alumni, the subway alumni or a lot of the players who played for him. Father Joyce speaking about Coach Devine said, "I would have hired him before Ara (Parseghian), but Devine wasn't available." Making Devine a bit more desirable was the fact that he was a Catholic. Undoubtedly Notre Dame's most successful coach was Knute Rockne, one of the next most successful coaches was Ara Parseghian. Neither Rockne nor Parseghian was a Catholic. While he was at Notre Dame, Devine won fifty-three games in just six years but his success was overshadowed by his failure to win over the players and the alumni, an uphill battle occasioned by the fact that he succeeded Ara. In fact Dan never got his due until Gerry Faust became head coach. The worse Faust did, the better Devine looked in retrospect. Devine was 53-16-1 in his six years. Faust was 30-26-1 over five years and his best season was 7-5. Devine's *worst* season was 7-4.

When Penn State chose the Orange Bowl and the challenge of stopping #6 Missouri's high powered offense, most Penn Staters, who would be sitting home watching the game, thought State should have chosen the Cotton Bowl, even though it would only prove who had the second best team in the country. Non-Penn Staters took the opportunity to engage in a bit of Penn State bashing since State opted to challenge #6 Missouri instead of #2 Texas. The adjective "shame" was dusted-off and hurled at the Penn State team.

The aforementioned adjective reminds the author of a classic Winston Churchill quotation. The quotation referred back to the *triumphant* return of England's Prime Minister Neville Chamberlain following a meeting with Adolf Hitler shortly before the out break of WW II . Germany had occupied land that rightfully belonged to Czechoslovakia, Austria as well as an area known as the Sudetenland. At the meeting with Chamberlain, Hitler, basically said, "If you let me keep what I have already taken, I'll sign a peace treaty that I won't take any more." Hitler had already proven that his word meant nothing, but Chamberlain chose to disregard that.

Upon his return from meeting with Hitler, newspapers everywhere carried a front-page picture of the Prime Minister emerging from an airplane with a sheaf of papers held high aloft in his left hand proclaiming, "We have assured peace in our time." This peace which lasted only months was achieved by selling out Czechoslovakia, Austria etc., and in so doing Poland was also sacrificed.

In a "Blitzkreig" (lightning war) Hitler overran Poland in September 1939. Now France and Great Britain could retreat no farther so they were forced to declare war on Germany and World War II was underway. When reminded of Chamberlain's rosy prediction, Sir Winston said, "They had a choice between war and shame. They chose shame. But war was what they got."

There is not meant to be *any* comparison by the author between far-reaching international decisions, which can result in World War, and the majority decision of a bunch of twenty-year-olds to go to the beach for the holidays. But why was Penn State so darn sure that they couldn't be #1? The existing mentality was clearly revealed in the November 24, 1969 issue of *Sports Illustrated* magazine.

At the conclusion of the 1968 season the Top Four teams were: in order, Ohio State, Penn State, Texas and Southern California. Now with the 1969 season almost over, *Sports Illustrated* was saying the best bowl game come January 1 would be Ohio State's offense vs. Ohio State's defense. Dan Jenkins was proclaiming "when Texas and Penn State are struggling to present their cases (we could) play us the game of the decade, which we would call the 'Woody Bowl.' We'll take that Ohio State offense...and we'll take the Ohio State defense... it might be the only way this dazed collegiate world of 1969 would ever find what (sic) the best team in the country is." But a funny thing happened on the way to the Rose Bowl. A Michigan team, which didn't read *Sports Illustrated* or possibly they read it, and recollecting the SI jinx, let it go in one ear and out the other, upped and beat the Buckeyes 24-12 and went to the Rose Bowl in their stead. And Ohio State was "Home for the Holidays."

All Penn State could do now was to put their best foot forward and try to keep McMillen, Moore and Staggers from lighting up the scoreboard like a pinball machine and then hope for the best. As a measure of Missouri's firepower consider that Penn State had scored 27 points again Kansas State; Mizzou had tallied 41. Missouri had also scored 40 against Michigan, the team that held #1, at the time, Ohio State to 12 points.

January 1, 1970 Thursday evening The Orange Bowl Miami, Florida

Terry McMillen, who had thrown for 300 yards three times this season and tallied six touchdowns in one game besides passing for four touchdowns in a contest, was held to 117 yards passing and threw five interceptions, in the January 1, 1970 Orange Bowl game against Penn State. Coach Devine even tried his other senior quarterback Ron McBride but the Lions intercepted him twice. All in all the Penn State defense garnered nine turnovers. Two of four Missouri fumbles were recovered by the Lions, while Onkotz, Neal Smith and George Landis deploying their vast array of defenses, gathered in two interceptions each and Gary Hull got one The seven interceptions were an all time record for any major bowl.

According to the 1970 Missouri University media guide, Dan Devine exclaimed after the game that Penn State's defense was far better than any other defense his team had seen. The Penn State defense held Missouri without a touchdown in a 10-3 win, a game in which the Tigers had the ball nineteen times, punted six times registered a field goal and turned the ball over nine times.

In the locker room after the game a newspaperman drew up a stool next to Denny Onkotz who had just played his last game of football in a Penn State uniform. Fishing for a line or some kind of story this sportswriter had come to the least likely source of some juicy quotes; our player of few words. Trying to raise an issue or put some words in Denny's mouth he said, "With all their speed and their high scoring offense how much longer do you think you could have held them without a touchdown?" True to form, Denny answered with a minimum of words when he said, "Forever" and then proceeded to take a shower, since the players were done dousing Governor Shafer.

Postscript: President Nixon stuck his nose into the college football situation when he said he would attend the Texas–Arkansas SWC final regular season game and proclaim the winning team the National Champions. Paterno, a Republican, screamed like a banshee and had two excellent parting shots. Regarding Nixon's self-appointed position as the highest authority in the land when it came to selecting the #1 team, Paterno asked, "How come he knows so much about college football and yet he knew so little about Watergate?"

When Nixon realized the fuss he had created he tried to placate Penn State by announcing he would present Penn State with a trophy acknowledging their outstanding non-losing streak. Neither Paterno, the team, nor the administration would accept the trophy and Paterno closed the issue when he declined to except an award for something they already possessed – the nation's longest non-losing streak.

After just four years at the helm, Paterno had a head coaching record of 35 wins 7 losses and 1 tie and his teams had tied a record set in 1922. His 1967-1969 squads had teed it up in thirty consecutive games and they hadn't lost one. Starting with the fourth game in the 1967 season and carrying through the Orange Bowl game against Missouri, January 1, 1970, the Lions had chalked-up seven wins and a tie and then back-to-back unbeaten, untied eleven-game seasons.

This accomplishment achieved by Joe's second, third and fourth squads exactly tied the record of Hugo Bezdek's second, third, fourth and fifth squads, 1919 –1922, that won six consecutive games in 1919, won seven and tied two in 1920, won 8 and tied two in 1921 and then won the first six games in 1922 for a total of twenty-nine games without a loss. Bezdek's 1922 Lions, in a game marking the debut of the Nittany Lion mascot, tied Syracuse in the thirtieth game and then faced Navy in game number thirty-one. In that thirty-first game, played in the rain at Griffith Field in Washington, D.C., on the first *Friday* in November, Navy torpedoed the Nittany Lions 14-0, snapping their streak.

Seeking his thirty-first consecutive non-losing game forty-eight years later, Joe Paterno's 1970 season-opening opponent would be…who else? Navy.

Hugo Bedzek and Joe Paterno's first four seasons as head coaches had some remarkable similarities such as the following:

1. Both coaches had unspectacular first seasons
2. Both coaches strung together thirty games without a loss starting in their second season.
3. Coach Paterno's record in his first four season's was 35 wins, 7 losses, 1 tie for a winning percentage of .82558. Coach Bezdek's record in his first four seasons was 23 wins, 3 losses, 5 ties for a winning percentage of .82258.

Penn State's 1969 Linebacker corps - Mike Smith, Dennis Onkotz, Jim Kates and Jack Ham. (Photo courtesy of Dennis Onkotz)

CHAPTER 16

Beaver Stadium Facts, a Brief History and a Story or Two

A. Football field locations

1887 through 1892 - Games were played on the lawn in front of Old Main.

1893 through 1908 - Beaver Field with a five hundred seat grandstand was inaugurated on November 6, 1893. This center-of-campus location was used through the 1908 season.

1909 through 1959 - New Beaver Field, located in the northwest corner of the campus near The Nittany Lion Inn, was home to Penn State football until 1960.

1960 through ? - Beaver Stadium is now located in the northeast corner of the campus.

B. Record crowds and selected homecoming games.

Year	Capacity	Record Attendance	Opponent	Score
1901	500	1,500 *	Dickinson	12-0
1912	3,500	4,000	W & J	30-0
1914	6,500	5,500	Michigan State	3-6
1920	8,000	6,000	Dartmouth**	14-7
1920		9,000	Nebraska	20-0
1922	12,000	17,000	Carnegie Tech	10-0
1923		20,000	Navy ***	21-3
1925		20,000	Notre Dame***	0-0
1939	22,000	20,000	Pitt	10-0
1947		20,313	West Virginia	21-14
1948		24,579	Michigan State***	14-14
1951		30,321	Michigan State***	21-32
1954		32,384	West Virginia***	14-19
1959	33,000	34,000	Syracuse	18-20
1960	46,284	37,715	West Virginia	34-13
1961		38,437	Navy	20-10
1961		45,306	Army	6-10
1962		48,356	Syracuse***	20-19

Year	Attendance	Opponent	Score
1963		49,383 Army	7-10
1964		50,144 Pitt	28-0
1968	48,284		
1969	48,344	51,402 Colorado	27-3
1969		52,713 West Virginia***	20-0
1972	57,538	58,065 Iowa	14-10
1972		60,465 Syracuse***	17-0
1974	57,723		
1975		61,325 Stanford	34-14
1976	60,203	61,645 Stanford	15-12
1976		62,503 Ohio State	7-12
1977		62,554 Houston	31-14
1978	76,639	77,154 Rutgers	26-10
1978		77,704 SMU	26-21
1978		77,827 Syracuse***	45-15
1978		78,019 Maryland	27-3
1980	83,770	78,926 Colgate	54-10
1980		84,585 Nebraska	7-21
1981		85,012 West Virginia	30-7
1981		85,133 Alabama	16-31
1982		85,304 Nebraska	27-24
1982		85,522 Pitt	19-10
1983		85,614 Alabama	34-28
1983		86,309 West Virginia***	41-23
1985	83,370****		
1991	93,716	94,000 Cincinnati	81-0
1991		96,304 BYU	33-7
1991		96,445 West Virginia	51-6
1991		96,672 Notre Dame	35-13
1992		96,704 Miami	14-17
1993	93,967	96,719 Michigan	13-21
1994		97,079 Ohio State***	63-14
1997		97,115 Pitt	34-17
1997		97,282 Ohio State	31-27
1997		97,498 Michigan	8-34

Footnote: * First recorded home attendance
            ** First football game at Penn State on Homecoming Week-
               end
           *** Homecoming
          **** Four new entry ramps reduced seating capacity to 83,370.

C. Miscellaneous Additional Facts:

1. Beaver Stadium – Home of the Penn State Nittany Lion football team was named in honor of General James Beaver a native of Bellefonte who served Penn State and the Commonwealth of Pennsylvania as President of the Board of Trustees and Governor respectively. He was a benefactor of Penn State athletics.

2. Beaver Stadium with a capacity of 93,967 as of 1999 was the fourth largest stadium in the country and the third largest one on-campus.

   1. University of Michigan   107,000
   2. University of Tennessee   102,544
   3. Rose Bowl Pasadena, California 102,083
   4. Penn State University   93,967
   5. Ohio State University   91,470

3. Penn State average home attendance:

   1960   31,003
   1970   48,211
   1980   83,045
   1990   85,204
   1991   95,846
   1997   97,086

4. The 1975 season was the last season when Penn State played before more fans away from home than at home.

5. Permanent lights were installed in 1984.

6. The 1991 seating capacity increase was achieved by adding an upper deck to the north end of the stadium.

7. A similar south-end addition was completed in 2001.

Following the conclusion of the 1959 season, New Beaver Field was replaced by Beaver Stadium located one and a half miles to the east beyond "Ag Hill." The appellation "Ag Hill" understandably was affixed to this portion of the campus since it was the domain of the School of Agriculture replete with its buildings, barns, pastures and animals.

The stadium was moved to the edge of campus to allow for additional expansion beyond the 53% seating increase incorporated into the move to the new site. Out there, in the rural aspect of the northeastern portion of campus, it was expected there would be virtually unlimited room for parking, stadium expansion, access roads, etc.

The concept of unlimited brings to mind a story George Preston Marshall, longtime owner of the Washington Redskins, told on himself. To improve the fortunes of his franchise he hired George Allen as head coach and general manager. Eight months after hiring Allen, owner Marshall said, "When I hired George I gave him an unlimited expense account and he has already exceeded it." Likewise the constraints of stadium expansion vs. the need for more parking along with access and egress roads around Beaver Stadium are already raising the question how long will it be until unlimited proves to be insufficient?

Following the 1959 season the New Beaver Field all-steel structure was dismantled, marked and the 700 pieces were then transported to their new Beaver Stadium location. There, the pieces were re-assembled under a new steel superstructure creating a stadium 70 rows high on each side from goal line to goal line. Steel men, at that time, said it was the largest all-steel stadium in the country and probably in the world. Doubling the number of rows from 35 to 70 between the goal lines increased the seating capacity from 30,000 to 46,000, which based on past crowds appeared to be adequate. After nine years in its new location, (1960-1968) and with the addition of some 2000 seats, Beaver Stadium's top ten crowds in those nine years ranged from 46,429 to 50,144 with two crowds over 50,000.

Following Penn State's 11-0-0 seasons in 1968 and 1969, Beaver Stadium's top ten now showed four crowds over 50,000. The addition of 9194 more seats in 1972 boosted the capacity to 57,538. In just two seasons seven of the top ten crowds exceeded the newly increased seating capacity, seats were being gobbled up as fast as they became available.

The increased attendance was a good news/bad news scenario. The increased revenue enabled Penn State football to be self-sufficient and beyond that, fund most of PSU's twenty-eight other varsity sports. However crowds of 60,000, made getting to Penn State on a Saturday morning and returning Saturday evening a headache. And hotel rooms in State College on football weekends were virtually non-existent. There was also an inherent problem with the stadium, which worsened with every expansion.

The original steel stands at New Beaver Field rose from first row to last at a very gradual angle. Since the number of rows at that time didn't exceed thirty-five, the people at the top were not *much* farther removed from the playing field than the spectators in the front row. However by the time the stands, continuing at this gradual ascent, rose to be 110 rows high, with a track and the bench area between the sidelines and the stands, the people in the upper reaches of the east and west stands would be a long way from the action on the field.

In 1959, had a decision been made to build a brand new stadium from the ground up, I'm sure the architects and engineers being free to think "outside of the box" would have questioned the negative factor of having a quarter-mile oval track between the playing field and the stands. The track location positioned the very first row of spectators that much farther away from the action for a football game, while providing seating for 46,000 people at a track meet which might draw 1500 fans. Even more importantly, the engineers would certainly have increased the angle of ascent when designing the stands. They might also have chosen to enclose the area under the stands to keep the frigid winds out during the later half of the season or even to have set the stadium down into the ground to insulate the field and the stands. Had they investigated the latter idea they might have located the stadium elsewhere which would have made future stadium expansion much less costly. However in an effort to save money the planners were not given the freedom to build a new stadium from square one. They were told, relocate this steel structure at the place we've chosen on the east side of campus, and increase the seating capacity by 50%. Thinking of the engineering involved in dismantling a stadium and to all intents and purposes constructing a new stadium just like the old one, recalls a true story.

On my first trip to San Francisco I visited Dr. Ed Foster, a classmate of mine at The University of Pennsylvania Graduate School of Medicine, and one of the nicest persons one could hope to know. As we were driving across the Golden Gate Bridge I repeated something my dad had told me about the bridge. The New Jersey Zinc Co., for whom my father worked, made zinc oxide, a vital component of quality paint products. Many years prior to my conversation with Ed, my dad informed me there were crews of painters who had the on-going job of painting the San Francisco Bridges. The life of the paint, under the prevailing conditions in the San Francisco area was such that by the time they finished the last bridge it was time to start anew on bridge number one. (Imagine if you were one of those retired painters and someone asked you, "What did you do, all of your working years?" and you replied, "Well, I painted the Oakland Bay Bridge and the Golden Gate Bridge three times then I retired.") Ed didn't dispute what my dad had said, but continuing to fix his gaze on the wet roadway ahead, he volunteered the following information:

"You know Ken, when they built this bridge they put enough steel and concrete into it to build another bridge just like it."

Well, I had heard of the San Andreas Fault and California earthquakes so the first thing that zipped through my mind was the safety factor. Wow! They built a bridge twice as strong as it needed to be, to make it safe even during an earthquake or something of that nature.

I can't tell you what my thought process was second by second or even minute by minute but I imagine it went something like this, "If not it took away the duplicate amount of concrete the double amount of steel etc., you could build another bridge like this and you would still have enough concrete and steel leftover to have a bridge like ... Whoa, wait just a minute, there would still be enough steel and concrete to build a bridge like this." I looked at Ed, and from the side I could see that sly grin of his toying with the corner of his mouth and I knew I had been had. Certainly, if you had enough of whatever it took to build this bridge, you would have enough materials to build another bridge just like this one. Of course you could do it – you just did it. As I told you, Ed is a peach of a guy, so he soothed my ego by telling me I caught on faster than most people did, in fact, he said he actually had to tell the "joke" to some people.

After five consecutive years in which all the home game tickets were sold out prior to the season opener in September (sometimes as early as June), the university bit the bullet and did a major make-over and enlargement of Beaver Stadium at the end of the 1977 season.

At first it was hoped that the track could be removed and the field could be lowered. This would make it possible to add seats, goal line to goal line, on both sides without tacking 30 to 40 rows on to the top of the stadium all of which would be even farther away from the playing field.

However, the bad news surfaced very quickly when the test borings showed the stadium to be sitting on solid limestone. Only blasting on a large scale would make it possible to lower the area between the east and west stands. There was a definite possibility that the extensive blasting would foster a slew of legal suits. Also, the fact that the State College area has a limited water supply, any action which might affect the water table and/or underground aquifers would be unacceptable.

Considering that it would be very costly, dollar-wise and politically, to abandon the present site of Beaver Stadium so soon and relocate the stadium elsewhere, the University had to decide on the next best approach. If it didn't make sense to move the stadium or to abandon it and the field couldn't be lowered at the present site, the next *easiest* approach seemed to be to *raise the entire stadium*. With such a daunting challenge facing the contractors, work was underway just days after the end of the 1977 season. The stadium was again dismantled, this time it was cut into sections and inch by inch each section was hydraulically raised *8 ½ feet*. The track, which encircled the field, was removed (and a new track constructed south of Beaver Stadium). The track removal and the raising of the steel superstructure made room for 20 rows of concrete stands in front of and below the existing steel stands. The temporary bleachers in the south end were replaced by 40 rows of concrete stands and the configuration of Beaver Stadium was changed from a horseshoe to a bowl.

The weather that winter wasn't favorable and by the spring of 1978 there was a possibility the stadium would not be ready for the beginning of the season. When this became apparent, Joe Paterno threw himself into the battle. No, he didn't pick up a shovel and pitch in physically, but he did stop by the stadium on almost a daily basis to give the workers in each phase of the work a pep talk to keep them psyched-up. With an all-out effort from the blue collar and the white collar workers and an attitude worthy of Penn State's blue and white teams, the construction team battled the elements and the clock and never gave up. Fortunately State opened the 1978 season September 1, at Temple. Given this additional time the necessary final touches were completed Friday, September 8, the afternoon before the Rutgers game.

On Saturday an area was set aside in the southwest stands for those construction workers who wished to attend the game. When Penn State took the field to warm-up, Coach Paterno made a point of going to the workers and shaking as many hands as possible. The construction team had overcome the opposition and the clock and scored a victory.

The home game against Rutgers drew a crowd of 77,154 which immediately surpassed the announced capacity of 76,639. But then so did all seven home games, with the Maryland gate topping 78,000. By the end of the 1978 season all seven 1978 home games ranked in the top ten of the Beaver Stadium all-time largest crowds.

With Penn State slated to begin playing a Big Ten schedule in 1993, Beaver Stadium was again expanded prior to the 1991 season by adding a seventy degree-arc upper deck over the north endzone seats. This, raised Beaver Stadium's seating capacity to more than 93,600. Penn State was now a member of the 90,000 club and as of August 2000, fifty-four of State's last fifty-five home games had been played in front of crowds of 90,000 or more.

Only five Universities in the whole country play their home games in a stadium with a constant seating capacity of more than 90,000 (Michigan, Tennessee, UCLA, Penn State, and Ohio State). Three of the above schools belong to the Big Ten, probably a "selling point" when Penn State was invited to join the Big Ten in the early 1990s. Four of these five stadia are on-campus. The Rose Bowl in Pasadena, California, which UCLA has used as their home field since 1982 is located miles from the suburban Los Angeles UCLA campus. Despite its lofty capacity UCLA averaged 60,000 fans per home game in only two seasons 1980 through 1995.

Prior to 1982, UCLA and USC both played their home games in the Coliseum. Interestingly when they met they both listed the game as a home game. USC continues to play its home games in the Coliseum which has a listed capacity for college football of 92,000. However for virtually every opponent other than UCLA and Notre Dame, 24,000 seats are covered and the capacity is reduced to 68,000.

Consider how times have changed since the 1940s. USC, drew home crowds of 102,050 and 104,953 against UCLA and Notre Dame in 1947 and 100,571 against Notre Dame in 1948. In those same two years Penn State's three biggest home crowds were Michigan State (24,579) in 1948 and West Virginia (20,313 and 17,814) in 1947 and 1948 respectively. More recently in the 1990s USC had only five home crowds of more than 90,000 in the six years, 1990-95, with the top attendance being 93,458. As of the end of the 1999 season 51 of Penn State's last 55 home games drew gates of 94,000 or more (with 36 crowds of more than 96,000) and an average home game attendance of 95,655 over the last nine years. With the conclusion of the 2000 season the Nittany Lions marked their tenth consecutive year in the Top Four in NCAA home attendance.

While we are on the subject of Beaver Stadium I will answer a question you may have asked yourself, if you have ever attended a Penn State home game. At Beaver Stadium the west side of the stadium which includes the press box is the home team side. Visitors are seated in the northeast corner of the stadium while Penn State students hold forth from the southeast portion of the stands to the southwest corner. Thus Penn State season ticket holders occupy all the seats from the southwest corner to the northeast corner including both decks of the north stands. The overflow Penn State season ticket holders also occupy several sections on the east side from the 30 yard line to the 30 yard line. Therefore if the majority of the home fans are on the west side why is the Penn State bench on the east side? When you consider that the Penn State bench has to squint, looking into the sun it's even harder to fathom. Here is one explanation as set forth by Coach Jim O'Hora.

In the '30s and '40s when State played its home games on New Beaver Field, games were rarely sold out. The westside seats were occupied by Penn State season ticket holders, faculty, alumni, etc. and the students sat in the east stands. In those days a large percentage of the student body attended the football games since there was little else in the way of entertainment or distractions and the students clamored for their Nittany Lion team to be on the eastside where they were, so their vocal support could be more effective. It would seem that the westside season ticket holders sat on their hands even then. As a concession to the students the home team bench was relocated to the east side and it remains there to this day.

We have discussed Beaver Stadium, its origin, its growth, its configuration etc., we would certainly be remiss if we didn't discuss Penn State's football field. If there were no field there'd be no reason to have a stadium. Penn State's football field is probably the best football field in the country and is used for only six to eight games per year. The all grass field is slightly crowned so it drains well and is softer and deemed to be safer than artificial surfaces.

Joe Paterno and his staff recognize that a superior football program must have players with a blend of speed, mental and physical toughness and size. Therefore they want a field that is kind to the legs, knees etc., of their players and caters to their speedy skill people.

Here's how the grounds crew readies the field for a Saturday game. Starting Monday with the long range forecast and by mid-week with frequent up-dates, the grounds keepers at Beaver Stadium are ready for whatever Mother Nature might throw at them. The most important factor week-in and week-out is precipitation. How much will State College, specifically Beaver Stadium, get before game time Saturday? What kind of precipitation will it be sleet, drizzle, driving rain, snow, will it be followed by windy conditions? When will the precipitation arrive, Thursday, Friday, Saturday morning? Of extreme importance, will the field have to be covered to prevent it from becoming too wet or to protect it from snow? And through the growing season as long as the grass on the field needs to be mowed, the mowing crew must know the amount of sunshine expected, whether the field might have to be covered and when will they be able to get on the field to mow. Based on the temperature, the humidity, the number of minutes of sunshine, Joe wants them to cut the field so the grass will be 1¼ inches high at game time, a height which favors Penn State's team speed.

Penn State defeats North Carolina State, 61-6 at New Beaver Field with its wooden grandstands (1929).

A Penn State football game, circa 1938, in New Beaver Field with steel grandstands. Note: non-participating players seated on benches, with coaches occupying folding chairs at midfield, between the benches (Photo courtesy of Ruth Toretti)

Beaver Stadium after expansion to 83,770 capacity. Permanent lights were added

Beaver Stadium following 1991 expansion. Capacity 93,967. Top Crowd - November 9, 1997, 97,498.

View of new triple deck, south end of Beaver Stadium. New capacity - 106,537 Crowd, for September 1, 2001 Miami game, 109,313.

Drawing of latest expansion of Beaver Stadium - 2001. (Courtesy of Penn State)

Statue and wall outside Beaver Stadium commemorating Joe Paterno's 324th win as Penn State's head coach. (Unveiled November 2, 2001.)

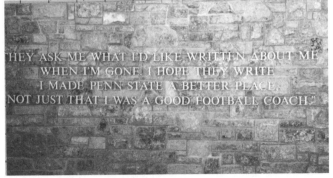

CHAPTER 17

Joe's Time for the Forty

In Chapter 12 we noted that football teams from the late 1960s through the 90s had twenty-two starters, eleven on offense, eleven on defense and since in the '60s, and '70s teams like Notre Dame, Alabama, Oklahoma, USC, etc., were generally three deep at most positions they never had to rebuild; all they had to do was reload, according to the sports pundits. But here going into the 1970 season Penn State truly had to rebuild. Returning on defense from the Orange Bowl team that dominated Missouri were only four-players—Jack Ham, George Landis, Mike Smith and Gary Hull. The players that graduated, Neal Smith, Pete and Paul Johnson, Ebersole, Reid, Smear, Kates, Onkotz had each played three years and most had started all of those years. There were no seasoned back-ups, as these warriors had gone all the way in every game for three years until the issue was decided. Now roughly 60 to 70% of that defense and seven-eighths of the crème de la crème of the defense was suddenly gone.

To further complicate matters there were some gaping holes on offense. Along the line co-captain, and a team leader, tackle Tom Jackson was gone and guard Charlie Zapiec had been moved to linebacker to plug one of the two gaps left by the departing Kates and Onkotz. In the backfield only Lydell Mitchell and Franco Harris were returning. Pittman and Abbey, who had teamed with Mitchell and Harris to give Paterno two tailback/ fullback tandems had graduated and it would be another year until Cappelletti and Donchez would appear on the scene. But the biggest offensive hole of all at least for the entire first half of the 1970 season, became apparent at a position where most on-lookers least expected it.

Gone was the much maligned quarterback, Chuck Burkhart, who threw only *one* touchdown pass his entire senior year. If records are kept in the category of fewest touchdown passes in a season it would be hard to beat Penn State's 1969 statistics; the Lions as mentioned threw one touchdown pass *and* their opponents threw *three*. Shades of the early 1900s, a total of four touchdown passes in an eleven game season by both the Lions and their opponents.

Despite the number of three-year starters lost, many Penn State fans expected the winning to continue unabated. Even road games at Colorado and Army didn't concern the faithful, with their rose-tinted glasses.

Only Wisconsin was expected to be a serious threat. After all hadn't State dispatched Navy, Colorado, West Virginia, Maryland, Ohio University, Pitt etc., very handily last year with no passing attack? Imagine what they would do with a quarterback who could throw more than one touchdown pass in a year.

Most Lion fans thought new quarterbacks, Mike Cooper, State's first African-American quarterback and rifle-armed Bob Parsons, would erase all memories of Burkhart after just a game or two. After all Cooper had quarterbacked William Penn High School in Harrisburg and their traditional rival John Harris' quarterback had been Jimmy Jones. Jones was so proficient that head coach John McKay came all the way from the West Coast to recruit Jimmy for Southern California, and some Penn Staters thought Cooper might be a reasonable facsimile. Jones ended up seventh all-time, through 1999, at the University of Southern California in passing and total offense. And despite playing on a team with two-time All-American running back Clarence Davis and college Hall of Fame receiver Lynn Swann, Jones, a three year letterman led USC in total offense in 1970 and '71. Didn't this mean that Mike Cooper would produce similar "numbers" at Penn State? Unfortunately the answer to that question was "No" and to add further insult, good-looking Bob Parson's arm was more shotgun than rifle. It turned out his right leg not his right arm was his "meal ticket" in the NFL were he played tight end and punted for Chicago Bears for twelve years. But it took a few games before the quarterback situation was resolved.

The opening game against Navy seemed to rubber-stamp all of the optimistic reports. The Lions scored 28 points in the second quarter and State won 55-7. Mike Cooper ran for one touchdown and passed for two (one more than Burkhart had all last year), Mitchell and Harris each scored and Parsons threw for one touchdown. This win established a new record for Penn State, thirty-one consecutive games without a loss and it was set against the same opponent, Navy, that denied the Lions in 1922. It was now time to visit Colorado's Folsom Stadium for what was expected to be a "Rocky Mountain High."

Disaster didn't wait until Saturday to strike. High over the Midwest Friday night, Charlie Zapiec became very ill and was taken to the hospital as soon as the Penn State charter landed. The next day, after the Lions were rudely pushed all over the field, one might wonder who was hurting more, Zapiec, who had to remain hospitalized when the team returned, having undergone an emergency appendectomy, or a Penn State team which had to leave the field on the short end of a 41-13 score, and return home, losers for the first time since its 1967 opener.

The Lions lost at Wisconsin, beat Boston College, where they intercepted seven passes (a repeat of the Missouri game), and they then readied themselves for a Homecoming game with Syracuse.

The Orangemen entered the game with just one win and three losses. In the three losses Syracuse was outscored by a total of seventy-one points. This looked like a good chance for the Lions to get well against a team which appeared to be foundering. A football season however can take some unexpected directional changes. Here was Syracuse, a one and three team playing against a two and two team, yet for sixty minutes the one and three team looked more like a three and one team and the two and two team could have been zero and four for all the offense and defense they showed in that game. Cooper and Parsons and their fellow backs turned the ball over to Syracuse repeatedly and when Syracuse had the ball they just ran, ran, ran. Fullback Marty Januszkiewicz (Jan-ess-kev-itch) carried the ball thirty-six times, the fourth-most carries of all time for a Syracuse back and Penn State went down to a 24-7 defeat that looked and felt like 35-0.

To the credit of the coaching staff they recognized this team did not need a tune-up or new tires, it needed a new driver and they chose the right one. Sophomore quarterback John Hufnagel started in the Army game and with his roll-out run-pass options and an emphasis on utilizing Harris and Mitchell lugging the leather, the offense cut down on the number of turnovers, especially interceptions and the Lions closed out the season with five consecutive wins, to finish seven and three. Hufnagel threw three interceptions in five games while Cooper and Parsons alternating at quarterback had thrown eleven in their five games. The Lions scored between thirty-two and forty-two points in each of the last five games, with "Huffy" at the helm, whereas after the Navy game the Cooper/Parsons-led Lions had averaged only sixteen points per game..

In many ways this was the end of an era, a short era but nonetheless a period of five years, where the first and last years were inauspicious, yet Penn State set a school record for consecutive non-losing games, won 32 lost 10 and tied 1 for a .756 winning percentage, had eight All-Americans and were ranked 10th, 2nd, 2nd and 18th in the nation in 1967-70.

Following this seven win, three loss 1970 season, Penn State did not play in a bowl game marking their only absence 1967-1983. The Lions were "Home for the Holidays" also in 1966, 1984 and 1988 which made a grand total of four years without a post season bowl game in Paterno's thirty-four years as Penn State's head coach (through 1999).

After his first five years as the head coach at Penn State, Paterno had registered forty-two wins in just fifty-three games. The following table is a comparison of the four Penn State head coaches who won forty or more games in their career and the number of seasons they required to reach the forty win mark.

Paterno reached 40 wins sooner than Engle, Higgins and Bezdek because he won a higher percentage of his games and he had three 11 game seasons. Engle and Higgins had only one 10 game season and Higgins had some seven game seasons. Bezdek had one 4 game season and only one year with 11 games.

| | | | | Through 2000 Season | |
| | | | | Career | Career |
Coaches	Seasons	Wins	Winning Pct.	Wins	Pct.
Paterno	5	42	.802	322	.780
Engle	7	41	.664	104	.679
Higgins	11	40	.489	91	.607
Bezdek	7	41	.738	65	.665

Despite the fact that this book started with Joe Paterno coaching Penn State to a victory over N.C. State, it isn't true that JoePa has been the head coach at State since the game of football was invented. There have been other coaches. It is however amazingly true that Paterno has coached (as an assistant and as the head coach) in *more than half of all the football games Penn State has ever played,* beginning in 1887.

A gathering of Penn State Halfbacks - Lenny Moore has some humorous words of wisdom for running backs Lydell Mitchell and Charlie Pittman who followed in his illustrious foot steps.

Fullback Franco Harris, 3 year letterman for the Nittany Lions and thirteen year NFL veteran; also part of famous Harris - Mitchell Penn State Backfield Tandem.

II

FIFTY YEARS, ONLY SIX HEAD COACHES

CHAPTER 18

Coaches Come and Go

As we mentioned before, in the early days of football it was common for one of the players to play and coach. Thus it was seventeen seasons (1904) until Penn State had its first full-time head coach, in the person of Tom Fennell. In 1909 Penn State tapped Bill Hollenbeck to succeed Fennell who had posted a 33-17-1 record in five seasons. Hollenbeck had just completed his senior year at Penn where he was the team captain and an All-American. At the age of twenty-three he became the youngest collegiate head coach in the nation.

Coach Hollenbeck's first season as a head coach was considered a definite success by everyone, as the Lions went undefeated (5-0-2) with ties against powerful Penn and the Carlisle Indians as the only blemishes on their record. In a surprise move, after just one season at Penn State, Coach Hollenbeck pulled up stakes and moved on to the University of Missouri for the 1910 season. Here, he replaced William Roper as head coach, after Roper had led the Tigers to their first and only undefeated season, and a Missouri Valley Conference Championship.

When Bill Hollenbeck left Penn State, he hand picked his brother Dr. Jack Hollenbeck, a graduate of The University of Pennsylvania and the University of Pennsylvania School of Dentistry, to replace him as head coach for just one year. Coach Bill promised he would return after one year at The University of Missouri. Despite his assurances, many people thought Bill Hollenbeck's move and his promise to return in one year were merely a deception to procure the Penn State head coaching job for his brother. But true to his word Coach Hollenbeck did return after just one year at Missouri. Like Bill Hollenbeck, Coach Roper had also been the head coach at Missouri for just a year but Hollenbeck and Roper weren't unique in their quick exits at Missouri University. From 1896 – 1923 Missouri had fifteen different head coaches with six staying just one year and only one head coach lasting as long as four years.

A modern day football fan looking back at Coach Hollenbeck's one year record at Missouri, might be puzzled when examining the scores of three games played that season, representing a win, a loss and a tie. The scores were 5-0, 5-6 and 5-5 respectively. The scores make much more sense when you realize that a touchdown was valued at just five points from 1898-1911, while a point-after touchdown stayed consistent at one point from 1898-1957. A field goal was worth five points originally, declined to four points in 1904, and in 1909 it dropped to three points where it has remained ever since. Touchdowns have been valued at six points since 1912.

Upon his return to State College, Coach Bill Hollenbeck continued his winning ways in 1911 with another marvelous undefeated season tainted only by a tie with Navy.

The following season, 1912, was probably Coach Hollenbeck's and Penn State's greatest year ever, if we consider the following:

1. Team record 8-0-0
2. Points scored, 285 in eight games, an average of 25.6 points per game
3. Points allowed, six in eight games, an average of 0.75 points per game
4. Scores of six noteworthy games:
   a. Washington & Jefferson   30-0
   b. Cornell   29-6
   c. Penn   14-0
   d. Villanova   71-0
   e. Ohio State   37-0
   f. Pitt   38-0

Penn State's chance to leave an unsurpassable legacy was thwarted when Cornell scored six points in a 29-6 loss to Penn State. Those six points were the only points scored on Penn State that year and those points deprived State of a very singular honor; being able at the end of the season to put those four little "u's" behind their record, which stand for unbeaten, untied and unscored upon.

Hollenbeck's 1909 team was tied twice, as mentioned before, and in those two ties surrendered a total of eleven points, the only points tallied against the Lions in that season. The 1911 team gave up six points to Penn, nine points to Colgate and the only game they didn't win was a 0-0 tie with Navy. Thus after three full seasons Coach Bill Hollenbeck was undefeated as a Penn State head coach, had racked-up twenty-one wins (while yielding just 32 points) and three ties in 24 games as he posted a winning percentage of .938. In *his* first three seasons Joe Paterno had a winning percentage of .766 and his charges had strung together nineteen consecutive non-losing games.

The 1913 Penn State football season began the same as the two previous ones. Bill Hollenbeck was at the helm, and his team was undefeated after two games. It appeared that the Nittany Lions were going to make it four consecutive years without a loss under head coach Bill Hollenbeck.

Perennial power Carnegie Tech had been routed 49-0 and Gettysburg had been vanquished 16-0. In twenty-six games to-date only five teams had scored on State. No one had scored in double figures; nine points by Colgate and eight points by the Carlisle Indians were the high water marks for the opposition.

One can only try to imagine what the team, the student body and the Penn State fans were thinking when the Lions traveled to Western Pennsylvania for an October 18, showdown against Washington and Jefferson, the third game of the 1913 campaign. What we do know is that Washington and Jefferson hung a 17-0 defeat on the Lions. While that loss must have been deflating, everyone knows that no team can remain unbeaten forever. Unfortunately the schedule wasn't going to get any easier as the next two games were at Harvard and Penn. The Lions were shut out in both games 29-0 and 17-0 respectively.

Finally there was a home game. The first meeting ever between Penn State and Notre Dame. This 1913 undefeated, Jesse Harper–coached Notre Dame squad was captained by Knute Rockne the man who would replace Jesse Harper as head coach in 1918. The Fighting Irish featured Rockne, who played end, and their quarterback Gus Dorais who was one of the early forward passing quarterbacks; the forward pass having been legalized in 1906.

Today, Rockne at 5' 8", 165 lbs., would be the size of a high school wide-out, not a tight end/defense end. But as a 1913 lineman he was bigger than his quarterback Gus Dorais who was 5' 7", 145 lbs. The biggest offensive linemen on the Irish team ranged between 180 and 190 pounds. Shorty Miller, the Penn State back from Harrisburg, Pennsylvania, whose record Bob Campbell almost broke, reputedly weighed 135 pounds. The Irish took the measure of the light and speedy Lions 14-7 in another big game for Penn State which was played in the rain.

State now faced Navy, then Pittsburgh on the road. The Middies tagged another defeat on the Lions 10-0 and finally the Lions scored for only the second time in six straight games, losing 7-6 to Pittsburgh as they closed out their season with their sixth consecutive loss, six games in which they scored a grand total of thirteen points.

A weak schedule enabled State to start the 1914 season, with four shut-outs, 13-0, 22-0, 13-0 and 30-0 over Westminster, Muhlenberg, Gettysburg and Ursinus respectively. But after those four home games the Lion's season ended with four of the last five games away from home. The first a 13-13 tie at Harvard in front of 22,000 fans, could almost be considered a victory, and a win at Lafayette 17-0 *was* a victory. However three straight season-ending losses to Lehigh, Michigan State and Pitt marked the end of Bill Hollenbeck's reign.

The next year 1915, saw Penn State with a new head coach. Dick Harlow who later was Rip Engle's mentor at Western Maryland, had played one year under each of the Hollenbecks and here in 1915 he became the first Penn State graduate to be the head football coach at his alma mater. Harlow's 1915, 1916 and 1917 teams posted records of seven and two, eight and two, and five and four respectively, giving Philadelphia-born Harlow a twenty and eight tally for his stay at State. Harlow also coached at Colgate and Harvard and was named to the Helms Foundation College Football Hall of Fame. With World War I thinning out rosters and curtailing schedules, Coach Harlow departed for the military service and Penn State went west to bring in an accredited football coach with a proven record. They found this head football coach in the dugout of the Pittsburgh Pirates' National League baseball team in the person of Hugo Bezdek.

The players weren't in place as yet because of the war. And next year's schedule would show but four games, however the curtain was ready to rise on an exciting, exasperating, exhilarating, frustrating, successful, disappointing twelve year span of Penn State football known as the Bezdek Era.

CHAPTER 19

The Bezdek Era Begins

To some extent he was a victim of his own early success but his cantankerous ways, his need to be in the spotlight and his passion for power probably would have brought him down even if he had never lost a game, much less losing nine and winning just once in twelve meetings with Pitt. Hugo Bezdek, Penn State's tenth football coach, and fifth full-time head coach was a hard-nosed tough disciplinarian born in Prague, Czechoslovakia. Prior to spending time on the University of Chicago football staff under the legendary Amos Alonzo Stagg, he was an All-American football and baseball player there. From Chicago, Bezdek moved to the University of Arkansas and in its football team's fifteenth year of existence he led the 1909 squad to an undefeated season. At a post-season rally Bezdek was credited with referring to his team as "a wild bunch of Razorbacks" and the epithet used to this day, quickly gained wide–spread acceptance.

Bezdek then became head coach of The University of Oregon Webfoots and there he coached his charges to a 14-0 win over Penn's Red and the Blue in the 1917 Rose Bowl game. Oregon's teams are now known as the Ducks because sportswriters are constantly searching for shorter team names. Actually the label Webfoots referred to the transplanted Massachusetts fishermen in the area and had nothing to do with ducks.

Then in 1918, Bezdek reversed directions. Having moved ever westward from Prague to Chicago to Arkansas to Oregon, he now moved to the East Coast, where he performed a unique balancing act. In 1918 and 1919 he was both the manager of the major league Pittsburgh Pirates' baseball team and the head coach of the Penn State football team.

World War I enabled Bezdek to accomplish this unique feat. In 1918 the major league baseball season was reduced from 154 games to 125 and the World Series was moved up, meanwhile the college football season was also curtailed and Penn State played only four football games that year, all of them in November. In 1919, Penn State played eight games all in the months of October and November and since the Pirates were not involved in the World Series there again was no real conflict. However in 1920 the Penn State season began in September and Bezdek because of the significant conflict in being a baseball manager and a football head coach, resigned his Pittsburgh managerial position and became the full-time head coach of Penn State's Nittany Lions. Bezdek left the major league baseball field despite the fact that he had taken the Pirates from eighth place where they finished in 1917 to consecutive fourth place finishes in 1918 and 1919. After he left Pittsburgh, the Philadelphia Phillies made a generous offer in an attempt to snare him as *their* manager. Penn State students lobbying against his belated acceptance of the Phillies offer carried signs on campus and on College Avenue imploring, "Don't You Go, Hugo." What clinched Bezdek's decision to stay we don't know but a look at the football talent on hand for 1920 and 1921 could have had only a positive effect.

As previously mentioned Bezdek's 1918 team played an abbreviated season of just four games. The Lions tied Wissahickon Barracks 6-6 in the first game and then lost to Rutgers and Pitt while beating Lehigh 7-6, the seven points being the most State scored that season. However they did manage to score in every game.

At the conclusion of World War I several Penn State players returned to State College to finish their education and to continue their football careers, a scenario that would be repeated after World War II. Among the returning veterans were a few future first team All-Americans who would be instrumental in getting Penn State's second extended non-losing streak off and running. Three of these players "Red" Griffiths, Charley Way and Glenn Killinger had their college football days interrupted in 1918 and/or 1919, but achieved All-American status upon their return. A fourth player, Bob Higgins was unique in the way his career evolved. He was an All-American in 1915 while earning four letters 1914-1917. He then returned to State in 1919 where he lettered for the fifth time and was an All-American for the second time, four years after he was first selected.

The Bezdek era rocketed off of the launching pad in 1919 and with booster stages in 1920 and 1921, Bezdek's football success at Penn State peaked in 1921 with an eight win season. After this, "Bez's" fourth season, he would never again win more than six games in a year and four of his subsequent eight teams would lose four or more games in a season.

In Bezdek's eleventh season, his 1928 team actually had a losing record, only Penn State's second since 1900, with the exception of the 1918 four game schedule. Prior to 1928 the most recent losing season was recorded in the next-to-last year of another Penn State head coach who had a meteoric rise to fame, the boy wonder Bill Hollenbeck. One year after the 1928, 3-5-1 losing season, Hugo Bezdek was replaced as head coach by Bob Higgins following the 1929 season. Bezdek continued to serve as athletic director until 1936.

Comparison of careers:

Hollenbeck			Bezdek		
First three years	21-0-3	.938	First four years	23-3-5	.823
Last two years	7-9-1	.441	Last two years	9-8-1	.528
Career	28-9-4	.732	Career	65-30-11	.665

CHAPTER 20

The Class of 1924 Arrives

George L. Werley, Class of 1919 at S. S. Palmer High School in Palmerton, Pennsylvania arrived in State College, Pennsylvania on an overcast day in September of 1920. Approximately three years and nine months later on Tuesday, June 11, 1924, after five days of graduation activities he would receive his Bachelor of Science degree in Industrial Chemistry and graduate with 515 classmates as The Pennsylvania State College's Class of 1924.

Born Friday, September 13, 1901, he was the oldest son of Granville and Libby Bachman Werley, both of whom left high school, years before graduation, to work on their respective family farms. Granville's father died in 1890 when Granville was fourteen and as the eldest child of six he left school immediately and became the man of the house. With the help of his mother who took care of the finances he was responsible for the survival and the well-being of his brothers, sisters and Mother. Later he would leave the farm, marry and begin a family.

When George graduated from high school he had an eight year old brother and his parents were expecting a child in October. (A sister, born in 1914 died three days before her third birthday, a victim of the influenza epidemic.) With young children at home it would not be possible for George's parents to pay his college tuition and incidentals even if he earned his room and board. This meant George had to postpone entering college for one year while he built up a nest egg.

George worked for the New Jersey Zinc Co. for fourteen months where his pay was twenty-nine cents an hour. His personal time book shows that he began work on July 1, 1919. From then until his last day September 9, 1920, George averaged approximately 9 ½ hours worked per day and twenty-six work days per month. He finished up in a flurry, working 73 ½ hours in seven days at the beginning of September to bring his total hours worked to 3428 ¾ hours and his total earnings for fourteen months to almost one thousand dollars. He was now financially able to enter Pennsylvania State College.

Today a freshman arriving on main campus at Penn State has probably visited the campus several times, and has been in contact with the university on numerous occasions regarding residence and roommate assignments, classes, dining hall and menu choices, etc. Things were different eighty years ago.

Even in 1920 some of the circumstances surrounding George's arrival in State College didn't conform with the majority of the new students arriving on campus. Difference number one, prior to this September day George had never been in State College, Pennsylvania, nor had he ever seen Old Main or any portion of the Penn State campus. The second circumstance that set him apart from most of his other incoming classmates was the fact the he still didn't have a place to stay that night.

Like many in-coming students from Northeastern Pennsylvania, George arrived in Bellefonte via the Pennsylvania Railroad. From there it was necessary to bus to State College using Johnston's Motor Bus. The two suitcases George carried and the trunk he checked at the bus depot in State College, were all the worldly belongings he had brought with him besides the clothing he was wearing. Walking along College Avenue he correctly identified it to be the main street east and west, so he decided to move his canvass a block or two to the south, where the real estate appeared to be mostly residential. With a purpose, George went from front door to front door. The questions he asked over and over were twofold: Would they take a roomer and could the roomer perform some tasks to earn his room and board? Block after block if the answer to the first question wasn't, "No," then that was the answer to the second question. After hours of fruitless bell ringing, knocking and querying a woman answered the front door at 125 Gill Street and replied as to how she might be agreeable to such an arrangement. To discuss the matter she invited George into the sitting room where he set down his suitcases and the woman began her interrogation. The widowed woman informed George that she rented out two floors of her home, providing room and board for ten male boarders as well as meals for another four who lived in the neighborhood.

It was now approaching suppertime and the scent of food and the sound of chairs moving on a wooden floor became increasingly more apparent in the sitting room. George and his landlady, Mrs. Oberly came to terms regarding his duties which included helping with dinner meals and cleaning the entire house weekly. When Mrs. Oberly asked, George stated he would like to begin his stay that day.

She thereupon showed him to the room he would be sharing with another boarder and pointed out the bathroom where he could wash up before joining the others at the dinner table.

A quick round of introductions left George with the impression that the other boarders were a reasonably friendly group. When the room turned silent, George bowed his head to pray and in his prayers he thought of his parents and his brothers Clayton and Ernest and pictured them at their kitchen table. He realized his day had been so busy that until now he hadn't had time to miss the folks at home. But here at the dinner table he wondered wistfully when he might see them again. Certainly Thanksgiving would be the earliest, but it would more likely be Christmas.

Picture of a Johnston's Bus Lines vehicle that could have brought freshman George Werley or Jim O'Hora to State College from Bellefonte.

CHAPTER 21

And the Streak Goes On

In the early days of football, a college varsity squad generally consisted of thirteen or fourteen players. The 1920 Penn State team numbered thirteen and showed a typical spread of youthful exuberance (two sophomores), five seasoned, experienced players (juniors) and six veteran, "been there, done that" seniors who weren't easily ruffled. And on this team many of the seniors first lettered in 1916 or 1917, making them very senior seniors.

The two sophomores, center "Newsh" Bentz, who would be, the team captain in his senior year, and end Ross "Squeaks" Hufford had the necessary talent to letter and start for three years, which both of them did (until Bentz ran afoul of Bezdek before the 1923 Rose Bowl Game). The juniors Stan McCollum, Ray Baer, and Joe Lightner were solid dependable players, while fullback/linebacker George Snell, a captain in his senior year, was an extremely tough and physical player. The fifth, Glenn Killinger, was one of Penn State's all-time greats.

A three year letterman in basketball, football and baseball, Killinger played professional baseball and football and coached all three sports on the college level for many years. On the football field he was a proficient passer and he possessed an ideal combination of evasive and straight-ahead power running. Besides all this, when "Killy" was on the field the other players looked to him as they would a coach.

The six seniors were end George Brown, tackle Clarence Beck, who later played professional football with the Pottsville Maroons, Captain Harold "Bill" Hess, guard and punter, and three All-Americans; guard "Red" Griffiths (1st team All –American, 1920) scat- back Charley Way, (1st team, All –American, 1920) and running back Henry "Hinkey" Haines (2nd team All –American, 1920) who later played quarterback for the New York Football Giants and was a member of the 1923 World Champion New York Yankees baseball team.

This squad was probably the most talent-laden of the four teams Penn State "fielded" while the author's father was a student at State, additionally it was probably the most colorful, as we shall see. The backfield had so much talent ("Hinkey" Haines, "Killy" Killinger, George Snell, Charley Way, Joe Lightner) that the captain, Harold "Bill" Hess, in his senior year had to switch from fullback to guard to get adequate playing time. All but Snell would be All-Americans. Snell, the captain of the 1921 club was deprived of his chance at All-American status when he became ill in his senior year and appeared in just half of that season's games, none of them at the end of the season when he could have impressed the voters.

Often the terms, *most talented, greatest potential*, etc., are associated with individuals or teams that are talented and have potential, but never put it all together and thus they fail to deliver what they promised.

Jerome "Dizzy" Dean, National League Hall of Fame pitcher, defined potential most succinctly when he said, "Potential means you ain't done it yet." On one occasion Dean, a major league baseball announcer at the time, received a highly critical letter from a high school English teacher branding him as a poor example for his teenage listeners, specifically his description of a player sliding into third base, when he said, "He slud into third." Dean, reading the letter over the air, replied to his youthful audience, "Don't be like me, you kids stay in school, and listen to your teachers, they'll teach you readin' and writin'. You listen to me and I'll learn you baseball."

But the 1920 Penn State football team more than lived up to its billing. Only a letdown at Lehigh where they had to settle for a come-from-behind 7-7 tie, and the 0-0 game against Pitt, blemished an otherwise outstanding season. Wins in those two games would have given the 1920 squad a nine-win season, a feat which no Penn State team achieved until 1947.

But let us start with the September Saturday when George Werley saw his first college football game.

September 25, 1920   New Beaver Field, State College, Pennsylvania

Freshman George Werley was part of a crowd of roughly 2,500 spectators who viewed an inauspicious season opener, a 27-7 victory over Muhlenberg. Ironically George had traveled 150 miles to Penn State to see the Lions beat a school that was located a mere twenty miles from his hometown. Nevertheless it was the first game of football he had ever seen and he was enthused, impressed and hooked on football right from the start. Penn State's Nittany Lions were now on a six game roll having won five straight games to close out the 1919 season; after a 19-13 loss at Dartmouth on October 18th.

In their second game of the 1920 season, the second of five consecutive home games, the Lions escaped with a narrow 13-0 victory over Gettysburg. At this juncture the 1920 team certainly had not been impressive, but they really hadn't been challenged either. (Having seen only two football games in his life, George didn't realize that the handful of basic plays the Lions were using weren't the complete repertoire of a good college team.) Bezdek was hammering on the basics and not tipping his hand by showing more than a few power running plays.

Two of the 1920 team's stars were, as we said, first team All-Americans, "Red" Griffiths and Charley Way. The two of them captured young freshman George Werley's imagination and no one else ever topped them in his mind. (We all know how lasting first impressions are.) In the Muhlenberg and Gettysburg games, Coach Bezdek kept Way "under wraps" giving him just a handful of carries, knowing full well what his capabilities were. George's other favorite, "Red" Griffiths, had lettered at center under Dick Harlow in 1917, however he was now playing guard and he definitely was one of the team leaders.

Charley Way, with his long gainers, was a game breaker, as many of his runs went for touchdowns. On those plays Way broke into the open and in ten seconds or less he was in the end zone and State had six points. Consequently one great run by Way for a touchdown would normally relegate him to the bench until Penn State went on offense again since Bezdek used Way only for spot duty both on offense and defense, deeming him to be undersized. Way at 5' 7" 145 pounds was only an inch shorter than "Hinkey" Haines and fifteen pounds lighter than Glenn Killinger, and those two played virtually every minute of every game, but Bezdek liked to pull the strings where his teams were concerned thus leaving no doubt as to who was in charge.

Griffiths however played defense as well as offense since this was one platoon football, therefore he had more opportunities to shine – and he and his red hair did. On defense Griffiths was generally in the middle of the action and since the team might be on defense for several three, even four-down series, his time in the spot light comprised many more plays than Way's six to ten carries per game. Griffiths' exploits might be evident play after play and could build to a crescendo on third or fourth down when the defense needed to stop the other team from making a first down or scoring. Additionally he had a unique way of rallying the crowd and thrusting himself into the limelight which he utilized when Penn State was in trouble and the game appeared to be on the line. George Werley thought he first saw Griffiths use his signature way of stirring up the crowd in the 1920 Dartmouth game, which would be the first of more than eighty football games played on Homecoming Weekend.

Scatback Charley Way, All-American in 1920.

ALL-AMERICANS

Bob Higgins, E, 1919
Percy W. (Red) Griffiths,
  G, 1920
Charley Way, HB, 1920
Glenn Killinger, HB, 1921
Harry (Light Horse) Wilson,
  HB, 1923
Joe Bedenk, G, 1923

*ABOVE: Head coach Hugo Bezdek
led the Nittany Lions to their first
Rose Bowl.*

k (far left) and Charlie Way took on foes at New

Coach Hugo Bezdek and All-American guard, "Red" Griffiths.

CHAPTER 22

The First Homecoming Game

During the week prior to the Dartmouth game, tension and school spirit built day by day. In the 1920s and '30s Penn State freshmen, George Werley included, were required to wear a green dink similar to a skull cap, when outdoors and to know the items in their freshman handbook. If requested by an upperclassmen, a freshman had to sing or recite Penn State's fight songs and/or the alma mater. Also along "Hello Walk" a freshman had to say hello to every upperclassman coming in the opposite direction and tip his dink. "Hello Walk" is still physically present. On Penn State's main campus it runs in a northeasterly direction toward Old Main. It branches off from the more easterly of the two parallel walks, which traverse the distance from College Avenue at Allen Street to the Pattee-Paterno Library Building.

Until World War II freshmen customs were a significant part of the fall semester as far as incoming students and their initiation into campus life were concerned. While freshman customs could last until mid-semester or the Christmas break, in the 1920s, customs ended early if a freshman team could win a tug-of-war against a team of sophomores.

Freshman customs were suspended during World War II and never resumed as post-war incoming freshmen classes included numerous ex-GIs many of whom were older than most members of the juniors and senior classes. As you'd expect, twenty-four to thirty-year-old servicemen who had put their lives on the line for their country and had taken orders from NCOs and officers were not about to take any guff from a nineteen-year-old sophomore or even a twenty-two-year-old senior. In fact they were not reluctant to question or challenge a professor if they disagreed with an answer or a grade.

The Saturday, October 9th game with the Dartmouth Indians, as they were known in those days, put Penn State squarely at a cross road. In the last nine years, State had played Harvard three times, Dartmouth two times, Cornell twice and Penn six times and all they had to show for those thirteen encounters were four wins over Penn and two over Cornell and a tie with Harvard. State had to prove it could beat an Ivy team, other than Cornell, not just come close, if they expected to enhance their football reputation. (Penn wasn't considered a full-fledged Ivy League school until they joined Columbia, Cornell, Brown, Harvard, Princeton, Dartmouth and Yale in 1954 as charter members of an official Ivy League.)

In the October game, Dartmouth jumped out to a 7-0 lead and State responded to deadlock the game going into the second half. As the momentum of the contest went back and forth the Lions fortunes seemed to be waning and they appeared headed for a loss in this inaugural Homecoming Game. As the outlook grew bleaker, State needed a stop like another Lion defense would provide forty-seven years later against N.C. State.

Then it happened! During a break in the action, "Red" Griffiths left the Penn State side of the ball and raced toward the Penn State bench. What could be the problem? Was Penn State's best defender hurt? If he was, how could he run so fast?

As Griffiths approached the bench at top speed, he had already unbuckled his helmet chin strap and just as he turned to head back to the action he hurled his helmet in the direction of the bench. This was done with such disdain for the helmet that it is hard to describe. It was as though the "stupid" helmet was at fault for interposing itself between Griffiths and the opposing players and interfering with the blow he was trying to deliver. Already on his way back to the line of scrimmage, his bright red hair flowing in the breeze, his verbal challenge to the opposing team announced his approach as he dared the offenders to try to run through him. The fans having been incited to a frenzy, then proceeded to yell even louder than they had been doing prior to "Red's" trip to the sideline. George Werley never lost this mental picture of Percy "Red" Griffiths with his bright red hair flowing in the breeze as he rallied the fans and his teammates. Penn Staters are fortunate that Matt Millen, Bobby Campbell and Chet Parlavcecchio couldn't do a reprise of "Red" Griffiths' flamboyant ploy. Had it been legal they might have tried something similar and never played again for Joe Paterno.

To the pleasure of a record home crowd of 6,000, some accounts reported the crowd at 12,000, the Lions responded to "Red's" rallying call and Penn State took the measure of Dartmouth 14-7, the first of 58 Homecoming victories, through 2000.

The following week, in the first of a four games series with North Carolina State which saw all the games played at Penn State, the Nittany Lions hung a 41-0 shut-out on the Wolfpack from Raleigh.

N.C. State had started to play football in 1892, five years after Penn State, and was then known as North Carolina State College A & M. Falling in line with the trend toward bright splashy colors, subscribed to by Penn State (State's first colors were magenta and pink) and many other turn-of-the –century college football teams, the "Aggies" chose pink and blue as their original school colors. The original choice was rescinded after three seasons and changed to brown and white. In 1896 the Athletic

Association and the student body voted to change the school colors to today's red and white and they adopted the name "Red Terrors." In 1907 N.C. State began using the nickname the Wolfpack, shortened in later years to the 'Pack.

The next week October 23, 1920, Penn State was involved in a headline grabbing 109-7 victory over Lebanon Valley. Although Bezdek cleared the bench and played all of his scrubs, it wasn't the scrubs that gave up Lebanon Valley's only touchdown. Lebanon Valley actually scored first in the game and thus led 7-0, before giving up 109 points.

The stage was now set for a crucial game at Franklin Field in Philadelphia where last year State had won for just the fourth time in twenty-three meetings. Could the Centre County lads score more than the 3.6 points they averaged in the previous twenty-three games against the Red and Blue? Penn State fans, including George Werley, were anxious to find out. For George there was one *big* problem; how could someone with no money for bus or train fare get to the game?

CHAPTER 23

Eastward Ho Young Man

The Red and Blue of Pennsylvania would be Penn State's sixth opponent here in 1920 and, as was the case in all forty-six meetings between the two teams, the game would be played in Philadelphia.

After losing to Penn in every one of their first fifteen contests, Penn State had finally managed a tie in 1909. Then in 1911 and 1912, under Coach Bill Hollenbeck, the Lions recorded consecutive wins. With their win in 1919, State now had another opportunity to register consecutive wins over their eastern big city rival. The Penn-Penn State rivalry was finally becoming competitive although the series, going into this game, had Penn clearly in the lead at eighteen wins to State's four, with one tie. State's traditional rivalry with its western foe Pitt, stood at thirteen wins for State to nine wins for Pitt. Starting this year the two rivalries would begin heading in opposite directions with State narrowing the gap in its series with Penn, and Pitt taking the lead in its series with the Lions. While the crowds for the Pitt-Penn State games would average about 34,000, 1921 - 1930, the Penn-Penn State crowds would grow over the years (reaching 65,000 in 1928 and peaking at 71,180 in 1948). The crowd at Franklin Field in 1919 was 20,000 – this year they were expecting a crowd of more than 27,000. The 1923 crowd would reach 56,000.

Young George felt he was doing well in school, therefore he could rationalize his overpowering desire to see the up-coming game by falling back on his superstitous nature. He easily convinced himself that his absence could jinx his adopted team and end the winning streak of ten straight games, half of which he had attended. So George made his plans to hitch-hike to Philadelphia to see this October 30th game which might draw a crowd twice the size of all five home games State had played this season.

After his Friday two o'clock class, George began his trek up Atherton Street (Rt. 322), the start of his two hundred mile hitch-hike journey to Philadelphia.

His first ride took him only as far as some farming country, miles from Lewistown; not a long hop. Prior to the end of his first ride, the ominous-looking clouds which had been visible to the northwest, when George began his ride, were already upon them and there was a good downpour in progress. The driver, in his effort to literally go the extra mile for his passenger, drove several miles out of his way to find shelter from the rain, a barn, and there he dropped his grateful hitch-hiker.

The downpour intensified and continued well past sunset precluding any effort on our traveler's part to resume his trip that day. With little else to do George ate the sandwich and cookies he brought with him and finding a spot where the roof leakage was minimal he settled down and quickly fell asleep. His last thoughts before he dozed-off, zeroed in on the unexpected bad weather. Come morning, if the weather remained unfavorable George figured he would hitch-hike back to State College, and be glad he hadn't gone farther to-day.

George's wake-up call was that of a rooster crowing and until he awakened more fully he thought he was back home. His parents always had a chicken-coop populated mostly by Rhode Island Reds to provide eggs and a Sunday chicken dinner when desired. But once his barn-surroundings became clearer, George knew where he was, as there was no barn on their property on Delaware Avenue.

It was immediately apparent that the rain had ceased and a quick look outside showed a sun that was trying to burn through the early morning haze.

Could he still get to Philadelphia in time to see his beloved Nittany Lions play those city slicker University of Pennsylvania Quakers? An oxymoron, if ever there was one. His immediate plan of action was very simple; brush off the straw, cup his hands together and get some water from the watering-trough spigot to refresh his face and to rinse his mouth out and then staying on the side of the barn where he couldn't see the farm house head for the main road.

George was now faced with a decision – onward to Philadelphia or back to State College? The beautiful day seemed to be a harbinger of good things to follow so George took his position on the west side of Route 322 and set his thumb to work.

From previous hitchhiking ventures, George was conditioned to the fact that many cars would pass before one would stop and offer a lift. It was his practice to count the number of vehicles that passed before he got a ride, a number he kept in his head and at the end of the trip he could, for future reference, come up with an average number of cars that he could expect would pass him by before one would stop and pick him up. George Werley played golf for more than thirty years after graduating. Over those thirty years he recorded every one of his rounds in a notebook he kept at home. At the end of every year he could tell anyone who was interested what his average score was for the year, for every group of ten scores, his lifetime average score etc. That was George Werley, the research investigator's approach, even where sports were concerned.

Unfortunately his statistics never made him a better golfer.

George's count had reached five. Vehicle number six was, in his words, a "snazzy" automobile, a Locomobile. The car was obviously new and that it passed him by was no surprise. But then surprise, surprise the automobile slowed, then stopped and the driver motioned George to "come-a–running, I'm waiting for you."

When George got abreast of the front door the driver said, "Where are you going, kid?" George replied "Philadelphia to see a Penn State football game."

"Well hop in," the driver replied, "I'm going that direction." Aware that the car was brand new and having just slept in a barn George began urgently brushing away imaginary straw, kicking one shoe against the other in case he had mud stuck to his shoes, reluctant to even put a foot on the spotless running board.

The driver gave a chuckle, "Get in, Kid, you pass inspection. My name's Dudley Brigham, here sit on some of this blanket and kinda keep your feet on the paper," pointing to the brown butcher paper covering the floorboards. During the next hour George had a nice conversation with Dudley, then without any warning Dudley pulled off the road into a parking area right in front of a diner.

"I know you haven't had breakfast and I could use a cup of coffee – you drink coffee George?" George nodded, "Yes."

"Good, let's go in and have some eggs or whatever you want. I've got the check, well, our dealership does."

To George's good fortune the driver was delivering the car to a customer in Philadelphia and he dropped George off at 33rd and Market Streets just a few blocks from Franklin Field. In addition he gave George one of the three sandwiches he had the diner make and pack for them. He pointed toward the west and said, "Franklin Field is over there, you can't miss it." George then asked his benefactor for one of his business cards. Quick to accommodate, Dudley handed George one of his cards and added "When you make your first $10,000 give me a call. I'll be happy to sell you a car. Well good luck – hope you win."

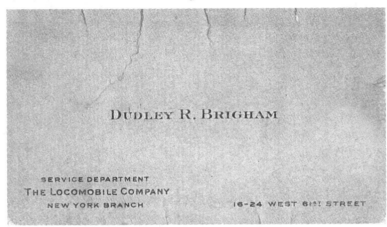

DUDLEY R. BRIGHAM

SERVICE DEPARTMENT
THE LOCOMOBILE COMPANY
NEW YORK BRANCH   16-24 WEST 61ST STREET

Business card of Locomobile representative who gave George Werley a ride to Philadelphia for the 1920 Penn - Penn State game.

George Werley exemplifying the 1924 "look."

George Werley (second row center), at 1927 reunion of Delta Sigma Chi fraternity, where he served as president, 1923-24.

CHAPTER 24

White and Blue Makes Red and Blue, Black and Blue

Coach Bezdek and his 1920 Lions were quite aware they were considered to be an easy mark by the Penn alumni and fans; however, they had proven the "experts" wrong several times last year and already one time this season.

Prior to every Penn State–Penn game the Philadelphia newspapers and fans would predict a Penn win. If Penn won the game, the next year Penn fans and students predicted more of the same. If Penn lost, the next year the Philadelphia papers would predict victory since State couldn't be that lucky two years in succession. Unfortunately the media, and the fan's perception of their mid-state rival was based on past history. Penn had won 16 of the first 17 games, with State managing just one tie from 1890 through 1910. But this year was 1920 and should the Red and Blue lose to their country cousins they would have lost four of the last seven games. Nonetheless conditioned by previous success, Penn fans tended to consider every State win an upset until the mid-fifties. (Starting in 1920 State won fourteen of the next twenty-four games played with three ties before the rivalry ended in 1958.)

In front of 30,000 fans Glenn Killinger scored the first touchdown of the game after Charley Way carried the ball to the Penn four yard line. Penn drove to the State one yard line late in the second quarter but failed to score and the first half ended with State ahead 7-0. Killinger played hurt the first half but he couldn't return to the field to start the second half which forced Coach Bezdek to make a halftime change at "Killy's " position. As the game progressed he would make several other changes. If there was one thing about Bezdek that *never* changed, it was the way he was *always* changing his line-up. Linemen were switched from tackle to guard and from one side of center to the other. A back might play well for several games but a fumble on his part could relegate him to the bench for the rest of the game or games, until someone else fell into disfavor. In a previous game before the start of the second half Bez told his quarterback Killinger, in front of the entire team, that he, Killinger, would return the kick-off and carry the ball on the first play from scrimmage since, "I know Killinger won't fumble." The remark was obviously directed at a back who had fumbled twice in the first half. Needless to say, on the first play from scrimmage Killinger fumbled.

Now, for some reason, possibly a first half fumble, whether it was lost or not, Bez announced that Charley Way would not return the kick-off. Since Killinger wasn't going to be in the line-up, who would return the kick-off? Singular among even the seniors, "Hinkey" Haines was one player who could question Bezdek directly, so Haines posed the question, "If not Charley, who Bez?"

Bezdek shot back, "You!"

Haines returned the kick-off for a touchdown and State was on its way. Two more touchdowns in the third period, closed out State's scoring and the Lions returned to Centre County with a 28-7 victory.

George Werley had gotten to Franklin Field, almost miraculously, in two rides, considering how short the first one was. He had seen his Nittany Lions beat the Penn team that got all the coverage in the Philadelphia papers he read as a boy and as a grown-up in Palmerton, and now it was time to consider how he would get back to State College. Dudley had used Route 30 and Route 3 as his routes into the city but George wasn't sure how to get back to Route 30, the Lancaster Pike.

Where should he begin hitch-hiking here near the center of such a big city? The thoroughfare which intersected with 33rd Street, where Dudley had dropped him, seemed like a major street, George could use it to get out to the suburbs; since he always had good luck on the open highways. Today was October 30th which meant it would be dark shortly – not a real comforting thought. Maybe he should find a bus depot, sleep there overnight and get a trolley to the suburbs at daylight tomorrow and then begin thumbing his way back to Penn State.

The crowd of 30,000 was filing out of Franklin Field on to Spruce Street and the numbered cross-streets. Only a few thousand of the departing fans were beaming with happiness and George was one of them, waving his pennant and smiling, but under the surface a bit unsure of his plans. Since the Penn State fans would probably be leaving the immediate area right after the game and heading back to State College, George headed toward the street Dudley Brigham used bringing him into the city. He regretted he hadn't asked Dudley what his best course of action would be when leaving the city but he had arrived long before game time and the sun had been high in the sky. Now the daylight was quickly diminishing and he began to realize that he was all alone in a very large and unfamiliar city. It wasn't a very comforting feeling.

Looking back over his shoulder searching for a friendly face, maybe another Penn State student, or possibly a car with a Penn State pennant, George continued to work his way toward Route 3 (Market Street).

Before George had walked two blocks a car pulled up next to him, and the driver leaned over and called out, "You looking for a ride?"

George answered, "Yes I am."

The driver replied, "Where are you going?"

George said, "State College."

The driver repeated a similar question but this time to another young man walking next to George, "How about you?"

The young man said "Harrisburg."

The driver said, "Well, hop in both of you."

The driver dropped the other young man in Harrisburg and as they were leaving the city he pulled over in front of a small cottage-type restaurant and offered, "C'mon George it's too far back to State College on an empty stomach, I'll buy you dinner."

After his second free meal in two days (and a sandwich), George and his host who lived in State College got back in the car and headed for their mutual destination. In State College, Marvin turned on to College Avenue and when they got to Gill Street, Marvin dropped George off leaving him less than two blocks from his rooming house.

Summarizing his trip, George had spent a total of $1.10, for a ticket, two five-cent drinks, twenty-five cents for a program and forty cents for a pennant. He had walked less than twelve blocks, up Atherton Street, to and from Franklin Field between rides and from College Avenue to his rooming house, covered the entire distance in just three rides and had two meals and a sandwich all at no cost. Talk about good fortune.

CHAPTER 25

Looking for Respect

Ewald "Jumbo" Stiehm a 1909 Wisconsin graduate broke into the head coaching ranks at Nebraska in 1911. There he led the Cornhuskers for five years, during which time his teams won outright or shared the Missouri Valley Conference title every year. Under "Jumbo's" direction Nebraska won thirty-five, lost two, both losses to Minnesota, and tied three for a .913 winning percentage. However, as a national football power, Nebraska was an early twentieth century Rodney Dangerfield, getting no respect. This situation existed partially because the 'Huskers beat teams with names like Kearney State, Bellevue, Adrian, Doane and Nebraska Wesleyan and by margins of victory that ranged anywhere from forty to one hundred and seventeen points. The other reason they garnered little respect was the fact that Nebraska rarely played anyone east of Iowa, Missouri or Minnesota. There were isolated games between 1911 and 1916 with Michigan and Michigan State, but even those games were all played in Lincoln. From 1915 – 1925 Nebraska did square off against Notre Dame in an eleven game series where each team won five games and there was one tie however all but two games were played in Lincoln.

In the five years under Stiehm, Nebraska tired of the lack of recognition and after finishing 7-0-1 in 1914 they declared *themselves* National Champions, after they vanquished Washburn, Kansas State, Iowa State, Morningside, Kansas, Michigan State and tied South Dakota. In 1915 they declared themselves repeat national champions reasoning if they were champions when they finished 7-0-1 with one tie how could they be less than #1 when they finished unbeaten *and* untied in eight games. But Coach Stiehm at season's end felt the personal sting of rejection and lack of appreciation when he was denied a $4000.00 raise and he promptly left Nebraska for Indiana.

The year of 1917, "Doc" Stewart's second year as head coach, saw Nebraska come as far east as Ann Arbor to play Michigan. In 1918 under head coach Professor William Kline who led a war-depleted squad, Nebraska was scheduled to play Syracuse and West Virginia but wartime travel restrictions forced the cancellation of four Nebraska games including those two.

Following WW I Henry Schulte, a Michigan graduate, in his second year as head coach decided to take his team to the East, "The Mecca" of collegiate football. Yale, Harvard, Princeton etc., continued to be revered and Walter Camp's All-American teams and all of his pronouncements about college football emanated from the East and were considered The Gospel. Also the best and most influential sports writers were in Boston, New York City, Philadelphia, Washington, D.C. and Baltimore. If Nebraska ever wanted to get the recognition it sought, it would have to leave the Mid-West occasionally and play some teams east of Chicago and preferably in the Boston, New York City, Pittsburgh proximity.

After traveling to New York City and State College, Pennsylvania, in 1920 and South Bend and Pittsburgh in 1921, Nebraska played only single games at Syracuse, South Bend, Pittsburgh and West Point 1922 - 1928. Nebraska however continued their series with Pittsburgh which ran from 1927 through 1942; a series that saw Pittsburgh win eleven times, lose twice and play to a tie on three occasions.

But here in 1920, when travel around the USA was not as commonplace, Nebraska's trip to New York City and then State College, Pennsylvania was certainly newsworthy. And while the 'Huskers – Rutgers game at the Polo Grounds didn't put "The Big Apple" on the map the meeting between Penn State and Nebraska brought State College front and center in the big city newspapers, when these emerging giants met at New Beaver Field the first Saturday in November.

Nebraska Partial Schedule
1920-1921

Year	Team	Game Site	Game Result Nebraska Score Shown first
1920	Notre Dame	Lincoln, Neb.	7-16
	Rutgers	New York City	28-0
	Penn State	State College, Pa	?
	Michigan State	Lincoln, Neb.	35-7
1921	Notre Dame	South Bend. Ind.	0-7
	Pittsburgh	Pittsburgh, Pa	10-0

CHAPTER 26

Man Killing Mastodons

November 6, 1920 Saturday A.M. State College, Pennsylvania

Centre County and more specifically State College were "center
stage" for Nebraska's second chance to impress Walter Camp
and the New York City/Boston/Washington, D.C. media. After
Nebraska's 28-0 thrashing of a good Rutgers Chanticleers team the scribes
were in State College to see more of the same or probably an even worse
beating administered to Penn State's Nittany Lions. The Cornhusker's
had stayed and practiced away from State College shrouding their personnel and practices in secrecy. The only whispers circulating about the
size of the Nebraska players, used adjectives such as, in alphabetical
order, Bunyanesque, enormous, gigantic, huge, hulking, immense, etc.
Eastern newspaper referred to them as "Mankilling Mastodons," not very
comforting for Penn State's fans, players or close relatives.

This contest had all the makings of a huge mismatch, a blowout of
embarrassing proportions similar to the one forecast almost forty–four
years to the day later when a Glenn Ressler-led Penn State team would
visit another heavily-favored Mid-Western foe. The two scores would
differ by a single touchdown.

November 6, 1920 Saturday Afternoon New Beaver Field State College, Pennsylvania.

The stands were filling quickly and the announced attendance of
9,000 was one and a half times as large as the record crowd that witnessed the Dartmouth game four weeks ago. There were patches of red
here and there in the crowd so one might guess there were some
Cornhusker fans present. Certainly there were Penn State fans here, some
fervent rooters, some fans just curious to see Penn State's football team
put their eleven game winning streak on the line against their third quality opponent this season. And then there were those who were curious to
see this vaunted Nebraska team in action. The town was a-buzz with
anticipation. Here, today, in little State College there were as many out-
of-town and out-of-state newspapermen as this town would normally
see in several years. No team from as far away as Nebraska had ever
visited State College.

Penn State's squad was already on the field wearing a variety of warm-up gear, while Nebraska had yet to make its appearance. The fans in the stands were almost breathlessly awaiting the appearance on the field of the Nebraska squad. Then it happened, almost simultaneously with a cheer from a few hundred people there was an audible gasp, from the balance of the 9,000 people who were in attendance. Onto the field in one long single file came a score or more Paul Bunyanesque football players. "They were all huge and well over six foot" (according to five foot nine inch, one hundred and thirty pound George Werley). Only a few of the largest Penn State players could match what seemed to be the average size of the first ten to twenty Nebraskans entering the field. Equally impressive was the fact that the Cornhusker's traveling squad seemed to number at least thirty. Thus the "Huskers had size and they had numbers but the crowning touch was the third part of the picture. Picture these players in their scarlet and cream Nebraska uniforms running on to the field carrying their helmets in their left hand. They all had their own long individual red blanket, with a large cream block "N," which they held securely under their chin with their right hand, the blankets trailing in the breeze behind them like a line of "Supermen." The fans, and probably the Penn State players in their assorted nondescript gear, were awe-struck.

As we noted, freshman George Werley was at the game and despite the passing of many decades his recollections of this game remained consistent regarding the following three points: First, the awesome sight of the Nebraska team coming on to the field "EACH player had his own blanket!" Second, the Nebraska team leaving the field, unwilling to believe the scoreboard which read PSC 20, Nebraska 0. Nebraska never expected to be beaten and certainly they couldn't believe they would be shut out and beaten by twenty points. In ten years only two previous teams had done this to a Nebraska team, Notre Dame under Head Coach Jesse Harper in 1916 and Michigan in 1917. Third but most dramatic according to George Werley's recollection Charley Way carried the ball on only six plays in the whole game for 165 yards.

As for the actual game itself, when the Penn State players took the field for the opening kickoff the partisan Nittany Lion fans must have been concerned with their eleven "Davids" vs. Nebraska's eleven "Goliaths." Penn State's team didn't have much size but they had athleticism and "pluck," an adjective in vogue at the time. Today we would certainly say they had "guts" or "intestinal fortitude."

From the opening kickoff the Cornhuskers marched relentlessly toward the Penn State goal but they came up empty–handed. Rather than being deflated by the long drive the Penn State boys took heart in Nebraska's failure to score. A later long drive early in the second quarter ended when a fourth down Cornhusker pass from the fifteen yard line hit the goal post, and "Red" Griffiths was already asking some of the Nebraska players whether they were tired.

According to Dad, with the ball on the twenty-yard line, Charley Way made his first appearance in the Penn State backfield. Several of the Nebraska players had already been needling the State players asking, "Where is this famous "Gang" Way? Does he only play in the easy warm-up games?" Griffiths and "Newsh" Bentz had each admonished the 'Huskers with words to this effect, "Save your breath, you'll need it."

Now Way was in the game. Quarterback/tailback Killinger ran two rather mundane plays out of the single wing with Way not even touching the ball. Now on third and long, Penn State came out in a double wing formation, which they had previously used this season only on passing plays. Way was the "wing" on the right. "Killy" took the snap and began running toward the right sideline, now Way came from his wing back position running across the formation toward the left sideline. Just in case Nebraska remembered that Penn State had run a reverse out of this formation last year, the wily Bezdek had slipped in a "new wrinkle." Instead of Way running behind "Killy" to get the hand off which is more obvious he ran inside "Killy," and hidden by his linemen he took the ball and lit-out toward the Penn State sideline. Way easily made the corner and now he was headed toward the Nebraska goal line up the left sideline to the 30 yard line, the forty, the fifty, down to Nebraska's forty, their thirty, their twenty... only the fact that the Nebraska safeties had read the play as a pass and at the snap of the ball had begun back-peddling, kept them from being left in the dust like the rest of the right side of the Nebraska defense. Charley put a move on the closer of the two safeties and sped right past him. Under today's rules, Way would have galloped into the end zone just inside the pylon on the east side of the Nebraska goal line, the score would be 6-0 and the Penn State Nittany Lions would be lining up for the point-after-touchdown try. However, under 1920 rules, at whatever point east to west the ball carrier crossed the goal line, as far as distance in from the sideline, that is where the ball would be spotted for the point-after-touchdown try. Thus if Way continued running straight ahead he would score but the angle for the point-after-touchdown would be very difficult. Instead he decided to cut back to the center of the field to cross the end zone there for a "head on" point-after-touchdown try. In his endeavor to do this, Way lost his footing or was "tripped-up" by the other safety and he was downed inside the five yard line. Some of the Nebraska linemen were a bit winded after their fruitless pursuit while Griffiths, Newsh Bentz along with Hess, Beck, Brown, Hufford and the other Penn State linemen, were all invigorated and ready to run the next play while Nebraska's behemoth linemen were just arriving. Griffiths with hands on hips chastised the late arrivals in a soft but stern tone of voice, "*Come on* gentlemen or we shall have to play on without you!"

The huge Nebraska line now dug their cleats in, glad there would be no more chasing on this next play, confident they could repulse any attempt to "buck" the ball into the end zone. Whereas most snaps go directly to the tailback this snap went to the fullback George Snell for what appeared to be a fullback buck. The fullback (Snell) took a step toward the line and then spun halfway around and lateralled the ball, one of the plays off of the buck-lateral series, to the tailback Killinger who gliding to the left threw a perfect strike to end "Squeaks" Hufford. "Squeaks" was so alone that he could circle around and put the ball behind one goal post for an easier "point after" try, as most of the Nebraska players were intermingled with Penn State players in one big heap of humanity at the line of scrimmage.

The score was still 7-0 when Penn State received the second half kickoff. With all the momentum on their side the Nittany Lions began a nice drive which had the big Nebraska team back on its heels. And then as quickly as a rainstorm can begin on a cloudy day, the tide of momentum swung into the 'Huskers favor. A Penn State ball carrier charged into a mass of humanity and out of the "scrum" came a Nebraska player with the football. First down Nebraska, in Penn State territory. The Nebraska team which appeared unable, since the second quarter, to take the fight to the Penn State lads now sprang to life with the quickness and the ferocity of one of Dr. Frankenstein's monsters after just one huge electrical charge.

It now seemed as though someone had rewound the game film and the contest was starting all over again. Nebraska was having its way with State and the Nittany Lions were unable to contain them. Penn State was finally forced to call time to re-organize. Both teams' water boys came out on the field with their water pails and metal ladles. All of the Penn State players were kneeling while dipping out quantities of water to drink. But more worrisome was their demeanor. It seemed as though the weight and power of the Nebraska onslaught had worn them down. Then halfway through the timeout the Penn State team stood up and formed a huddle. And out of the huddle racing toward the Penn State bench came a single Penn State player. As he ran he unhooked the helmet chinstrap, removed the helmet and with clenched teeth he heaved, the offending item at the bench. With his bright red hair shining, "Red" Griffiths raced back to his teammates who, in concert with the fans, seemed to have been so totally recharged that you could image you felt the electricity in the air. The Penn State defense rose up and staged an almost fanatical defense and then proving how fickle the fates can be Nebraska fumbled and Penn State recovered.

Going into the fourth quarter the score was still 7-0. At this point Charley Way reentered the game and "Killy" wasted no time putting him to work. On a straight-ahead carry into the line from the ten-yard line Charley spotted his "hole" right where it was supposed to be. Bentz and Griffiths had put a high-low block on the big Nebraska tackler with Griffiths throwing himself at the legs of the 'Husker. Way came out the other side of the hole and he carried the ball almost to mid field. On a subsequent carry Way went 57 yards to pay dirt for a 14-0 Penn State lead. Later in the fourth quarter Way went twenty yards, to go with a previous 55 yard run, to register his second touchdown. Ahead 14-0, Way later said he felt scoring the third touchdown to make the score 20-0 was more important than the point-after, so on this end sweep he crossed the goal line where he could. Because of the angle of the kick the point-after was missed and the final score was 20-0 in favor of State.

At an alumni affair in the 1970s Charley Way confided to my dad that he felt *that* one game, gained First Team All-American Honors for "Red" and him. He felt the presence of Walter Camp and the Mid-West and East Coast big city sports reporters at a game where he had some big runs and "Red" had some flamboyant moments along with a win over a quality opponent got them the necessary voter exposure.

As often happens with football teams after a big win – they have a let down the following week. The Nittany Lions, fresh from their victory over Nebraska, traveled to Bethlehem, Pennsylvania, where they played to a 7-7- tie with Lehigh.

As for the Pitt game, a year ago the Nittany Lions won for the first time, since 1912 under Bill Hollenbeck. Thus Penn State fans were extremely optimistic about winning two years in a row, as this veteran team had beaten Dartmouth and overwhelmed Penn and Nebraska with its speed. As far as common opponents, Pitt had played Penn and had come away with a close 27-21 win, while State had beaten the Red and Blue 28-7. However, as always, this game was to be played in Pittsburgh. In a muddy Forbes Field quagmire the speedy Penn State backs Charley Way, Glenn Killinger and "Hinkey" Haines were unable to break loose due to the condition of the field. Whether accurate or not, George Werley always said, the word around campus was that in both 1920 and '21, the night before the Thanksgiving Day meeting of these two rivals the Pittsburgh Fire Department chose to flush their fire hydrant lines in the area, including those inside Forbes Field. The result was a sloppy, muddy field the next day. Might there have been any truth to such a campus rumor?

The author can't answer that question but the table at the end of this chapter will show that going into their Thanksgiving Day game with Pitt, in five of the seven years, 1919-1925, Penn State's record for that season was as good as or better than Pitt's yet State managed only one win and two 0-0 ties.

After 1919, State did not beat Pitt until 1939 when Pitt played at State College for only the second time in that twenty-one year period. The 1939 victory led to a reported confrontation between a Penn State alumnus from back in "the twenties" and a senior undergraduate student who immediately after Penn State had sealed its 10-0 victory, let out a loud yell and stated, "I've been waiting for this for a LONG time." The alumnus who had seen virtually every Pitt-Penn State game through the "twenties" and "thirties" grabbed the student by the coat lapels, almost lifting him off the ground and shouted into his face, "YOU'VE been waiting a long time?" and his voice jumped an octave, "YOU'VE been waiting a long time? You have no idea what a long time is!"

It's little wonder that long time Penn State fans can't get enough when it comes to beating Pitt. A Penn State pin/badge that sells very well year after year voices the prevailing sentiment when it proclaims, "My two favorite teams are Penn State and whoever is playing Pitt."

	Season record before game		Team with	Team	Season record after game	
Year	Penn State	Pitt	better record	that won	Penn State	Pitt
1919	6-1-0	6-1-1	Even	State	7-1-0	6-2-1
1920	7-0-1	6-0-1	State	Tie	7-0-2	6-0-2
1921	8-0-1	5-3-0	State	Tie	8-0-2	5-3-1
1922	6-3-1	7-2-0	Pitt	Pitt	6-4-1	8-2-0
1923	6-1-1	4-4-0	State	Pitt	6-2-1	5-4-0
1924	6-2-1	4-3-1	State	Pitt	6-3-1	5-3-1
1925	4-3-1	7-1-0	Pitt	Pitt	4-4-1	8-1-0

CHAPTER 27

Cartwheels, Handsprings and Backflips Announce the News

U ntil Penn State began playing football in the Big Ten in 1993, the Lions had always gone their independent way. Such independence, as is usually the case, had advantages and disadvantages. Probably the biggest disadvantage was reflected in Penn State's football schedules, beginning back in the 1920s. Examine for example the imbalance between home and away games when we look at the 1921 – 1925 years. Yes, there were twenty-seven home games and only twenty-two non-home games but basically the home opponents were the likes of Lebanon Valley, Gettysburg, Franklin and Marshall, Middlebury, William and Mary, Marietta and the away opponents were Penn, Pitt, Harvard, Washington, West Virginia and Southern California.

In five seasons, 1921-1925 State had five home games against name teams - Michigan State, Georgia Tech, Navy, Notre Dame and Syracuse. They had twenty-two games away or at neutral sites, *all* against marquee teams. State didn't play a major football opponent at home, earlier than October 20, in any of those years. Thus the schedule was top heavy with early home games against lightly regarded opponents and then the Lions ended their seasons with away games against highly regarded teams.

Had State been in a conference their schedule would have had better balance in regard to the distribution of the home and away games over the season. Also the schedule would not have crammed all the toughest opponents into the tail end of the season.

No matter when the season starts the football team returns to campus before the main student body. This enables them to get their conditioning and "two-a-days" in before classes begin, since these practices are so demanding physically and take such a big chunk of time out of each day. As the first two or three days generally are light practice days, the players register for their classes on these days. From that point on, time is too precious a commodity, to be spent standing in line. Registering early also enables the players to get the classes they need, in time slots that don't interfere with football practice.

According to George Werley, back in 1920-1923 football players who hadn't taken the course previously, and other students who could fit it into their schedule, signed-up for a particular fall semester religion course. There were many reasons, including the fact that the professor made the course very interesting. Also, he liked football and he liked to talk about football to the extent that the bull sessions about football often consumed up to one quarter of the allotted class time. Another big reason was the small amount of out-of-class study time needed since the final exam format was the same every year. There would be some true and false and some multiple choice questions but one could achieve a passing grade by answering the final essay question comprehensively. Obviously the more true and false and multiple choice questions you answered correctly the higher your grade would be, but you had several months to put together a slam bang dissertation on the essay question which would earn you a passing grade. The big question was to name and to write about The Twelve Kings of Israel. When George managed to schedule the course in his senior year, several football players in his class had academic problems at the end of the fall semester because the old reliable Religion 101 proved unreliable. During the semester the professor was hospitalized and didn't return to teaching for almost a year. One of the advanced degree post-grad students took over the class and completed the semester for the ailing professor. Unexpectedly the replacement "prof" removed the pivotal question "Name the Twelve Kings etc." and replaced it with "Name the major and minor prophets of the Old Testament." Any football player or other student who was counting on this gimme question to pass the course was in big trouble. However, at least one player really did give it the old college try when he answered thusly, "Far be it for me to say who in the eyes of the Lord were the major and who were the minor prophets, but as for the Twelve Kings of Israel they were as follows."

The Lions began 1921 looking just as strong as they were in 1920. The defense didn't yield a touchdown until the fourth game of the season, as they blanked Lebanon Valley, Gettysburg and N.C. State 53-0, 24-0 and 35-0 respectively. In Penn State's second homecoming football game, Lehigh dented the Nittany Lion goal line for the first-time but the Lions left the "alums" happy with a 28-7 victory. Gone from last year's team were Charley Way, "Red" Griffiths, Carl Beck, "Bill" Hess, "Hinky" Haines and George Brown. It was not likely that any underclassman would step up and replace a fiery leader like Griffiths or a game breaker like Way. It would be as difficult as replacing Matt Millen, Keith Dorney, Karl McCoy and Curt Warner all at once from the 1978 team. But Coach Bezdek's cupboard was far from bare. The backfield had Joe Lightner returning, and he would be a second team All-American in 1921, along with fullback Captain George Snell an outstanding three-year letterman. There was a sophomore halfback, with the intriguing nickname of "Light Horse Harry" Wilson who was already getting rave reviews from the coeds and the sports writers, and sophomore lineman Joe "Dutch" Bedenk who would be a second team All-American in his first year on the varsity. Last but far from least was Quarterback/Halfback Glenn Killinger. "Killy" would cap-off a meteoric rise to fame when in his senior year he would be chosen by Walter Camp as a First Team All-American.

Killinger had not even gone out for the freshmen football team when he came to State because he didn't think he was good enough. One source informed the author that Killinger didn't play high school football, but another source said that wasn't correct, it was "Hinkey" Haines who never played high school football. Regardless Bezdek convinced Killinger he might have the requisite talent to play collegiate football after observing him play basketball and invited him to "try out" for the team.

In assessing the 1921 backfield, the loss of "Hinkey" Haines and Charley Way seemed to leave a huge void but Harry Wilson moved up to the varsity to take up some of the slack and Bezdek expanded Killinger's offensive role. Killinger could pass, run and punt and he could think. He was an excellent leader and the proverbial "coach on the field." In this his senior year he was the team's star. Besides lettering three years and being a Walter Camp football All-American, he lettered three years in baseball and basketball. All this from a young man who thought he might not be good enough.

Looking next at the linemen, Bezdek had two fine ends returning, in Stan McCollum and "Squeaks" Hufford, and center "Newsh" Bentz who would be the team co-captain as a senior was in the second of three seasons as a letterman. Ray Baer was at one guard while Joe "Dutch" Bedenk, just a sophomore, was debuting at the other. Penn State's two tackles, 6' 7" "Tiny" McMahon and intercollegiate heavyweight boxing champ "Rags" Madera, were stalwarts. Although the 1921 squad was again faced with a schedule that had them playing five of their last six games on the road, they had the personnel to win them all. And if they did (win them all) they could receive a Rose Bowl bid, and with a win there, this Lion team should be the #1 team in the country.

About the time of the Civil War the Head of the U. S. Patent Office made a statement which has to be one of the worst predictions ever made. Our expert said that the Patent Office would have a dim future in the 1900s as everything worth inventing would probably have been invented by the turn of the century.

My father proudly contradicted that prediction by stating on numerous occasions that he lived through the greatest age the world has ever known, and since he wasn't born until 1901, I would go out on a limb and say that there were a number of substantial inventions after 1900. To very briefly give credence to George Werley's statement consider that the following advancements were made during his life time:

1. Travel went from horse, ships and trains to automobiles, airplanes, jet propulsion, supersonic speed, rocket ships, space travel to the moon and beyond etc.
2. The invention of electricity led to electric lights, stoves, refrigerators, air conditioning, portable heaters, electric washers and dryers, toasters, hot water for showers, electric irons, the radio, wirephotos, electric clocks, x-ray machines, vacuum cleaners, adding machines, copiers, medical and dental advances etc.
3. The unveiling of the world of communications – telephones, television, portable radios and phones, computers, printers, motion pictures, phonograph records, tape recorders and players, CDs, cell phones, fax machines etc.
4. Mechanized farm implements, tractors, electric and gas trimmers, chain saws, tillers, chippers and shredders, in fact any equipment in use on a farm today which isn't wind, water, horse, mule, etc., or human powered didn't exist in 1901.

All of those advances and too many more to list occurred in one man's lifetime.

Readers of this book might question the relevance of enumerating the above inventions when discussing State's next football game, an away game at Harvard. However something we use virtually everyday and possibly assume was always available, was absent in the early 1920s.

In 2000, an avid Penn State fan might elect to travel to an away game, probably by automobile or airplane. The less venturesome in 2000 might stay home and watch the game on TV or as a last resort listen to the game on radio at home, at work, in their auto or almost anywhere indoors or out. In 1921 automobile travel from State College to Cambridge, Massachusetts was probably attempted by only a few hardy souls. In fact those who owned an automobile in the early 1920s probably didn't travel more than twenty-five miles over a weekend. Even in 1924, after graduation, when George Werley had resumed working for the New Jersey Zinc Company he recalled the two standard Monday morning questions were, "Where did you go (with your car) and how many flat tires did you have?" For those remaining in State College there was no TV, and there wouldn't be for thirty or more years. And in 1921 radio stations broadcast almost exclusively from studio sites and were "on the air" only a fraction of a twenty-four hour day.

What recourse was available to some loyal fans sitting in State College who wanted to know the fate of their beloved football team in real time? An enterprising person, or persons, would reserve Schwab Auditorium for the length of the football game plus some warm-up time before the scheduled 3:00 kick-off. They would then sell all the seats in Schwab Auditorium for thirty-five cents each. Next they enlisted the talents of the Penn State cheerleaders, all males, who didn't make the trip. Utilizing the proceeds from the ticket sales, they rented time at the Western Union telegraph office on South Allen Street and the Western Union office in Cambridge, or Boston, Massachusetts.

With those preliminary arrangements seen to and Schwab Auditorium packed at forty minutes before kick-off, eleven young men in white "ducks," white shirts with dark blue bow ties, blue sweaters and black and white saddle shoes carrying their white megaphones, bearing a big blue block "S" came running down the aisles and up onto the stage. As they lined up across the stage, the head cheerleader prepared to speak into a megaphone which was affixed to a tripod standing before him and positioned very nearly at the center of the stage, from left to right. He had to pause for a period of time as the crowd had spontaneously erupted into a chant of "Go State." When the noise abated the head cheerleader made a few announcements after which the squad and the audience went through all of the Penn State cheers. Then, with piano accompaniment, the auditorium reverberated to the sounds of "Fight On State" "Hail To The Lion" and a moving rendition of the Alma Mater.

With everyone seated, including eye-witness George Werley, the head cheerleader began to announce the starting line-ups for both teams and when he read the fullback position the crowd learned for certain that Captain George Snell did not make the trip due to a severe throat infection. As the line-ups were being posted on a blackboard the cheerleader farthest to the audience's right, on a signal from the head cheerleader, raced down the steps and up the aisle and disappeared out the rear of Schwab Auditorium. After a reasonable interval the next cheerleader was dispatched, All, out-going cheerleaders, departed stage left. Within a few minutes the cheerleader who departed first came running down the left aisle (left in relation to the audience). The slightly "winded" young man ran up the stairs on to the stage and handed the head cheerleader a thin strip of paper. The head cheerleader announced to the crowd that Penn State won the coin toss and chose to "take the wind." The response from the crowd was mixed, at best. The crowd obviously desired to have the ball to start the game. However, Hugo Bezdek probably wished to provide his defense, which had given up but one touchdown all year, a chance to set the "tone" for the contest and he chose a goal to defend, virtually assuring that Harvard would choose to receive.

The Schwab Auditorium crowd which was disappointed at kick-off, went from disappointed to discontented to disenchanted to disconsolate as the Western Union messages continued to arrive. Harvard seemed to have no trouble solving the Penn State defenses as they drove the visitors back scoring a touchdown to lead seven to nothing. Then the news arrived that Penn State tackle "Rags" Madera, had suffered a broken leg and was carried off the field and taken to the hospital. He was replaced by Lee Hill, an undersized player, who gamely did his best, but his ability was probably reflected in the fact that he lettered only this one year. Back Pete Redinger was the next Penn Stater to go down, and very quickly the score discrepancy doubled to fourteen to nothing in favor of the Crimson. The young and relatively untested Harry Wilson had to step in for Redinger in a backfield that was already missing its best blocker and most physical player, fullback George Snell. The veteran Harvard team continued to pummel the Lion players and soon Newsh Bentz and several of his teammates were bleeding and bruised. But Bentz was indefatigable, the more punishment he appeared to absorb, the harder he flung himself into the next play.

At last in the second quarter Penn State seemed to stem the tide and finally the Lions got on the scoreboard when Joe Lightner plunged into the end zone and State kicked the point after, making the halftime score 14-7. Penn State's drive for the touchdown and Lightner's score resulted in several of the cheerleading relay runners doing cartwheels down the aisle as harbingers of the good news they were carrying.

To start the second half (this time it was Harvard's choice) the Crimson elected to receive, figuring a quick touchdown or two would put the game out of reach. The Penn State cheerleaders at Schwab after the halftime break now seemed to have gotten their second wind and the ongoing cycle of cheerleaders departing stage left was quickly mirrored by a returning cheerleader stage right. However the little strips of paper were at best some good news, some bad news. Penn State was now the team piling up the statistics and getting its fans at the game and in Schwab up out of their seats hootin' and a hollerin' but they were unable to score. With Penn State monopolizing the ball Harvard could not get their desired two touchdown cushion. As matters stood now a single Penn State touchdown could tie the score. But time was fleeting.

According to George after an exchange of punts in the fourth quarter, instead of punting on third down from its own ten yard line State ran the ball and Wilson got the first down. This brought another cheerleader cartwheeling down the left aisle to give the announcer the strip of paper which contained the crucial happening. Such a gamble so deep in your own territory signaled great confidence or a desperate calculated gamble;

whichever, the Schwab crowd loved the move and they exploded in a huge roar. The windows at Schwab were open and there was a throng of people who, for financial reasons or lack of space for them, had gathered on the steps and on both sides of the building and they too roared when the news was passed outside to them. There were a few more positive but not exciting reports. Killinger gained three yards and Lightner got two more. But the next cheerleader, virtually brought down the house before his message was even announced. He cartwheeled once or twice in the aisle but as he came on stage he did not go directly to the announcer. Without breaking stride he motioned everyone back and then he did some handsprings and finished it off with a back flip. At this point the crowd went wild as the announcer read, "Wilson goes off left tackle, running down the sideline he goes out-of-bounds on Harvard's 3 yard line – a 62 yard run." It's bedlam in Schwab! More cartwheeling messengers carry the news that the Lions have scored working the ball toward the center of the field. And from that position "Killy" kicks the point-after and the score is knotted at 14-14. Just as the pessimistic Harvard fans had feared, the momentum had changed hands and Bentz and his rugged teammates were taking the fight to Harvard.

Later in the fourth period a series of acrobatic maneuvers by a succession of relay runners brings the news that "Killy" has run the ball to the Harvard eight yard line and two plays later Joe Lightner has his second touchdown of the game and Killinger kicks the point after.

The surprising Lions now lead 21-14 and in Schwab the joint is jumping.

Since kick-off numerous people who hadn't bought seats, but wanted to join in on the festivities, had crowded inside the building. Some on the main floor and more in the balcony. Despite the protests of some of the college maintenance people, students were boosted up by people on the main floor and pulled up by rooters already in the balcony. When Penn State scored, the expression "the joint was jumping," was used and as it was told to me this was no exaggeration. The balcony literally was flexing under the weight of the fans jumping up and down. Then, with a sharp "CRACK" the right side of the balcony dropped two to three feet pitching some of those in the front rows over the railings and down on to the unfortunate people directly below. There followed a creaking groaning sound as the balcony rubbed against the wall and then it appeared to stabilize. People on the main floor were tending to injured people, clamoring to get out the rear exits or pushing and shoving toward the stage in case the balcony should fall the rest of the way. Persons in the balcony, either froze where they were, fearful their movement might trigger a more complete collapse, or panicked and bolted for the stairs.

The auditorium was evacuated with no loss of life, although persons who fell from the balcony and those upon whom they fell suffered a variety of injuries.

The fact that Harvard came back to tie the score at 21-21 under such dark conditions that lighted matches could be seen across the field, was partially over-looked in the aftermath of the episode at Schwab.

Newspaper reports called the game a Penn State moral victory as they outrushed Harvard almost three to one and had double the number of first downs the Crimson registered, nineteen versus nine.

The balcony at Schwab was "roped-off" that day and all the seats under the balcony and in the balcony could not be used until repairs and structural changes were made As I recall, Dad thought it stayed in that roped-off state of disrepair for quite some time.

CHAPTER 28

Playing the Best, from East to West

The Harvard come-from-behind tying touchdown pass in virtual darkness, left the Penn State squad on a huge downer. They had allowed a victory to slip through their fingers after valiantly fighting back from the battlefield losses of Pete Redinger and "Rags" Madera and the absence of Captain George Snell. Before entraining for the trip to Cambridge, Coach Bezdek and the entire team had visited Snell in the hospital where his worsened condition had confined him to bed. He had tried his best to motivate his teammates before they left but his throat infection made talking very difficult. The team definitely missed his fierce defensive play and leadership.

For the Nittany Lions, and their five away games at season's end, it was one down and four to go, with just the Carnegie Tech home game interposed among the road games. Despite the preponderance of away games State had hoped to go undefeated through these six games as a spring board to a #1 ranking. The Harvard tie technically meant they could still go undefeated but there would be a slight blemish – a tie. However, if your team had to play a tie game with any team on its schedule, a tie with mighty Harvard on their home field would be the easiest to justify.

But there was no time to dwell on the tie. Friday the Lions had to travel to New York City to meet Georgia Tech's Golden Tornado at the Polo Grounds the next day. (They weren't the Yellow Jackets yet.) It must have taken a bit of persuasion on the part of Penn State or New York City to get Georgia Tech to leave their home cooking and their Atlanta confines where they enjoyed tremendous success. From 1913 through 1921 Georgia Tech had the following won-lost-tied records:

1913	7-2-0
1914	6-2-0
1915	7-0-1
1916	8-0-1
1917	9-0-0
1918	6-1-0
1919	7-3-0
1920	8-1-0
1921	8-1-0

For the years 1913 – 1921, Georgia Tech won sixty-six games, lost ten and tied two for a winning percentage of .859. For those nine years Tech averaged seven wins and one loss each year. And during those same nine seasons the Engineers played just twelve away games including the 1921 game with Penn State; which actually was held at a neutral site. That amounts to four away games every three years, which is very favorable scheduling.

John Heisman, for whom The Heisman Trophy was named, became Georgia Tech's first full-time head coach in 1904. He directed the Golden Tornado, as they were known until 1930, to a 102-29-7 record over sixteen seasons, 1904-1919. In his last five years at Tech, Heisman had his greatest success, compiling a 37-4-2 record which included selection as the INS Co-National Champions in 1917. During that year Georgia Tech beat Penn 41-0, Washington and Lee (not to be confused with Washington and Jefferson) 63-0, Vanderbilt 83-0. Carlisle 98-0 and Auburn 68-7, while yielding just seventeen points in the entire season. However two seasons later John Heisman left Georgia Tech and Bill Alexander took over as the head coach in 1920.

With "The Wizard," as he was dubbed in his later years at Tech, enjoying even greater success 1915-1919, than he had 1904-1914, one would speculate that Coach Heisman was lured away to become the head coach at a more prestigious university, Harvard or Yale perhaps? If we were playing twenty questions, it would be one down, nineteen to go.

Maybe financial inducements were involved or the combined position of coach and athletic director at a school where John Heisman the athletic director would be in charge of scholarships, budgets and schedules for Head Coach John Heisman's varsity football team, a cozy arrangement. Was this the reason? No. Two down, eighteen to go.

An excellent guess would be player revolt, since all season long Heisman had the hot water to the locker room showers shut-off Monday through Friday making all the players take a cold shower after every practice. Hot water was available only for post-game showers. Was this the reason he left? No. Three down, seventeen to go, but let's go directly to the correct answer.

John Heisman left Atlanta after the 1919 season because he and his wife divorced and they agreed never again to live in the same city. Mrs. Heisman chose to remain in Atlanta so John Heisman left Georgia Tech.

That was 1919. Here in 1921 Bill Alexander was in his second season as the head coach at Tech. Under Coach Alexander Georgia Tech had lost but one game in 1920. At the start of this, the 1921, season, Tech had beaten Wake Forest, Oglethorpe, Davidson and Furman by a combined score of 222-0. These numbers 222-0 will re-surface later, so retain them in your memory.

The week prior to the Penn State game, Rutgers had traveled to Atlanta and for their trouble they were rewarded with a 48-14 trouncing. As a result, the Golden Tornado was now heavily favored for its game, against Penn State. However those persons making Georgia Tech a huge favorite should have reflected back to last year when Rutgers was supposed to be a measure of the strength of Nebraska's Cornhuskers and we all know what happened then.

October 29, 1921 Saturday, New York City, New York, The Polo Grounds
This was the first of four football games Penn State would play in New York City. State would play Georgia Tech and Syracuse in the first two in 1921 and '22 at the Polo Grounds home of The National League New York Baseball Giants. The next two Penn State football games in New York City, would be against West Virginia and Georgia Tech in 1923 and '25 and they would be played in Yankee Stadium. Had George Werley been at the 1921 Georgia Tech game he would have witnessed another first, possibly as memorable as the Nebraska game where each player had his own blanket. When Georgia Tech came onto the field they ran between the two goal post uprights and between two *female* cheerleaders. The two distaff cheerleaders probably shocked the Penn State team and fans, almost as much as the Georgia Tech football team did. Tech on its first possession fumbled. But they got the ball right back when State couldn't sustain a drive, and on their second possession featuring their Heisman Shift and legendary backs Buck Flowers, Red Barron and Judy Harlan they marched right down the field to jump out to a 7-0 lead. Just like the odds makers and the Golden Tornado fans expected.

It was now Georgia Tech's turn to kick-off. After the game, Bezdek proudly proclaimed the Lions executed the kick-off return just as he diagramed it. According to Bezdek, the return was supposed to give every appearance of being a middle return, but the blockers suddenly veered off to the right and set up a wall two yards from the right sideline and behind this protection Glenn Killinger returned the kick eighty-five yards for a touchdown. While this touchdown merely tied the score, Penn State took control from this point on. With "Light Horse Harry" Wilson, Joe Lightner and "Killy" adding three more touchdowns, one each, and the defense holding Tech scoreless, State recorded its second 28-7 win of the 1921 season.

State's unbeaten streak was now at twenty, breaking the record of nineteen straight established by Bill Hollenbeck's 1911 – 1913 teams.

In the final home game of the year on November 5, 1921, the Lions recovered from a fifty-yard touchdown by Carnegie Tech on a triple pass trick play. State put together two long drives with Wilson scoring both touchdowns and the Lions won 28-7 for the third time.

Away from home the Lions were often the underdog, however, they proved to be an excellent draw on the road. Home crowds averaged close to 3600 per game. But on the road State drew 30,000 at Harvard and 30,0000 at the Polo Grounds. Navy at Franklin Field attracted 25,000, the Pitt crowd was 34,000 and the December 3rd game in Seattle had a gate of 35,000.

The Penn State – Navy game was played in the mud at Franklin Field, Philadelphia, on November 12th and State won 13-7. One neutral sportswriter in his report said, "under good conditions Penn State would certainly have won by a greater margin." However it *was* a win. State now had thirteen days to prepare for Pitt. The Lions however had more on their minds than just the Pitt Panthers. But Pitt would be focusing on Penn State and Penn State only in their practice.

Penn State was scheduled to play Pitt, at Pittsburgh on Thanksgiving Day a dual arrangement which persisted virtually every year from 1907 through 1930. The Lions were then slated to play the University of Washington Huskies in Seattle on Saturday December 3rd.

For the ordinary traveler a coast to coast train trip in the 1920s took the better part of four days. A football team had two options – one option was to travel a day, work-out one day, travel a day, work-out one day, etc., or they could travel straight through during which time the players would lose their legs and their "wind" and conditioning. To regain those requisite physical attributes, so they could play up to their capabilities in an ensuing game, required the better part of a week upon reaching their destination.

Penn State didn't need thirteen days prior to the Pitt game to prepare for Panthers, therefore some of the practice time was devoted to preparations for Washington. After the Pitt game, State would be traveling straight through to the Seattle area meaning the time after they arrived would be spent on conditioning, timing, and "getting their legs back." So the act of scheduling the Washington game on December 3rd, the blame for which should most likely be laid at Bezdek's feet, affected two games – the Pitt game, and the Rose Bowl game which never happened. (How often does a team play a worthy opponent, beat them by two touchdowns and cost themselves a Rose Bowl trip? Penn State managed to do that.) Besides the division of the practice time and the diversion of the squad's and the staff's oneness of purpose the common departure from State College diffused the squad's concentration on Pitt. When the team left State College for the Pitt game they were also in fact leaving for the Washington game. They would not be returning to State College after the Pitt game to practice for Washington with a separate departure for Seattle, in fact the two games would be further commingled since the team would be boarding the train for Washington, in Pittsburgh, just hours after the Pitt game ended.

If we begin to compile a list of reasons why State would *not* beat Pitt in the up-coming game we could start with the Pittsburgh jinx, State had beaten Pitt only once since 1912, add in the distraction of a trans-continental four day train trip to The University of Washington after the Pitt game and then for good measure have Coach Bezdek not only be awakened Thanksgiving morning by the sound and sight of rain, but get him to predict to some sportswriters at the breakfast table that the final score for the day's game would be 0-0 and you have a can't miss recipe for an unhappy outcome. Then and now, one needn't be an ex-head coach or a Sports Psychologist to predict that the Nittany Lions weren't going to win their eighth game of the season, this day. When a coach 'fesses-up that he doesn't expect his team to score, you know this attitude will pervade his game plan, his play calling, his use of his personnel and it will rub off on the squad. A wise person once observed that when faced with an undertaking, if one person says, "I can do it" and another person says " I can't," chances are they are both right.

Sure enough Bezdek shelved many of the plays and formations State had been practicing to use against Pittsburgh; and Bezdek instead of playing to win, played not to lose. The strategy almost backfired as Pitt was deep in State territory on two occasions once on the three yard line, while State threatened only once when Pitt fumbled near their own twenty five yard line. But Bezdek's self-fulfilling prophecy of a 0-0 tie came true against a team that previously lost to Lafayette, Nebraska and Washington and Jefferson and just squeaked by a 5-4-1 West Virginia team and an even worse Cincinnati team.

Thursday evening following the 0-0 tie with Pitt the Penn State squad boarded their train for Washington and despite the more or less continuous journey they didn't arrive at their destination until Monday. Bezdek kept the squad away from the inquisitive press by housing the team and putting them through their paces outside of Seattle.

On Saturday, December 3rd the Huskies and the Lions met for the first time, and with the Lions going to the air repeatedly Penn State scored two touchdowns rushing, and one passing as Killinger completed twelve passes, eleven to end Stan McCullom in a 21-7 win.

It might not have been the straw that broke the camel's back but it certainly didn't help when someone decided that the Penn State team would not high-tail-it for home after the Washington game, instead they would take a leisurely one week sight-seeing return trip. This meant the team would not be back at Penn State ready to resume classes until the twelfth of December, having been away from campus nineteen days.

In what appeared to the public to be an affront to the Penn State team, Washington and Jefferson was invited to play the University of California on January 1, 1922 in the Rose Bowl. Predictably Bezdek was vehement at this oversight. However if we just look at the logistics and the overall situation at State we can pose the question, should the same squad that just took a trip to the State of Washington that involved being away from campus for nineteen days turn around and approximately ten days later take another four-days-out, four-days-back and six days-in-California trip to the West Coast? Might not this trip be better allocated to another Penn State team since no other football team in Penn State history except this 1921 team, had traveled farther west than the State of Ohio? Also this trip would mean that everyone making both trips would be away from home for Thanksgiving, Christmas and New Years.

Rumors have it that, the Rose Bowl committee approached the Penn State administration unofficially to find out if Penn State would be receptive to an invitation to play in the January 1, 1922 Rose Bowl game. The answer they were given was that such an offer would be held in the highest esteem but it would be respectfully declined. Naturally the Rose Bowl committee did not wish to be publicly rebuffed, so no invitation was proffered and Washington and Jefferson was invited instead.

The Washington and Jefferson players acquitted themselves quite well battling The University of California to a 0-0 tie in the 1922 Rose Bowl. One story and one game statistic received attention then, and bear repeating to-day; first the statistic. In the January 1, 1922 Rose Bowl game, Washington and Jefferson head coach Earle "Greasy" Neale did not make a substitution throughout the game. All eleven Washington and Jefferson players played the full sixty minutes.

Regarding the story, as you might expect Washington and Jefferson College was little known west of Ohio. Therefore when the news broke on the West Coast that W & J would be the University of California's New Year's Day opponent there was a scramble among the newspapers to find newsworthy information about this mystery team. A sports editor at a Berkeley, California, newspaper called one of his sports reporters into his office and said, "Doug, I want you to write a series of articles leading up to the game to familiarize our readers with these Easterners. What do you know about Washington and Jefferson?"

In a classic reply the sports reporter said, "The only thing I know about Washington and Jefferson is – they're both dead."

CHAPTER 29

"Wrong Way" Riegels, John Heisman and the Ramblin' Wrecks from
Georgia Tech

The January 1, 1929 Rose Bowl game involved Georgia Tech and
the University of California, in one of the most memorable Rose
Bowl games ever played. The 1929 Tech team came into the Rose
Bowl game as the undefeated 9-0-0 Southern Conference Champions,
having beaten VMI, Oglethorpe, Vanderbilt, North Carolina and Tulane
as well as Alabama, Auburn, Georgia and Notre Dame and there was a
possible National Championship in the offing.

Early in the second quarter of the game "Cal" got an apparent big
break in what had been a scoreless battle. Tech halfback "Stumpy"
Thomason fumbled the football at Tech's own 36-yard line. For Roy
Riegels, California's center and captain, fate had given him a wide -open
opportunity to scoop up the football and run for a touchdown, for the
first score of the game. Had Roy Riegels been just an average football
player, someone else might have beaten him to the football, or were he a
less confident player he might have just fallen on the ball and it would
have been "Cal's" ball at Tech's thirty-six yard line. But Roy Riegels was
an above average player (why else would he be the team captain?) so he
scooped up the ball and set off to score. As Roy ran with the football, one
of the fastest players on the California team, Benny Lom, set out in pursuit of Riegels.

As Lom drew abreast of Riegels he yelled, "You're running the wrong
way," but with the entire Rose Bowl crowd yelling as loudly as their
lungs would allow, Riegels couldn't make out what Lom was saying
through the tiny ear hole in his helmet.

"I thought he wanted a lateral," Riegels later explained, "but I told
him, get away this is my touchdown." Finally at the 10-yard line Lom
tried to stop Riegels by tackling him but Roy was too determined and he
pulled away. Lom had however slowed Riegels down sufficiently so
that he and several other California players brought Riegels down at the
California three yard line. As yet no damage had been done. "Cal" had
the ball. Tech hadn't scored, there were no points on the scoreboard so
nothing irrevocable or irreversible had occurred. In the "Cal" huddle
there wasn't mass hysteria. All Captain Roy Riegels muttered was a quiz-
zical "Why would I do something like that?" California still had the ball,
and four downs to attempt to extricate themselves from this situation.

Lady Luck still had a chance to smile on the California Golden Bears and Roy Riegels. Had "Cal" chosen to run one or two plays to regain their composure they might have moved the ball out of danger and then punted or they might even have driven the ball deep into Georgia Tech territory or scored. Had any such thing transpired, Roy Riegels' fifteen seconds of notoriety would have long been forgotten.

However the "Cal" brain trust made a very poor decision. After an unsettling or momentum changing occurrence it is not wise to immediately call a play where one missed assignment can bring disaster. But this is what "Cal" elected to do. Instead of running one or two safe plays and then punting on third down if the offense has not been able to make a first-down, the head coach panicked or went ultra-conservative, and ordered a punt on first down, not giving his offense a chance to get organized. With Lom back in punt formation to kick the ball out of danger, Riegels made a perfect snap to Lom. But the whole left side of the California line collapsed and Tech's tackle Vance Maree broke through to block the punt which went out of the end zone for a safety and a 2-0 Georgia Tech lead.

Both teams traded touchdowns in the second half. "Cal" made their point after touchdown for seven points while Georgia Tech missed their point-after for six points but with the two points from the safety, Tech prevailed 8-7. And Roy Riegels was ever after known as "Wrong Way" Riegels.

Upon due reflection wasn't the left side of the "Cal" line equally culpable? Also why didn't Benny Lom tackle Riegles sooner rather than running stride for stride with him trying to yell over the roar of the crowd? But no one bailed Roy Riegels out and his "wrong way run" cost California the Rose Bowl game. The play has lived on and Riegels had to bear-up under the adverse notoriety the rest of his life. However, Roy Riegels didn't "cash in his chips," in fact maybe that incident made him a better, stronger person. Maybe the notoriety helped him to get a better job, or helped him to further his career because he was the one and only "Wrong Way" Riegels. I first heard of Roy Riegel's run more than fifty years ago and never forgot his name. However prior to doing this research the author had never heard of Benny Lom, Vance Maree, the Georgia Tech player who blocked the punt, or the other nineteen players on the field with Roy Riegels at the time of his run.

Incidentally, Georgia Tech was named the INS Co-National Champion for 1928.

While John Heisman had a reputation as an innovator in football who invented, refined, and/or popularized some trick plays, (the lateral pass, the onside kick, the reverse and the pulling guard) he also engaged in some subterfuge and some borderline unethical ploys. One of his trick plays which was later declared illegal involved the quarterback taking the center-snap then slipping the ball under his uniform jersey, while faking to hand it off to a back. He then bent down to tie his shoelace and after the defenders were off chasing the presumed ball carrier, the quarterback would produce the ball and run for a touchdown.

The same John Heisman was the head coach at Clemson before he held the same post at Georgia Tech and in 1902 in that capacity at Clemson he pulled a scam which made the author wonder why he wasn't persona non gratis at Georgia Tech for ever after. A full day prior to the Clemson-Georgia Tech football game that year, Heisman and his squad checked into an Atlanta hotel and proceeded to party in the lobby, in the restaurant, in the men's bar and on the two floors where the team was lodged. The boisterous noise and rowdyism brought numerous complaints from other guests in the hotel as the partying didn't die down until the sun came up Saturday morning. Since betting on football games was done openly across the country, the word-of-mouth news of the all-night revelry spread like wildfire and everybody who could find a patsy, bet big bucks on Tech.

What those bettors never did see was the Clemson varsity arrive Saturday morning on a second train (not the one that brought the decoy scrubs the previous day). The varsity arrived fresh and well-rested after a quite night in Lula, Georgia and Clemson trounced Tech 44-5.

On October 7, 1916 one of the strangest football games of all time was played in Atlanta, Georgia. Some say Georgia Tech sought revenge on the football field, for the 22-0 trouncing Cumberland University had handed Georgia Tech in a previous *baseball* game. Others say John Heisman was trying to build Tech into a national power and having seen the Cumberland team practice, he recognized an opportunity to schedule a team Tech could beat by any score he would choose. To get Cumberland University to leave Lebanon, Tennessee and travel to Atlanta, Heisman offered them a $500.00 guarantee. In those days $500.00 was a very attractive "pay day."

At some point prior to game day, the Cumberland team became aware they were in over their heads, therefore on their train trip to Atlanta they stopped in Nashville and tried to recruit some Vanderbilt players to bolster their team. One can only imagine how lacking in skill the Cumberland team must have been if they tried to recruit players from a team, which the next year would lose to Georgia Tech 83-0. As it turned out when Cumberland University's team arrived in Atlanta they discovered that not only hadn't they been able to recruit any "Vandy" players, but they actually lost three of *their* players in Nashville.

Georgia Tech kicked off to Cumberland to start the game. Beginning with their very first possession and continuing throughout the game, on every series of downs, Cumberland University showed negative yardage. They didn't make a single first down in the whole game and the score at the end of the first quarter was 63-0 in favor of Georgia Tech.

As the game progressed the Cumberland players became aware that blockers and ball carriers took the most punishment so they punted early and often or fumbled giving Tech the ball. If the defenders had sufficient numbers they would attempt to tackle the ball carrier, single tacklers probably used the bullfighter's "Ole" technique.

Georgia Tech didn't throw a pass in the whole game but racked up 509 yards on end runs. Despite shortening the quarters to 12 ½ minutes and clearing the bench, Tech scored 63 points in the second quarter to lead 126-0 at halftime. Another 54 points in the third quarter broke the record for the greatest number of points scored by a college football team in one game (152 points by Michigan in 1912) and 42 more points in the fourth quarter made the final score 222-0.

The Cumberland Bulldog players collected their $500.00 and reportedly took in the sights of Atlanta before returning to Tennessee.

CHAPTER 30

The Last Bowl Game for Twenty-Five Years

The destiny of the Penn State 1922 football team was inexorably altered by the 1921 football game at Washington which resulted in the Rose Bowl invitation that was never proffered. The next year in what may have been a record for an early bowl invitation, Penn State was offered and officially accepted a Rose Bowl berth after their fifth game of the 1922 season. Actually reliable sources say the offer was made and accepted by Penn State *before* the season began. Even more amazing other reliable sources say the invitation might have been made as early as April or May and unofficially accepted at *that time.* Unfortunately for Penn State's reputation, and it's won-lost record, the early invitation, as is often the case, backfired.

Relative to Penn State's football reputation the pendulum had gone as far in the favorable direction as it would go in 1920 to mid-1922 after which it would reverse its swing. The 1919 –1921 teams were better than they were acknowledged to be, but the 1922 squad wasn't as good as the Rose Bowl Committee and outsiders thought it was. It is not uncommon for a football team to lose their next game after a big win or upon clinching a league title or a Bowl bid. But the 1922 Penn State team, once it had the bulls-eye on its back, just didn't have the leadership or the players to right the ship when things began to go badly.

The bowl bid was officially announced on the eve of the Syracuse game at the Polo Grounds in New York City This was the initial game in an annual rivalry between the Orangemen and the Lions extending through 1990, missing only one year, the 1943 war year. Even though this was the first meeting between the two teams the final score a 0-0 tie was a precursor to the early competitiveness of the rivalry. A series where Syracuse had three, four and five game winning streaks before 1960 and State had an eight game and a three game winning streak in the same time period. The series stood at 17 to 16 in favor of State (with 5 ties) through 1960. After two PSU wins in 1961 and '62 and four Syracuse wins 1963 – 1966, the series swung heavily in favor of the Lions as they defeated the Orangemen 21 times in the next 24 meetings.

Penn State, following the 1922 Syracuse contest, had now played 30 consecutive games without tasting defeat. When a team is on a roll they don't like to have their routine altered. But like it or not the practice week between the Syracuse and Navy games would be shorter than normal as the Navy game was not only an away game, but due to a scheduling conflict at Griffith Field the game had to be played on Friday instead of Saturday. While Penn State won the battle of the statistics, two hundred and thirteen yards to one hundred yards, and nine first downs to just four, Navy used two State turnovers and a fake punt to score twice and the Midshipmen ended Penn State's streak with a 14-0 win.

What had caught up with State was the fact that the Lions simply couldn't overcome the loss of Snell, Lightner, Redinger, and above all Killinger from their 1921 backfield. Redinger was supposed to return along with Wilson, but after the 1921 season assistant coach Dick Harlow and head coach Bezdek acrimoniously parted ways. Harlow became the new head coach at Colgate and he took Redinger and several other players with him. Bezdek complained about this treachery privately for months, but after the Navy loss, "Bez" went public, practically accusing Harlow of "gutting" his team.

Despite the loss, the students welcomed the team home and, in a remarkable show of support, turned out in large numbers for the week's practice sessions. That Saturday a large and enthusiastic crowd cheered the Lions to a 10 – 0 win over Carnegie Tech. (Every November home game 1921 – 1923 was against a "Tech" team. The 1921 and '22 games featured Carnegie Tech while the 1923 contest show-cased Georgia Tech on its only visit to Penn State.)

The new "winning streak" ended one week later when the Lions lost to Penn 7 – 6 and the new losing streak doubled when Pitt topped the Lions 14 –0. This loss to Pitt was the first of fourteen consecutive losses Penn State fans would have to endure. Thus the Rose Bowl-bound 1922 Penn State team ended up losing three of their last four regular season games and went to Pasadena as badly damaged merchandise.

There was public criticism of Bezdek's management of the team personnel, with some experts stating that Mike Palm wasn't the man to be quarterbacking the team, that the only bonafide star and leader was Harry Wilson and that the team needed him at quarterback. When Bezdek finally did make a change, he made what seemed to be a desperation move when he took "Squeaks " Hufford, a third year starter at end, and moved him to right halfback. He also promoted sophomore scrub Barney Wentz to starting fullback, keeping Wilson and Palm at their previous positions.

January 1, 1923 The Rose Bowl, Pasadena, California

The most memorable moments in this replay of a Pennsylvania team vs. a California team occurred before the game started. In a classic blunder, Penn State was not provided with a departure time sufficiently in advance of the announced kick-off time. This was the first game played in the new stadium at its present site and that coupled with a huge traffic jam after the Tournament of Roses Parade resulted in the taxi cabs transporting the Nittany Lions to the game, being caught in traffic that couldn't move. Finally, after being threatened by "Bez," the cabs drove across people's front lawns, but they still could get no closer than one mile from the stadium. That necessitated the team hiking the remaining distance, arriving some thirty minutes late, requiring a forty-five minute delay in the start of the game. Bezdek felt he had been sandbagged, but USC Coach Elmer "Gloomy Gus" Henderson was not at all sympathetic, he thought it was an intentional psychological ploy on Bezdek's part and the two coaches almost came to blows on the field before the game began.

Southern California in their first Rose Bowl game took the measure of State 14 –3 and many USC people credited the Trojan win against State to their freshman coach Harold "Bill" Hess the captain of the 1920 Penn State team. It was Hess who helped head coach Henderson devise a defense to stop Bezdek's short pass offense. This was *another* knock against Bezdek. It was said that he was reluctant to give anyone on his staff credit, keeping all the glory for himself and thus he failed to inspire any of the people around him with a strong sense of loyalty.

As if State didn't have enough problems Captain "Newsh" Bentz ran afoul of Bezdek during the week preceding the game and "Bez" held him out of the game until it was too late. With the game's late start, State had its second contest in two seasons that ended in near darkness. Sportswriters said they had to strike matches for sufficient light to finish their accounts of the game.

Penn State's 1922 Varsity Football Squad. Front Row (left to right), Wilson, Hufford, McMahon, Bentz, Bedenk, Frank, Palm. Back row Coach Bezdek, Logue, Hamilton, Artelt, Flock, Wentz, Parsons, Manager.

Commencement Booklet for Class of 1924 graduates.

CHAPTER 31

"Light Horse Harry" Wilson, the Seven Year Letterman

We might compare the 1923 Nittany Lion to a male African lion about to lose dominance over his pride and his territory. He will soon be driven out by a younger lion or lions, and the King of Beasts will be destined to wander for the rest of his declining days. At least in college football there is a chance for the vanquished "King" to reclaim his throne. But for this majestic Nittany Lion of Centre County its reign had peaked between 1919 through 1921, and by 1925 it was apparent that its days were numbered. There would be a few good years, 6-2-1 in 1927, and 6-3 in 1929, but there would be no more undefeated years or bowl games for two decades.

While the 1923 team boasted some outstanding players such as "Hap" Frank and All-Americans Joe Bedenk and Harry Wilson, the wealth of talent trickled down to just an occasional drop by the 1930s as Penn State went "Simon Pure" and stopped giving any football scholarships. However for this 1923 season, George Werley's senior year, "Light Horse Harry" would saddle up for the last time at Penn State and with the help his teammates could provide, Wilson did his best to carry the team to a lofty finish reminiscent of prior teams. Despite any other versions, my father insisted that Penn Staters never referred to Harry Wilson as Harry "Light Horse" Wilson, it was *always* "Light Horse Harry" Wilson.

State laid shutouts on Lebanon Valley 58-0, North Carolina State 16-0 and Gettysburg 20-0. Now came the tough part of the schedule Navy, West Virginia, Syracuse, Georgia Tech, Penn and Pitt with only Navy and Georgia Tech being home games. In the season's last six games State beat Navy 21-3, tied West Virginia 13-13, lost to Syracuse 10-0 beat Georgia Tech 7-0 and Penn 21-0. The Pitt game was played (where else?) in Pittsburgh, on (what else?) a muddy field and State lost 20-3. In those six games, his last at Penn State, "Light Horse Harry" scored *every touchdown* Penn State recorded, a total of nine.

Surprisingly, considering how Harry Wilson carried the Penn State team, Walter Camp only selected him to his second team. Camp at times lacked objectivity when it came to his dearly beloved Ivy League. Red Grange and two Ivy League backs edged out Harry for the quarterback/halfback slots. Equally unjust, the immortal Ernie Nevers, Stanford's fullback, was relegated to the 3rd team. Harry did make several other first team All-American squads in '23 and many others including Knute

Rockne's in 1926.

"Light Horse Harry" never had a serious injury in seven years of varsity collegiate football. Most remarkable. Some people said that he had a little trick of just getting his foot or his feet off the ground when he was going to be tackled and brought down and this ability helped explain his injury free career. There were also people who said that the last person you wanted to be tackled by was the now-graduated George Snell, as he could hit you three times before you reached the ground. So we probably shouldn't believe everything we hear.

However back to Wilson and what constitutes an injury; it's the old story – it depends "whose ox is being gored." Early in the 1922 Georgia Tech game with the score 7-7, Wilson was kicked in the mouth, which "knocked-out" one tooth and completely broke off another. When "Light Horse Harry" rushed over to Captain Glenn Killinger and showed him what happened (probably expecting "Killy" would call for a time-out,) he was confronted by a very stoic Killinger who with almost a hint of disdain said, "Well, Harry we can't do anything about that now can we?"

As we mentioned previously the 1922 Navy game was played on a Friday with the result that a number of Eastern head coaches attended the game. As the story goes, Army had, prior to the Navy game, approached tackle "Tiny" McMahon about attending West Point, but McMahon wasn't interested. "Tiny" supposedly told his recruiters "that fella over there might be interested," "that fella," being Harry Wilson. Possibly head coach John McEwan saw Harry play on November 3rd, with the result that Harry was offered an appointment to the Military Academy. "Light Horse Harry" Wilson, who obviously had the moniker long before he entered West Point Military Academy where a cadet might pick-up a nickname of that nature, became a career Air Force officer who always held Penn State first in his heart. At Penn State – Army basketball games, boxing and wrestling matches, while a cadet, he drew a lot of flak from his fellow cadets because he couldn't make himself "root" against Penn State.

Harry's accomplishment of lettering *seven* times in football, three at Penn State and four at West Point while somehow managing to avoid "burn-out" and/or injury was an amazing feat. His intelligence and experience enabled him, especially on defense, to be at the right place at the right time with seemingly a minimum of effort. According to Ridge Riley a photograph of an Army team "digging in" on defense just a yard or so away from their own goal posts (at that time goal posts were made of wood and were positioned right on the goal line) showed "Light Horse Harry" leaning against one of the goal posts. I wonder if Wilson ever met Dennis Onkotz. They both seemed to be able to conserve their energy for those times when it mattered the most.

At Army out of 1500 lettermen over one hundred and six years (1890-1995), Harry is one of only ninety-one football players to win four letters. He was elected to the National Football Foundation Hall of Fame and he accomplished something matched by few, if any. He was named to the All-Time Teams of two schools, Penn State and Army.

A final note about "Light Horse Harry" and his teammate, also a four-letter-winner, halfback Christian "Red" Cagle. Wilson was the Captain of the 1927 team, a team that went 9-1 losing only to Yale 10-6. In the final game of his career, when "Red" Cagle's number was called down on the Navy goal line, Cagle twice refused the carry and insisted that "this is Harry's game and he should get the call." Wilson scored both touchdowns as Army beat Navy 14-9. Even though Cagle over-shadowed Wilson and was selected an All-American in 1927, '28 and '29 while Harry was selected only in 1926 the two were good friends. Ironically in 1928 and 1929 when it would have been his turn to score against Navy, Cagle never scored. Why?

For years Navy had complained of Army's recycling of football players who had played several years elsewhere and then played three or four more years at West Point. When Army refused to alter their eligibility rules Navy refused to schedule Army in 1928 and 1929. It finally took an act of Congress to renew the rivalry in 1930. Army did change their eligibility criteria and the two teams have met every year since then. (Navy has been the last regular season opponent on Army's schedule every year since 1930 except in 1933 when Army closed their season against Notre Dame the week after the Navy game. Army lost that game 13-12 to end their 1933 season at 9-1.)

CHAPTER 32

Penn State Subscribes to the Carnegie Report

Beginning with the 1904 season, when Tom Fennell became Penn State's first full-time head coach, Penn State compiled a won-lost-tied record of 59-19-5 through the 1912 season. After losing seasons in 1913 and 1918, State rebounded in 1919 - 1921 with 22 wins no losses and four ties for a .720 winning percentage through the 1921 season. This winning percentage dipped to .682 by the end of the 1929 season and the decline continued through the 1938 season. This decline of fortunes was precipitated by the infamous 1927 Carnegie Report. The Report was the end product of an investigation into the excesses resulting from, and attributable to college football. The Report, in summary, found that football led to rowdyism, contributed to professionalism (vs. amateurism), gambling and excessive drinking and had an adverse effect on the academic aspect of colleges where football was emphasized. Some schools, and Penn State was one of them, elected to accept the findings and in response abolished all future football scholarships. By 1932 Penn State football had seen all but two of the former scholarship players graduate or leave school. The now toothless Nittany Lion was so weakened that the eighteen meager wins it could manage in the years 1930 through 1935 came against the likes of Lebanon Valley, Niagara, Marshall, Sewanee and Lehigh. From 1930 through 1935 (six years) Penn State *did not win one* of the twenty-two games the Lions played against Bucknell, Colgate, Temple, Syracuse, Waynesburg, Pitt or Penn. They did manage to tie Penn and Syracuse once each.

Even *if* the big city schools like Pitt, Penn, Temple, Syracuse etc. did accept the report and also stopped giving scholarships they still had many more football players going to high school, living and playing football within a ten-twenty mile radius of their university than was the case at Penn State. The area surrounding State College was, and still is, small towns, open countryside and no city with a population of 100,000 within 75 miles. This sparsely populated landscape didn't then and doesn't today turn out large numbers of Division 1 football players and does not have many AAA and AAAA schools where the highest levels of competition exist.

On the other hand, schools like Pitt, Penn, Fordham, NYU, Georgetown and Temple had huge numbers of football players within a bus, a subway or an "el" train ride of campus. These young men could more easily get-by without a scholarship, if they had to, since they returned home at the end of each school day and their only college cost was tuition, since they slept and ate at home. Pittsburgh, among others, had one additional ace up its sleeve. Pitt's coach at one time was Jock Sutherland who was really Dr. "Jock" Sutherland a dental school graduate. "Jock" and other big city coaches took numerous kids from coal-mining towns and after their college football days were over expedited their entry into Pitt, Penn, etc., dental schools giving them a life-time profession in lieu of, or after a pro football career. These were living examples of what football could do to take a tough high school kid away from a life of labor as a coal miner and these success stories were powerful recruiting tools. Penn State still doesn't have a dental school "pipe line" but it now has law school and medical school affiliations, which are helpful.

As recently as the late 1940s and early '50s football coaches at these more rural high schools found that some of their biggest and hardiest male students lived on farms. They also found very few fathers of these young men were willing to let their sons play football on weekends and practice football after school on weekdays (at a time of the year when there was precious little daylight after school). Especially not when there were crops to be harvested, fields to be tilled, chores to be done and cows to be milked etc. After all, when this young man finished with his schooling he was going to inherit the farm - there was no talk of "Pro" football. Many a high school coach's jaw "dropped," like a kid looking at a store window display of electric trains, upon seeing an in-coming freshman who could pick up two fifty-pound feed bags hold them out at arm's length and toss both on to a flatbed truck, only to learn that the young men in that family didn't play football, they had farm work (chores) to do before and after school.

The legendary University of Minnesota coach Bernie Bierman however worked these rural areas very successfully 1932-1941 probably with the help of scholarships, during which time his teams won National Titles in 1936, '40 and '41 and finished fifth and tenth in 1937 and 1938 respectively. Tall-tale tellers said Coach Bierman did his recruiting simply by driving through the country-side looking for a strapping young man plowing a field with a one-man plowshare. It was said that Bernie needed just one question to decide if he wished to recruit the young man. Coach Bierman would ask him to point in the direction of Minneapolis. If the teenager took his hands off the plowshare and pointed, Bernie drove on. When he found a young man who just raised the plowshare and used *it* to point he gave him a scholarship on the spot.

(Minnesota incidentally plays for four Division I football rivalry trophies. The "Little Brown Jug" rivalry with Michigan dates back to 1903 while the rivalries with Iowa for "Floyd of Rosedale," Wisconsin for "Paul Bunyan's Axe" and Penn State for the "Governors Victory Bell," date back to 1935, 1948 and 1993 respectively.)

However all through the 1930s and until WW II intervened, Penn State, with no football scholarships to give, was playing against a stacked deck and its record showed it . Penn State's twelve year record 1930 through 1941 was forty-seven wins, forty-four losses and seven ties, a winning percentage of just .515. (With eighteen of the forty-seven wins coming in 1939-41.)

CHAPTER 33

The Thirties and the Depression

Prior to World War II, and shortly-thereafter, many people, Pennsylvanians included, had only the vaguest idea where State College and Penn State were located. The following story, which took place in the mid-1930s, was related to me by one of the three young men in the story and he said their naivete was not at all uncommon.

Three Penn State College incoming freshmen of stocky build and with that rolling gait that says, "football player/athlete on the move" were ambling along College Avenue toward Allen Street. The leader J. J., flanked by Mac and Red, each with a suitcase in each hand were making the familiar trek from the bus depot. They had arrived via the Pennsylvania Railroad, and the Bellefonte to State College Johnston's Motor Bus Line, just as George Werley had done approximately 15 years earlier. Like George, none of the three had ever been in State College prior to disembarking from the bus.

It was a Chamber of Commerce State College September day, with the sun just losing its hazy appearance. While J.J. and his buddies were not walking with any urgency they were walking more directly than George Werley had years prior, because *they* had rooms waiting for them. All they had to do was find Penn State and the Main Building. As they approached Allen Street they still didn't know where, in State College, Penn State was located. And what the heck was Penn State supposed to look like anyway? Having been raised in two of the towns, which blend right into the City of Scranton, these three frosh didn't expect that this college educational collection of buildings would be out in some farmland. Thus when they reached the corner of College Avenue and Allen Street they looked to the side where most of the urbanization and building seemed to have taken place and there they saw a building with an American flag in front of it. They guessed "this must be Penn State and the Main Building," the place where they were supposed to report. As they proceeded up Allen Street a man who had witnessed their indecision asked if he could help them.

The leader J. J., said, "Well, we're freshmen here and we're going to report to the Main Building at Penn State." Now, pointing at what in actuality was the U. S. Post Office, he asked, "Is that it?"

"No", replied the good-natured gent, "You just turn yourself around and go back where you came from on the corner. Across the street you see the road that runs between those two stone pillars with the walkway on each side? You just follow either walk up the hill and the Main Building is to the right behind that stand of trees - it's a six-story building with lots of windows. That's Penn State over there among all those trees."

Jim O'Hora and his two fellow athletes were attending Penn State through the efforts of Jim Gilligan, a high school official and a Dunmore, Pennsylvania, resident. There still were no football scholarships, but Gilligan in Northeastern Pennsylvania and Casey Jones in Southwestern Pennsylvania arranged to get financially strapped football players of good character, with the necessary academic background into Penn State. These two men through their contacts found jobs for the players, arranged to get them free books from recent graduates, alumni, etc. The jobs were real, Mrs. Ruth Toretti told the author that her husband made up beds as one of his jobs. Today such actions, getting free books and jobs for players would bring the NCAA to the offending school like moths to a light. But considering that Penn State had voluntarily and unilaterally ceased giving athletic scholarships what charges would an outside agency make? Should Penn State be accused of being devious for saying they would not give athletic scholarships and then having some well-meaning Penn Stater circumvent, to some degree, the policy the Administration had voluntarily imposed upon itself?

Casey Jones and Jim Gilligan were responsible for at least two of the following four assistant coaches being at Penn State and lettering as players in the 1930s: Earle Edwards who played in 1928-1930 and coached 1936-1948, Al Mikelonis, who changed his name to Al Michaels, played in 1933-1934 and coached 1935-1952, Sever Toretti played 1936-1938 and coached 1949-1962 and Jim O'Hora 1933-1935 who coached 1946-1976. We will take an in-depth look at the careers of two of these men.

While Penn State wouldn't have a winning season until 1937 and Coach Bob Higgins wouldn't get his won–lost percentage above .500 until his twelfth season, the efforts of Casey Jones and Jim Gilligan began having an effect by the late 1930s. Then came World War II.

If World War II had not happened what would our world be like today? Would it be a better world or might it be much worse, with anarchy and no strong governments after decades of worldwide depression? With all of the suffering and loss of life occasioned by World War II we'll still never know with 100% certainly that the world might not be worse than it is. One cannot have the absolute certainty that an Alcatraz inmate expressed, upon being transferred to another facility when Alcatraz was closed. The inmate, a Mr. Thompson, said, upon boarding a boat to leave the island, "This place never done nobody no good." But World War II did do Penn State considerable good, bringing football players and other young college persons to State College from other colleges and universities who otherwise would never have been exposed to Penn State. Many of these players participated on Penn State teams during the 1942-1946 era and many who left to go off to war returned to play and study at Penn State at a later time.

When Jim O'Hora graduated with the Penn State Class of 1936 he had a degree in Physical Education. However, the market was top-heavy on the supply side and sorely lacking in demand. Jim was just one of hundreds of grads with no experience looking to get a teaching/coaching position at the height of the Depression. But the bleak outlook turned rosier when Coach Bob Higgins asked O'Hora if he'd like to take a graduate assistant coaching position and work on his Masters degree. O'Hora, the man later known to his players as "The O," said he didn't see how he could manage that, his college funds were pretty well depleted. He couldn't ask his mother to keep sending him $5.00 each week for food when things were so tough back home.

Coach Higgins said, "Oh, you'll get a stipend of $1,000.00 for one year and your books and tuition will be paid."

O'Hora thought, "Holy smokes, I've been living on $5.00 a week. I can sure as heck live on $20.00 a week and send money home to the family." He said, "I jumped at the opportunity before he had a chance to take the offer back."

Given this terrific opportunity Jim worked hard and studied conscientiously and a year later he now had a leg up on the competition. He was older than the new graduates, he had more than an ordinary Bachelors Degree, and on his resume he could show he had been on the Penn State Football Coaching Staff, something not many applicants could equal or top.

O'Hora got a head coaching position in the western part of the state where he had a very successful two years. Despite his success, he had his eyes and ears open for a position closer to his hometown of Dunmore when the perfect position at Mahanoy Township High School became available. It was perfect because it was close to home, but not too close, and because Mahanoy City High School was turning out great basketball and football teams some of this success and notoriety was rubbing off on the Township High School team. O'Hora made the switch and along with his coaching success at Mahanoy Township it was there he met and fell in love with his lifelong mate Elizabeth "Betts" Miller. Like many others in his age group O'Hora's career was put on hold while he gave Uncle Sam and the U.S. Navy several years of his life. During this time he became an officer and a husband.

At the end of the war Coach O'Hora returned to his job at Mahanoy

Township. But now, the "Phys.Ed" major who was too young and inexperienced to get a head coaching position in 1936, was in his mid-thirties and wondering when he would get a chance to be a college coach.

And then it happened. Bob Higgins called again, asking O'Hora if he'd be interested in an assistant coaching position at his alma mater. O'Hora wasted no time accepting this offer of "The Hig's" either.

Coach O'Hora's first year on the Penn State staff started well when State opened with a 48-6 win over Bucknell. The tide had turned in this rivalry and State had now won eight games in a row over the Bisons. Two more wins and the rivalry with Bucknell would end, since the two football programs were obviously heading in opposite directions.

Opponent number two was Syracuse, against whom State didn't win a game in six years, 1930-1935. Then when the pendulum paused to change direction State won two, lost one and tied two. Now it was payback time and Syracuse wouldn't win a game 1941-1949. The game at Syracuse was a night game and according to Ridge Riley this 1946 Penn State 9-0 win was more than just a Williams to Durkota touchdown pass and an Ed Czekaj field goal. Syracuse head coach Clarence "Biggie" Munn, prior to the start of the game, complained to State's coach Higgins that Penn State was wearing all white uniforms intentionally, since the football used for night games in those days was all white; and this put his Syracuse team at a severe disadvantage. The average football fan probably is aware that in Division I football the home team wears the colored uniforms and the visiting team must wear a contrasting color generally white. Interestingly in Division I basketball the situation is reversed, the home team wears white and the visitors wear dark uniforms. What many people do not realize is that the visiting team must bring both light and dark uniforms just in case the home team should choose *not* to wear the dark uniforms. LSU is a home team which chooses to do exactly that. They consider their white "away" shirts to be their lucky uniforms, possibly pre-dating night games when white would have been cooler under the Louisiana sun. Since they wear their away uniform at home they get to wear them all the time. Well *almost* all the time. Recently in a game at The University of Florida the Gators chose to wear their "away" uniforms at home forcing LSU to wear their less-lucky dark "home" uniforms on the road.

But back to the Syracuse game. The teams went to their respective locker rooms with Coach Munn figuring State would not change uniforms and Coach Higgins feeling Syracuse might protest the game if State stayed with their all-white uniforms. Therefore State switched to their dark uniform tops and when they came onto the field Coach Munn went ballistic since he had come to the conclusion that Higgins wouldn't give in, so he had the equipment managers darken all of the footballs. After a baseball score 6-2 win over Colgate, the Lions beat Fordham 68-0. A follow-up 75-0 win in 1947 would end that rivalry also. Two more wins 26-0 over Temple and an unexpected 12-7 win at Navy preceded the Pitt game. Navy and Army were two of the powerhouse teams during the war years but following the war's end in August, Midshipmen and Cadets who wished to return to civilian life were allowed to have their commitment waived and many did, leaving both academies considerably weakened.

Once again Penn State was favored in the Pitt-Penn State game which was no longer being played on Thanksgiving Day. Pitt came into the game having won only two games, a 33-7 victory over a 5 and 5 West Virginia team and a 7-6 victory over Marquette. The Panthers had scored more than eight points but once all year however, they put a season high fourteen points on the scoreboard which was sufficient to make State it's third victim in nine games, 14-7.

Coach Jim O'Hora's 1940s' Mahanoy Township football team. (Coach O'Hora left rear.)

CHAPTER 34

The Sitting Hen Play Almost Cooked State's Goose

The 1947 season began with Penn State playing Washington State in Hershey, Pa. on September 20. Penn State won 27-6 but the game obviously wasn't much of a "draw" as the announced gate was just 15,000.

In the next three games State scored 169 points to the opposition's (Bucknell, Fordham, Syracuse) zero. A 21-14 win over West Virginia closed out the month of October and November 1 Penn State's Lions would meet Colgate's Red Raiders for the eleventh time. Interestingly the first Colgate team to use the nickname Red Raiders found the new sobriquet to be a good luck charm until the season ended. The Red Raiders attained that most coveted of all season records, the four "U" season, unbeaten, untied and unscored upon. However that's where Colgate's good luck ended because they collected the dreaded fifth "U," uninvited (to a bowl game). The 46-0 walloping "The Nits" hung on the Raiders, enabled State to move ahead of the Michigan Wolverines in offensive production. Now, they were not only the number one defensive team in the country, but they were also number one offensively. The Lions, who were loaded with returning servicemen, several of whom played and lettered four years at State, had terrorized all but two opponents through the first six games of this 1947 season. The Nittany Lions averaged almost fifty-four points per game in their four lopsided victories and forty-four points per game in all six contests. Of all of their opponents to date, only West Virginia and Washington State scored.

During the week preceding the Temple game, the fact that Penn State was now ranked first in the country offensively *and* defensively was a hot topic in and around State College. *The Daily Collegian* and other football prognosticators fearlessly predicted Temple's Alumni Homecoming Weekend would be washed away by a Blue and White tidal wave, or words to that effect. This adoration and all the number one hoopla was very heady stuff for a football program which ten years previously had recorded its first winning season since the 1920s, a program which won just thirty-four games, lost forty-one and tied six in the ten years, 1930-1939. Penn State's faculty, administration, students and State College borough inhabitants had not seen a Penn State team win its first four games in any season since the ill-fated 1923 team, and none of these fans were experienced in coping with such a situation. An unbeaten team must be ever vigilant, especially where opponents with poor records are concerned. Teams with superior records try to play well in every game; to maintain their superior record they have to win all or most of their games. They can't point toward just one game. Teams with poor records can and do. A team with a disappointing season can erase all that frustration, disappointment etc., with *one* big win over a superior opponent or a traditional foe. Such a win can be savored, cherished, and remembered for years to come when all other "hurts" are forgotten. Coaches know, anything can and does happen; that is the reason coaching staffs often say, "The only thing worse than a team that believes it can't win, is a team that "knows" it can't lose." It was true Temple had lost to Holy Cross, Oklahoma A&M (now Oklahoma State University) and Syracuse. Syracuse had beaten Temple 28-12 the week before Penn State dominated Syracuse so completely that Syracuse ended up with minus yards rushing and minus forty-seven yards in total offense, an NCAA record that stands to this day. Thus the mind-set among the Lion players and fans was one of unbridled optimism.

While Temple was only a .500 team when they met Penn State, they did have a solid head coach in Ray Morrison and a number of accomplished football players. Most impressive of these footballers was Phil Slosburg, a three year letterman (1945-1947), who had played several positions. Ray Morrison had installed the T-formation at Temple when he arrived in 1940. Prior to 1939 (Fred Swan was Temple's head coach for one year), "Pop" Warner was the head coach and he was definitely not a T-formation advocate. "Pop" was a proponent of the single wing, the short punt and the fullback buck lateral and spinner series, to which he added some nuances of his own. Glenn Scobey "Pop" Warner took Temple to its only major bowl game; the January 1, 1935 Sugar Bowl where they lost to Tulane 20-14 and he was one of the legends of collegiate football coaching. But the coming of the 1940s, his age and the T-formation, which would be the offense of the second half of the decade, had done him in. The 1947 Temple team starred the aforementioned fullback Phil Slosburg who was leading the East in yards gained and total offense. It's unusual for a 187 pound back to be a fullback, it's more unusual for a fullback to be his team's leader in yards gained, and it's even more rare for a fullback to be his team's total offense leader. Slosburg did all of this under the auspices of a T-formation coach. (In 1945-1946 Slosburg was listed as a halfback.) There were two other Temple players on the 1947 team who deserve mention. One was Joe Lee, an end who would gain some notoriety in the Penn State game. Lee was part American Indian, however he carried no nickname referring to his heritage; he lettered four years (1945-1948). Two of those years (1946-1947) he had an older teammate, "Indian Joe" Nejman who first lettered in 1942, and in 1946 played fullback while Slosburg played halfback. Odd as it may seem, "Indian Joe" Nejman was of Polish descent and had no Indian ancestry.

In the category of ancestry, heritage and bloodlines Penn State was happy to proclaim that a member of its first-ever football team would be present for Saturday's game. *The Daily Collegian* announced that Charles C. Hildebrand, one of six living members from State's first football team (he was a sophomore in 1887) would attend the game, and most Penn State fans expected the 1947 team to show Mr. Hildebrand how the face of Penn State football had changed over sixty years. The weatherman however had other plans.

The game was a night game, and hours before kick-off Mother Nature unleashed a "tidal wave" of her own which threatened to "drown" both offenses. By game time the field was soaked, still the rain continued unabated. The field soon became a quagmire, uniform numbers were obliterated and the contest became a slipping, sliding affair that reminded onlookers of "mud wrestling" rather than football.

Unfavorable weather conditions of this magnitude tend to limit the scoring, making it possible for the underdog to score once and come away with a win or a tie. That's why bad weather is termed the "great equalizer." If the favorite team can be held to just a field goal, a touchdown, or less, then just one lucky score can enable an underdog to pull off a huge upset. In a game under these adverse conditions there is a certain rhythm that sets in and both State and Temple seemed to settle into a routine of three plays and a punt, three more plays and a punt. The favored team waiting for the weaker opponent to "crack," or make a mistake upon which it can capitalize and in so doing its offense becomes passive not offensive. In this hypnotic back and forth play which continued into the second half, neither Temple nor State had completed a pass (nor would they) although three passes were intercepted. Temple had twenty-five yards of offense, two first downs (one of which we will discuss) and Phil Slosburg was held to minus twenty-one yards. End-of-the- game statistics found Penn State, which had been averaging four hundred yards of offense per game, with a total of just one hundred and seventy two yards and nine first downs. These sets of figures cost Penn State their number-one in-the-country offensive rating and Phil Slosburg his first place total offense ranking in the East. Far into the third quarter the score remained 0-0, and it looked as though no one would score if they played all night. It was at this point that Coach Morrison and his staff resurrected a play which Morrison's alma mater, Vanderbilt, used in the 1930s aptly called "The Squatting Hen Play."

First some thoughts about this genuine "Academy Award Trick Play." This trick play was not just a simple reverse, a double reverse, a double or triple pass or a halfback option pass. It was a play people would talk about for weeks and thus Temple would not be able to use the play again for years, due to all the publicity it generated.

Before we get into the actual play itself there are two main criteria that must be met before a head coach should consider using such a play. First of all if it is true that when you use the play you won't be able to use it again for years because every future opponent will be looking for it, then the play should be saved for a critical time in a critical game. Don't waste it early in a game that you might win or lose by forty points without the play. Secondly look for the most favorable weather conditions such as impaired visibility, rain, mud, standing water, etc.

Considering the above, Coach Morrison felt the use of the play was indicated because one score could win this game and this play could produce that winning score. Secondly, the weather conditions weren't just favorable, they were perfect, they would never be better. It was raining, the field was soggy and sloppy, pieces of turf were torn up, everyone's uniform was wet, dirty, and mud-caked, and the game was a night game. The wind-driven rain was descending at an angle which enhanced the glare of the artificial light from the light towers and was further augmented by its reflection off the wet grass. which glistened as though it were ice-covered. Altogether an array of distracting factors which favored the successful implementation of a trick play. The stage was set for "The Sitting Hen" nee "Squatting Hen Play."

If you were the head coach considering the use of such a singular play what items would you and your staff want to be sure to address before you would actually call the play in a game situation? If that question were asked of a group of knowledgeable football fans I would expect they would give us the following suggestions:

#1. The team must be able to "run the play" successfully.
#2. The play must be successful virtually every time you use it.
#3. The play must be a well-kept secret.
#4. The play must be used when both game conditions and field position are favorable.
#5. The play should be used in an important game, preferably against a superior opponent when the game is on the line.

Number 1 is very obvious, if you can't execute the play properly it won't work.

Number 2 is a matter of practicality. Why bother to keep a play in your repertoire if you use it only once every five years and half the time it doesn't work.

Number 3 is common sense, if your opponent knows you have a trick play and what it is, it won't work. This is why the play can't be used more often that once or twice in a decade.

Number 4 makes sense since certain game conditions – rain, mud, etc., are distracting factors, and in regard to field position springing a trick play too close to the opponent's goal line means all twenty-two players are near to the ball and any one of the eleven players on defense may see the trick and expose it. Optimally you want the opponents spread out over the field. This way when the subterfuge ends and it's discovered who has the ball, hopefully there isn't a tackler close enough to stop the play.

Number 5, If you had a movie pass good for one free movie every five years you'd want to see the biggest and best blockbuster movie of the half decade. Here too if the play succeeds, you want it to win a blockbuster of a game for you. An additional point is that a superior opponent will, on defense, be playing you pretty much straight up. And if they are well-coached and disciplined as a very good team is, while they will be more intelligent and more athletic, they will also be more predictable.

This still leaves us with one item that must be tended to otherwise your well-conceived, beautifully executed, Academy Award trick play may be derailed. You need to alert the officials who are working the game that you have this trick play in your repertoire. If you fool the opposition, but you also fool the officials, they, like the opposing players, may follow a player who doesn't have the ball and when he goes down or goes out-of-bounds they will blow the play dead. Blowing the play dead (blowing the whistle to end a play) means *that* play is over right then, even if your runner with the ball is behind all of the opposing players and running unimpeded for a touchdown but hasn't crossed the goal line yet.

The stage is set. Coach Morrison and his staff have rehearsed the play often enough that they feel the play will be well executed and it will fool Penn State. The officials were alerted before game time and the conditions and the field position are right. So here it comes, "The Sitting Hen Play." The Temple Owls break the huddle and the center comes up to the line of scrimmage and positions himself over the ball. Slosburg, in the game as the T-formation quarterback, sets his line down, then reaches in under center and starts calling signals. The ball is snapped and after turning his back to the defense the quarterback retreats one step and still crouched-over hands the ball off to one of the backs who begins running toward the far sideline. At least this is the way it appeared to all on-lookers because the quarterback holds both arms outstretched well away from his body and its obvious he doesn't have the ball (in either hand). For the next five or more seconds the attention of all the spectators is fixed on the vast majority of the players who are running across the field toward the far sideline. All at once there is an outcry, followed by pointing of arms and turning of heads in a direction 180° from where the action is supposed to be happening. A Temple player is running down the field pursued by just one or two Penn State players. It's not possible to tell who the Penn State pursuers are but one might be co-captain Johnny Potsklan one of Penn State's ends. It is now apparent the Temple player, Joe Lee has the football. How the ball got to the Temple end, running down the near sideline no one knows. My best guess was a forward shovel pass but I never saw the ball in the air or any arm movement indicative of a pass. It was as though a magician made the ball disappear over there and then miraculously appear over here. But here was the Temple ball carrier sloshing his way toward the Penn State goal line and two Penn State defenders motoring after him and gradually narrowing the gap. From our seats it looked like the ball carrier was finally pushed out of bounds inside the ten-yard line.

It was now first and goal to go for Temple and should they get the ball into the end zone, that score might hold up for a 7-0 Temple upset win. Under normal circumstances a play like this should have given Temple momentum and a surge of confidence. In turn, Penn State should have been deflated, and back on their heels. Temple could be thinking we didn't score on that play but we certainly will on one of our next four plays. If they should score, then this team which wasn't nearly as big and/or talented as State, could end the Lion's perfect season. Then again maybe, just maybe, the Temple team wasn't supremely confident. Maybe they were thinking, "Shoot, we missed our chance. Here we make one of only two first-downs we're destined to get and we might come up empty-handed. If only Lee were a faster runner."

Meanwhile on the other side of the ball Penn State might be thinking "Hey they bet the whole ball game on that one trick play – they can't beat us straight-up. The dramatic trick play since it didn't score had a very common counter-effect. The Penn State team had gotten a "wake-up call." Not only did they stop the Owl's offense "stone cold" but when they went on offense, with every play a running play, the Lions marched down the field on the legs of tailback Bob Williams, a former V-12 Marine now playing his fourth year at State and fullback Fran Rogel, the human battering ram, to score the first and only touchdown of the game. And when Ed ("Eye-chart") Czekaj (pronounced Check-eye) kicked the point after touchdown, Penn State slipped out of North Philly with a 7-0 win.

Postscript: It wasn't until days later that the mechanics of the "Sitting Hen Play" were exposed. One version said the quarterback took the snap, faked the pitch to the right and "sat" on the ball until virtually everyone was running to the right and then slipped the ball to the right end on a reverse to the left. The version I believe to be more accurate stated that after the snap when the quarterback turned his back to the defense he slipped the ball between his thighs. He then made the very obvious and dramatic motion with both arms that *he was pitching* the football and "showing" he no longer had the ball he remained half-crouched over. Later he slipped the ball to Joe Lee the right end coming across the formation in the opposite direction from the general flow of the play. I think the first theory is less believable since sitting on the ball could draw attention to the ball. If the quarterback slipped even for one instant and his butt or a knee touched the ground while in contact with the ball the play would be dead right there. Actually sitting on the ball, I think would be more contrived, more unnatural, and more awkward. Regardless, the play was well timed, well executed and the weather conditions were ideal and only the fact that some Penn State player(s) "stayed home" prevented an almost certain touchdown and a crushing loss. The surprise element was there and the officials weren't fooled. So the only fault I can find in this well conceived and well-executed play is that the Temple brain-trust should have waited until they were ten yards closer to the Penn State goal line before they used the play. My observation is similar to the answer to the question, "How long should a person's legs be?" "Long enough to reach the ground."

The 1947 Nittany Lions were not Paper Lions and they showed it by beating Navy for the second year in a row and by blanking Pittsburgh 29-0. This win over Pitt came after three consecutive losing efforts during which time the Lions scored a grand total of seven points. This time it was Pitt that was embarrassed as the Lions scored in every quarter and held Pitt to minus twenty-six yards rushing and seventy yards passing.

Coach Higgins' 1947 squad boasted the best players "The Hig" ever had on one team. Penn State was still not giving scholarships but all of the ex-servicemen could attend college under the G. I. Bill which paid their tuition, books, room and board just as a scholarship would. The team had men in their mid-twenties, some of whom had been through the blast furnace of war and emerged as tempered and hardened steel, others were in their fourth year of varsity football. These were the men of the 1947 Cotton Bowl team and during this season which promised a return to better times for Penn State, they set some team and NCAA records which stand to this day. A partial listing goes as follows:

1. Most points scored in a half, 55 against Fordham, first half. (team record).
2. Most points scored in a quarter, 40 against Fordham second quarter (team record).
3. Fewest points allowed for nine game season, 25 (team record).
4. Fewest yards total offense allowed one game vs. Syracuse October 18, 1947. Forty-nine plays: a total of plus 60 yards passing, minus 107 yards rushing, total offense minus forty-seven yards (NCAA record).
6. Fewest yards allowed rushing per game for a season 17.0 (NCAA record).
7. Fewest points allowed per game for a nine game season 2.8 points/game (team record).

Despite winning nine games and going undefeated, Penn State was still lobbying for a bowl invitation after the Pitt game was over. Coach Higgins made it clear the team would not agree to play in any bowl that wouldn't allow their two African-American players, Wally Triplett and Denny Hoggard to participate. This meant State wouldn't be invited to play in the Orange or the Sugar Bowl games, two of the four legitimate bowl classic games. Since the Rose Bowl had an annual arrangement calling for the Big Ten champion to play the Pacific Coast Conference champion, the only other Bowl of any consequence in those days was the Cotton Bowl and the chances there normally would not be good. Fortunately Southern Methodist University won the SWC championship and SMU had already played one or more teams that were not all-white so they were not adverse to playing State.

The final AP Poll Top Ten had Notre Dame as #1, followed by Michigan, SMU, Penn State, Texas, Alabama, Penn, Southern California, North Carolina and Georgia Tech. In those years the final AP poll was taken at the end of the regular season rather than after the bowl games were played. There were probably two reasons for this. Number one there were only four bowls of any importance which meant that only a select eight teams had an extra chance to impress the pollsters. The second reason would be that Notre Dame refused to play in any bowl game from 1926 through the 1968 season and thus they would have been one of the teams at a disadvantage. Consider the 1947 season. Notre Dame didn't play in a bowl game, but number two Michigan did. And in a poll after the bowl games Michigan, on the strength of its 49-0 thrashing of

Southern California, might have moved up to #1 since Notre Dame was idle.

Sadly the post-WWII era saw the demise of some storied football programs – St. Mary's, Santa Clara, Georgetown and Fordham University. The once mighty Fordham Rams football program which was ranked #3 in the country in 1937 and #6 in 1941 produced a number of All-Americans including, Vince Lombardi of Green Bay Packer coaching fame. Lombardi, one of Joe Paterno's heroes was a stand-out player on a Fordham line forever immortalized as "The Seven Blocks of Granite." This appellation is second only to Notre Dame's "Four Horsemen" in terms of backfield and offensive line football lore. But by 1947 Fordham's football fortunes had fallen so far that they were setting records for margin of victory for their opponents, witness Penn State's 75-0 win. The only remaining highlight of their football games was one of their cheers; "One dam, Two dam, Three dam, Fordham." However the Roman Catholic order in charge of Fordham University banned the cheer. Possibly the powers-to-be should have done a "one-eighty" like MIT students did. When MIT took up football late in the century, they too had a pitiful football team that was "blown away" by one opponent after another. However their student body chose to cheer after each *opponent* score, "That's all right, that's okay, you'll be working *for us* someday."

Undefeated 1947 Cotton Bowl-bound Penn State football team still holds NCAA records for fewest yards allowed in a game (-46) Syracuse October 18th and fewest yards allowed rushing, per game 17.0 and per rush 0.64, for a season.

CHAPTER 35

The Cotton Bowl Paradox
Invited? Yes! Welcomed with Open Arms? No!

Participating in Penn State's first bowl game since 1923 should have been a very special and joyous achievement for the 1947 squad. The key word is "should."

The Cotton Bowl had broken with tradition and invited Penn State, with its two African-American players, to play Southern Methodist University in the January 1, 1948 Cotton Bowl. While the selection committee had broken the color barrier, which seemed to put Dallas in the vanguard of integration, the Penn State team, coaching staff and administration were naïve however, to think that this meant during their stay in Dallas, the populace would be color blind. Some segregationists immediately labeled the game the Chocolate Bowl and Penn State found out very quickly that the city of Dallas was still segregated, and no Dallas hotel would accept the team because of its two non-white players. This was the beginning of a very unhappy stay in Dallas.

The closest the team could stay to downtown Dallas was the Dallas Naval Air Station which was on Federal property well out of the city and the players had to be escorted and bussed to and from Dallas for all of the social events. There was no laundry service at the base, except do-it-yourself and for the most part the food was mess hall chow. For those ex-servicemen on the team, each day was a recurring nightmare, there was the sound of reveille every morning, the mess hall chow, the fenced-in compound with Marine guards manning the gates and the overall haunting feeling that they were back in the service. There was no warm, sun-bathing-type weather in Dallas to compensate for the cold practices in State College. And in the mother of all negative motivational moves, Coach Higgins held a scrimmage on Christmas Day and the players had a cold turkey Christmas dinner.

After dinner in town one evening, a mini-revolt took place when a number of the players did not board the busses returning to the Naval Air Station. Instead they went out and did the town. It was ironic that virtually all of the player discontent sprang from the fact that the team couldn't be housed in the city, because of the two African-Americans. Thus during their stay in Dallas, the team's stand against racial discrimination ended up with the white players suffering, while the two African-

American players reportedly were dined and entertained at every opportunity by the black populace for their part in bringing down another color barrier by playing in the Cotton Bowl.

The game was played on a freezing cold day and SMU jumped out to a two touchdown lead. None of the SMU rooters was concerned that SMU's All-American Doak Walker missed the second extra point because it was still the first half and the Mustang fans expected more than two additional touchdowns in the second half. However as the clock clicked down to less than one minute in the half Penn State scored, to make the score 13-7, on a Woody Petchel to Larry Cooney pass and an Ed Czekaj point after touchdown.

At halftime the Penn State team was just as unfocused as they were at the start of the game and the locker room resounded with shouts, accusations etc. The players still weren't mentally prepared to play a good game as most of them weren't in concert about anything – except possibly their dissatisfaction with "The Hig" and the whole Cotton Bowl fiasco. As one of the team captains said upon the team's return to State College, "There's not a man on the team that would have voted in favor of playing this game had they (sic) known" (what was in store).

In the second half State scored the tying touchdown near the end of the third quarter. Now came the play for which Ed Czekaj has been long remembered, the PAT to put State ahead. With Bob Williams holding, Czekaj booted the ball high above the cross-bar and the uprights. The referee made no signal for what seemed to be ten seconds but he finally signaled the try was no good leaving the game tied at 13-13. Williams was adamant that the try was good. When Higgins asked Czekaj, Ed replied, "Hig, I don't know, you always told me to keep my head down."

On the next to the last play of the game Petchel hit Bob Hicks for a first down near the SMU 30 yard line. Then on the last play of the game, end Denny Hoggard broke free in the end zone, but by the time Petchel's pass approached him, an SMU defender loomed in front of Hoggard to bat the ball down. In preparation Hoggard was on his toes prepared to dive for the ball whichever way the defender deflected it. As luck would have it, the defender "whiffed" on his attempt to bat the ball down and it went cleanly between his hands. The ball struck the startled Hoggard, who was ready for anything except this, in the chest and the ball fell to the ground before he could react; and the game ended 13-13. Many Penn Staters, while disappointed, thought they had the better team and with the number of underclassmen on this squad their feelings were best expressed in the old cry, "Wait'll next year!"

Jim O'Hora had been on the Penn State staff just two years when the 1947 Penn State went undefeated, played in the Cotton Bowl, and finished fourth in the country in the AP Poll. This would be another plus on his resume. Unfortunately this success came a bit too soon in Jim and Betts' four year plan. When O'Hora took his first high school head-coaching job in Western Pennsylvania, he had put in only two years when the Mahanoy Township positioned opened up. Then W W II came along after he had served only three years as the Township head coach. After W W II O'Hora returned to Mahanoy Township but he was there just a short time when Bob Higgins called, giving O'Hora an opportunity he couldn't pass up. Now he felt he had to make a concerted effort to put in a total of four years at State so that his resume didn't give the impression that every two years he was looking to jump to another job. But there was no assurance what the next two years (1948-49) would bring.

It's preferable to leave a program when its fortunes are up, not down, because an assistant coach gets the same can tied to his tail as the head coach when a program is not successful. If the head coach is labeled a loser then by virtue of association the assistant suffers the same stigma. Equally so, a program that's a winner reflects favorably on the head coach and the whole coaching staff. Unfortunately when you're with a winning program and your resume looks its best, you rarely need another job. It's when the program nose-dives and doesn't pull-out of the tailspin that an assistant coach is most likely to be cut loose. Either the athletic director cleans house and fires everyone, or even worse the head coach tries to deflect the heat he's taking, away from himself and he fires an assistant or two as scapegoats. The head coach surely won't give those departing assistants a glowing recommendation. Regardless, O'Hora felt he must stay at least one – maybe two more years.

CHAPTER 36

"The Hig" Retires
Who Will be His Replacement?

The 1948 season which spanned only two months, October and November, ended up with four of the last five games on the road. (dé jà vu 1921-1923) as State had only four home games in their '48 nine game schedule.

There were three satisfying wins to open the season, a 35-0 rivalry - ending win over Bucknell, and 34-14, and 37-7 wins over Syracuse and West Virginia. The fourth game was against the always formidable Michigan State Spartans.

Penn State first played Michigan State in 1914 when it was known as Michigan Agriculture College, and lost the inaugural game 6-3. In 1925 MAC became Michigan State College and the Aggies changed their nickname to Spartans. Penn State beat the Spartans, to even the series but the Lions wouldn't win any of the next eight games played between 1945 and 1966. (Since joining the Big Ten in 1993, PSU has won six of the eight games contested between the two schools, 1993-2000.) But here in 1948 the Spartans were two and two on the season having lost to Michigan and Notre Dame 13-7 and 26-7 while beating Hawaii and Arizona 68-21 and 61-7. Michigan State always presented a match-up problem for Penn State and many other less talented teams than Michigan and Notre Dame, because of their team speed and the ability of some of their personnel to dominate the action; players like Lynn Chandnois, Don Mason, Everett (Sonny) Grandelius, Ed Bagdon, and future stars, Bubba Smith, George Webster, Don Coleman, Leroy Bolden, Norm Masters, Herb Adderley and Gene Washington.

As game day neared, everyone was talking about MSU's great scat back George Guerre who had rushed for one hundred and fifty-two yards on fourteen carries in the 1946 meeting, shades of Charley Way. In 1948 Penn State held Guerre to just sixteen yards but the Spartans got eighty-two yards from running back Frank "Muddy" Waters as the two teams battled to a 14-14 tie.

Sandwiched between two lopsided wins over Colgate and Temple was a classic football game in which State beat Penn 13-0 in front of 71,180 fans including the author, his brother, Carl, PSU '56 and George Werley, PSU '24, who was reliving a twenty-eight year old reprise of his first Penn-Penn State game, except he didn't have to hitch-hike to the game. The Quakers came into the game on an unbeaten streak dating back to the Army game in 1946 while State hadn't lost since the Pitt game in 1946, a string of fifteen games. The Red and Blue were led by Chuck Bednarik who has to rank along with Dick Butkus, Ray Nitschke and Jack Lambert as the most feared middle linebackers in pro football. On the collegiate level Bednarik could dominate a game from his middle backer position and if you were a running back you had best know where #60 Bednarik was at all times when you were carrying the ball since tackling you, was just a by-product of his main objective, to render the ball carrier senseless. State, playing like the 1947 defense, held Penn to less than twenty yards rushing and less than one hundred yards combined rushing and passing. The big play on offense for State was Fran Rogel's forty-four yard touchdown run where he lowered a shoulder into Bednarik bounced off and went all the way for the score. On defense, besides Chuck Drazenovich playing all sixty minutes there was Wally Triplett the Philadelphia native, on one goal line-stand batting down a pass, almost intercepting the next pass and on fourth down tackling the pass receiver and holding him just short of the goal line to prevent a score. When Penn came knocking on State's goal line door late in the game, a fourth down pass headed for an open Penn receiver in the end zone was deflected away by the speedy Triplett to help preserve the victory. Triplett a wingback and defensive halfback was the first African-American football player at Penn State who starred and then went on to play in the NFL. Denny Hoggard was on the same team but he wasn't nearly as gifted athletically as Triplett. Penn State actually broke the color barrier when they recruited David Alston and his twin brother Harry in the early 1940s. After spring practice and some, legal-at-that-time, summer scrimmages the word was that Dave had run and thrown for a dozen touchdowns showing All-American potential, as well as drop-kicking extra points. Everyone connected with Penn State football could hardly wait to see Dave at tailback for the next three years. In a tragic medical accident David died of anesthetic complications while undergoing a supposedly routine tonsillectomy the summer before his sophomore year. His brother Harry left school and an expected assault on the Penn State record book ended before it started.

Another brother act, Chuck and Joe Drazenovich, did not start and complete their careers after 1950 thus they are not mentioned in Chapter 71, "They Numbered among State's Best". But they do bear mentioning. Chuck, number 23, was bigger than his older brother Joe, number 66, and thus it may seem odd that Joe played guard while Chuck was the quarterback on offense and a tough-as-nails linebacker on defense. Number 23 however was not a T-formation passing and running quarterback but rather a single-wing formation quarterback who was basically a blocking back. As you would suspect "Draz" drew his biggest "aahs" and "oohs" from the crowd for his hellacious hits from his linebacker spot.

The author saw Joe and Chuck often at lunchtime as the Brownsville, Pennsylvania brothers usually ate together in the Allencrest Tea Room on Beaver Avenue, an unlikely place to associate with these two burly "bruisers." Joe, shorter than Chuck, had a round cherubic head and he seemed to be the less intense of the two, grinning frequently. Chuck had handsome chiseled features somewhat similar to the movie-star Victor Mature, but he didn't laugh as easily as Joe. The two brothers sat across from each other at a square table in the middle of the tea room, semi-hunched-over and they rarely interrupted their eating and hushed conversations with each other to talk with anyone passing by. They came and left very inconspicuously with very few people bothering them as they seemed to prefer their privacy. Besides being an outstanding football player who went on to play ten seasons with the Washington Redskins as a linebacker, Chuck was also an NCAA heavyweight boxing champion. Few opponents lasted three rounds with Chuck who was an intimidating figure in the ring. While he must have taken some "shots" that hurt, he never showed it and he never seemed to retreat. He had several classic toe-to-toe slugging matches with Syracuse's Marty Crandall but as the author recalls, Chuck won each time. Had "Draz" played at Notre Dame, USC or some similar place he would probably have been an All-American once or twice.

The Temple game, State's last home game of the season, was not a "cliff hanger" like the 1947 contest. The Lions chewed up the Owls 47-0 holding Temple to seven net yards on the ground. The next, but not the last, game on the schedule was Pittsburgh. Recalling State's emphatic 29-0 win over Pitt in 1947 some Penn Staters were anticipating two wins in a row for the first time since 1912. But that was not to be.

Pitt in 1948 under Coach Walter Milligan, whose three year record at Pitt was 13-14, had been beaten by SMU 33-14, Notre Dame 40-0 and Ohio State 41-0. They had one touchdown wins over Purdue and Indiana and wins that ranged from a ten point margin against West Virginia to a 20 point win over Western Reserve. All of Pitt's opponents were from the Midwest or Southwest except for West Virginia and State. Coming into the Penn State game the Panthers had scored a total of just 112 points with Robert Becker leading all scorers with five touchdowns for thirty points. Lou (Bimbo) Cecconi was Pitt's leading rusher (292 yards) and leading passer with thirty completions good for 542 yards and five touchdowns. On the other hand, Penn State had posted 212 points and their leading rusher, fullback Fran Rogel would rush for 602 yards and five touchdowns, tailback Elwood Petchel would pass for 628 yards and nine touchdowns while wingback Wally Triplett would lead all scorers with six touchdowns. The game, true to form for Pitt-Penn State games, was a low-scoring affair, with neither offense registering a touchdown. The Panthers whose offense never came closer than State's thirty-yard line scored their only touchdown when Pitt tackle Nick Bolkovac gathered in a deflected Woody Petchel pass and ran 25 yards for the only score of the game. Penn State's hopes for an unbeaten season and a second consecutive bowl game ended on Pittsburgh's one-yard line where Fran Rogel was stopped as time expired. (Fran Rogel was so important to the Penn State offense that the game plan was often joking summarized by fans in a nursery rhyme, "Hi diddle diddle, Rogel up the middle.")

For only the sixth time since 1903, the Pittsburgh game was not the final game on the regular season schedule. (Not counting 1932-1934 when the two teams didn't meet.) As in 1921, the last game on the 1948 schedule would again be played in the State of Washington but this time the host team would be the Washington State Cougars. Rather than a transcontinental train ride, this team would be treated to the first airplane trip to an away regular season game involving a Penn State football team. Some of the players and staff had flown during World War II, while others had never been "off the ground" in their life other than on a roller coaster or a ferris wheel. However, whether crossing the continent by rail or in the air somethings never change, the travel party still had to bus to Pittsburgh to fly west to Washington. The propeller driven DC-6 Northwest Orient flight was routine until the plane encountered turbulence over the Rocky Mountains. At this point some players and coaches became ill. The trainers and the team doctors were trying their best to tend to one and all, but some of them, especially team physician Dr. Griess, were "under the weather" too. In fact when the plane landed and the squad and official party went to the team hotel, Dr. Griess did not accompany them. Instead he went directly to the railroad station and purchased a ticket for a Sunday departure back to Pittsburgh.

Sunday morning following Penn State's 7-0 victory, the Northwest Orient "prop-job" made a lot of people wish they were accompanying Dr. Griess home on terra firma. The aircraft, from the moment the wheels were up, labored as it circled ever upward seeming as though it were being forced to climb a circular staircase so challenging that the plane might not make it to the rim of the crater and escape to the East for the return trip. The laborious rise went on for what seemed to be ten minutes. The plane had no more than cleared the Rocky Mountains, and a mild encore of turbulence, when the pilot was notified the plane couldn't land in Minneapolis, where the team was supposed to have a sumptuous Thanksgiving meal, because the airport was snowed-in. The flight would have to be diverted to Rochester, Minnesota. In the first of a series of aggravating occurrences, upon landing in Rochester the coaching staff discovered that the amount of food available at the airport was woefully inadequate for a plane load of football players. To make matters worse the flight crew having landed would not be permitted to take-off again because of the number of hours they had flown in the past twenty-four hours. They had to be replaced by a fresh crew. However the nearest crew was in Minneapolis meaning the team, hungry or not, couldn't depart until the replacement crew *drove* from Minneapolis to Rochester, since the Minneapolis airport was snowed-in. A take-off was tentatively scheduled for 1 A.M. However after getting everyone at the hotel ready to go to the airport, the entire group was sent back to their rooms to get up at 7 A.M. for an 8 A.M. take-off.

The following morning the aircraft took off without a hitch however by the time the airplane was over Ohio, the pilot received word that Pittsburgh was now snowed-in by the same snowstorm that forced the team plane to be diverted to Rochester. The plane was now re-routed back to Willow Run, Michigan. Finally, late that day the team and official party reached Pittsburgh by plane only to face a snowy bus ride back to State College. Bad as the situation was for those on the flight - the friends, families and relatives of those on board, had received little information regarding the aircraft's diversions, lay-overs, delayed departures, re-routing etc. This must have been more nerve-wracking for those safely on the ground back in Centre County than those on the flight because those on the flight knew they hadn't crashed and that they were alive, whereas those in State College may have feared that tragic news was being withheld.

The tie with Michigan State coupled with the Pitt loss had bumped State out of the Top Ten and any chance of a bowl bid. However after the unsettling round trip air flight some people may have heaved a sigh of relief.

In a move that caught many people by surprise, Bob Higgins, who had a history of heart trouble, resigned at the end of the 1948 season simply saying, "I want to live long enough to see my grandchildren grow up." Virginia and Bob Higgins' daughter Ginger had married one of "The Hig's" All-American players, guard Steve Suhey. Steve and Ginger would have three sons who would win ten letters in football at State – Larry 1975-76, Paul 1975-78 and Matt 1976-79.

Unfortunately Bob Higgins passed away in 1969.

CHAPTER 37

A One Year Investment Yields Fifty Years of Dividends

In 1949 Penn State remained a college with no seeming urgency to shed its college status and become a University. The Penn State of that time period seemed to exist in a world of its own before cable television impacted and compacted the nation.

If you were familiar with this Penn State family feeling, you understood when Coach Higgins resigned, why it was taken for granted that his successor would be one of the assistants on his staff and no one else. Since Jim O'Hora and Earl Bruce had just recently joined the staff it was expected that the new head coach would have to be Joe Bedenk, Earle Edwards or Al Michaels. Bedenk had the most seniority but he was a line coach who played all of his college football as a lineman. Also in the spring he seemed more interested in baseball, where he was the head coach, than he was in spring football.

Earle Edwards was last in line as far as seniority was concerned, but this actually seemed to be to his advantage since he was seven years younger than Bedenk, and his peers thought he was more in tune with the times and had a more up-to-date grasp of current football tactics and formations. While Penn State was still a single wing team, and had been at least since Bezdek's time, Edwards probably had some knowledge of the T-formation which was sweeping the country. The third prospect, Al Michaels graduated after Edwards but he had been an assistant at State one year longer than Earle. His support base was basically the same as Edwards' and for that reason Michaels probably did not hold himself out as a candidate for the head coaching vacancy. In fact Earle Edwards was the only avowed candidate and the only one openly seeking and being mentioned for the job. As ex-coach Higgins later remarked, when he went to bed the night before the announcement was to be made, he was sure the job was Earle Edwards' and no one else's.

As was apparent the next day, when Joe Bedenk was announced as the new head coach, the real campaigning had gone on behind the scenes and not out in the open. Most people felt Bedenk had "politicked" for the job behind the scenes or that Bedenk had played the loyalty card pointing-out that he had been at State longer than Edwards or Michaels, and the good old boys had gotten Bedenk the post. Someone who was in a position to know, told the author that Joe Bedenk did not want the job and only took it because of pressure from a faction who did not want

Earle Edwards as the head man.

There is an old adage about investing in the stock market which is true now and probably always will be which states, "It's better to be in the *right* stock for the wrong reasons, than to be in the *wrong* stock for all the right reasons." Thus Penn State's choice of Joe Bedenk for it's new head football coach, although done for the wrong reason, turned out to be a fortuitous choice in the long run.

Joe Bedenk assumed the helm in 1949 with more than a bit of trepidation. By the end of spring practice he had to have a handle on what the hold-over material could do and whether the holes created by graduation could be filled, or at least smoothed over. Gone was punter-fullback Joe "Bells" Cologne, and all of the speed in the backfield in the persons of "Woody" Petchel, Larry Cooney, Larry Joe and Wally Triplett. The best passer, Petchel, and the best receiver, All-American Sam Tamburo, were departed along with guard John Simon and tackle John Finley. Six of the eight departees were not replaceable by any back-up currently on the depth chart, so Bedenk had to expect a definite fall-off in production. Bedenk was already finding that being the head coach involved much more administrative and organizational work than he had to deal with in the past. And more and more he was possibly wishing Earle Edwards had gotten the job, and the headaches that came with it. However, after the surprise selection of Joe Bedenk, Earle Edwards quickly put out some feelers and one of the respondents was "Biggie" Munn the Syracuse coach in 1946, who after just one year there, moved to Michigan State. At East Lansing, "Biggie" replaced Charles Bachman who had held the post for fourteen years after succeeding "Sleepy Jim" Crowley, one of Notre Dame's famed Four Horsemen. Interestingly Crowley left Michigan State after the 1932 season to take over the reins at Fordham where he coached "The Seven Blocks of Granite" creating a unique link between those two immortal groups, the "Four Horsemen" and the "Seven Blocks of Granite." Edwards joined Munn's staff in 1949 and later became the head coach at North Carolina State in 1954, taking Al Michaels with him at that time as an assistant coach. Prior to Edwards there was a PSU-MSU connection in the person of Albert M. Barron, MSU's head coach 1921-22 and also a PS letterman.

Fortunately for Bedenk, assistant coach Jim O'Hora still had aspirations of becoming a head coach someday, so O'Hora volunteered to do some of Bedenk's paper work, an offer Bedenk gladly accepted and he allowed O'Hora to do the work with no interference. Jim O'Hora had played for Bedenk for three years as a center, had been a graduate assistant on the staff for one year and had served as a fellow assistant coach with Bedenk 1946-1948, so they were good friends and had known each other for more than fifteen years. This was a win–win situation as it took a load off Bedenk's shoulders and it gave O'Hora some excellent on-the-job training.

After spring practice, but before the 1949 season even started, Bedenk told his boss, athletic director Dr. Carl Schott that his stay as head coach was going to be for one year only, he would not return for the 1950 season. This information found its way to the assistant coaches' ears, possibly directly from Bedenk, or it could have filtered down from the athletic director's office. Or Bedenk's approach to certain items or decisions might have made it obvious that he wasn't looking any farther down the road than the end of this season. If Bedenk would be leaving at the end of the season, of the three assistants who were considered as replacements for Bob Higgins only one, Al Michaels remained. But the word was the administration and the Board of Trustees, this time, would be more involved in the process and there would be no more intra-family in-fighting and/or power plays. The Board would solicit applications, interview candidates and carefully, with considerable thought and investigation they would choose the best man for the job wherever he might be, not just the best man presently on the staff.

For the assistant coaches what was known and what was surmised wasn't very comforting. It was rather certain that the new coach would be coming from outside. Since the new coach would be someone who had been successful at his present school, they assumed this coach would demand to bring most, if not all, of his present staff with him to maintain the continuity of his winning "team." This unfortunately would mean that many of the assistant coaches would lose their coaching positions. However, in stark contrast to most universities in Division I football, they would not be fired. Most universities hire their head coach and his staff as outside independent contractors, thus the school can terminate their services simply by not renewing one or more of the coaches' contracts. At Penn State from the 1930s and into the 1970s, all coaches taught a few classes each week and were tenured professors and employees of the university. So while one or more of the assistant coaches might be replaced on the new staff, they would still have a job in the School of Physical Education and Athletics.

Now, September was here and with it came the September 24 *opening* game with Villanova; supposedly a tune-up and a chance to smooth out the rough spots before the big game at West Point on October 1. The Villanova Wildcats however did not come to State College to be a scrimmage opponent to warm up the Lions for their battle with the Cadets. Penn State wasn't in the game after the third quarter and scored its only touchdown in the fourth quarter. Bewildered Nittany Lion fans couldn't believe their eyes when the scoreboard posted the final score Villanova, 27 and Penn State, 6.

The following week, the author and many other Nittany faithful made the long drive to the U.S. Military Academy which required a 5 A.M. Saturday morning departure. The game itself had the look of a possible upset as the Lions went to the locker room leading 7-0. However Army scored 42 unanswered points in the second half as the Lions wilted and suffered their second crushing and humiliating loss.

The Lions returned home, first to host Boston College and then Nebraska, the latter on Homecoming Weekend. Boston College featured their typical potent passing attack and their quarterback Ed Songin was 1948's Eastern collegiate passing champion. But in a turn-about State scored on three touchdown passes and recorded their first win of the season by a 32-14 score.

The Homecoming game against the Cornhuskers (labeled the Corn Huskers by the LaVie Yearbook) was not a marquee attraction as other match-ups between these two teams would be, but rather a meeting of two teams one of whom would end its season with a 5 and 4 record, while the other would finish at 4 and 5. The Lions won the contest 22-7. Penn State now went to East Lansing Michigan where the Lions were a decided underdog against Michigan State. The "Nits" didn't have the requisite power or the speed and they were shut out 24-0.

This was "Biggie" Munn's third season at the helm of the Spartans and it had started the same as the previous two, with a loss to Michigan. Although all three were losses, the scores those three years showed that Munn had the Spartans on the right track. In 1947 in his first game of his first season at Michigan State, Munn's Spartans were steamrollered by Michigan, 55-0. The next year Michigan won again, but this time the score was much closer, 13-7. In 1949 the Wolverines in Ann Arbor eeked-out a 7-3 win. Even though the next three games were all at Michigan, the Spartans came out on top 14-7, 25-0 and 27-13. All of the games except the 1948 tilt were played in Ann Arbor and they were all the first or second game on the Michigan State University schedule. To the reader the circumstances surrounding the games might seem a bit strange. Why would an important Big Ten game be played so early in the season and why did the Big Ten make State play five of the six contests at Ann Arbor, home of the University of Michigan? As is often the case, when you have all the pertinent facts the answer is simple. Michigan State joined the Big Ten in 1949 but was not integrated into the football schedule until 1953. (The Big Ten had in effect been the Big Nine since the University of Chicago left the conference in 1946.) But Michigan State had the biggest laugh. In 1953 their last season under "Biggie" Munn and their first season in the Big Ten in all sports, they beat Michigan, Ohio State, Iowa, Minnesota and Indiana, in league play, losing only to Purdue and went to the Rose Bowl as the Big Ten Champions and beat UCLA. Obviously Earle Edwards had cast his lot with a winning team.

Following the loss at Michigan State, Coach Bedenk, the 1949 football team and the Penn State football program were looking at some pretty hard numbers. After next week's home game against Syracuse the last three games would all be away games. Also if one were to go with the odds, one would have to predict that Pitt would win the Pitt-Penn State game and this would give State four losses. The Lions would therefore have to beat Syracuse, West Virginia and Temple, in succession, to keep intact their record of consecutive winning seasons, which started in 1939.

Happily the '49 team rose to the occasion and beat Syracuse, West Virginia and Temple, and, as predicted, lost to Pitt to end their season with five wins and four losses. In so doing they saved Joe Bedenk from the stigma of being the only Penn State head coach in the Twentieth Century to have a career losing record.

While Penn State certainly hadn't hired Joe Bedenk expecting he would be the head coach for just one year, his one year term as head coach was definitely the only way that Penn State would have ended up with a certain head coach, who would stay at the helm more than thirty-five years (1966-2000) and bring the school more than 300 wins and so many other peripheral honors and favorable national recognition. If you question that statement consider; had Rip Engle stayed at Brown, he would never have hired Joe Paterno, since his staff was intact with no vacancies, the coaches were all well-versed in coaching the Wing-T and Joe had absolutely no coaching background. Rip Engle prevailed upon Paterno to accompany him to Penn State "just for one year" since Engle's quarterback coach remained at Brown to succeed Engle and because none of the other assistant coaches would agree to leave Providence. R.I. for rural central Pennsylvania. Had Joe started law school or gone out into the business world, even for one year, I feel sure he would have found a position that paid more than the $3500.00 an assistant coaches' position paid in 1950, and once he was in law school he would not have quit school to start at the bottom of the ladder in a career where he had no training or experience.

Penn State 1946 coaching staff (left to right) Earle Edwards, Al Michaels, Bob Higgins, Joe Bedenk, Jim O'Hora (Photo courtesy of Penn State Sports Information)

CHAPTER 38

Sever "Tor" Toretti: Sportsman, Gentleman, and True Blue
Competitor

Joe Bedenk's one year term as head coach provided Penn State with the opportunity to hire "Rip" Engle which in turn resulted in the hiring of Joe Paterno. Joe Paterno would never have become Penn State's head football coach under any set of circumstances other than Bob Higgin's successor serving for one year and one year only. On Bedenk's watch there was another fortuitous happening and Bedenk should get full credit in this instance since all of the benefits that accrued were attributable to his decision to hire two young coaches.

One of the new assistant coaches, Frank "Pat" Patrick, had played fullback for the Pitt Panthers and lettered in 1935-1937. He remained on the Nittany Lion staff long after Bedenk and Engle were gone (1949-1973) during which time he coached the defensive backs and punters and was an academic advisor. "Pat" never lost the Midwest big city inflection in his speech but he was very friendly, and popular with both the players and the "alums" and he fit in well with the rest of the staff, becoming over the years, a true blue Nittany Lion.

The other addition, Sever "Tor" Toretti, was a Casey Jones recruit. The Monongahela High School product was a three year letterman who returned to Penn State in 1949 to be an assistant coach, scout and lead recruiter. Tor's importance as a recruiter necessitated that he stop coaching after the 1962 season and become a full time recruiter, and goodwill ambassador for his beloved University. His contacts with high school coaches across the Commonwealth and his reputation as a pillar of honesty made him of immeasurable value to Rip and Joe during their years at the helm, and even after Tor retired in 1979. A keen judge of talent and character and an all-around "class" individual he was a prime factor in getting Rip and Joe the material from which they assembled their highly successful teams.

Toretti was no stranger to hard work and diligence. The seventh of eight children, his father died when he was twelve. After working his way through college, he graduated in 1939 a time when the nation was still in the midst of a terrible depression and there were virtually no teaching jobs to be had. Therefore, Toretti returned to the Monongahela steel mills and worked there until the middle of the school year when he was appointed Physical Education teacher and boxing and football head coach at Brockway High School in Central Pennsylvania at an annual salary of $1100.00. Mrs. Toretti when relaying this information to the author emphasized "that was eleven hundred, not eleven thousand dollars."

Nonetheless if Casey Jones had not gotten Toretti the help he needed to attend Penn State who knows where "the path untrod" might have taken him. Tor was always grateful for all the good things State did for him, especially introducing him to his one true love Ruth Kistler. Ruth and "Tor" met when she was a sophomore at Penn State, and he was a senior, working part-time at the University golf course. Ruth was a Health and Physical Education major with well above average athletic ability but she was relatively new to the game of golf and Toretti, a good athlete himself, was on his way to becoming a very accomplished golfer. This gave "Tor" a chance to give Ruth some golf lessons and a chance to exhibit his male superiority. Toretti did make a mistake when one day he suggested playing tennis for a change. He was not aware that Ruth had taken lessons and was a strong player. After absorbing a thorough drubbing, "Tor's" words in defeat were, "You're going to have to learn to play golf," indicating they as a couple would not be playing a lot of tennis. By June 1941 Tor felt confident enough about his job in Brockway to pop the question. Ruth had removed the only objection her parents had to her marrying Tor (or anyone), that she finish college and get her degree. With her acceptance they decided to be married that summer. There was however one problem, Ruth's older sister already had a July wedding planned. To give Mrs. Kistler's nerves and her Penn State professor father's bank account a chance to recuperate there had to be a hiatus of two months. But this created another problem, the football season at Brockway High School. Fortunately Brockway had one Saturday open date in September so that date was set as the wedding day, the church was reserved and all the plans were set in motion.

But we all know life has its little surprises, especially when you're going to marry a football coach. As a skeptic might have predicted, the Brockway athletic department found Kane High School in Kane, Pennsylvania had the same open date, so they both filled the opening in their schedule with a Friday night game. For Coach Toretti this meant that instead of a Friday night rehearsal and bachelor's party, he would be taking his football warriors on the road to Kane, Pennsylvania, forty miles from Brockway to play a Friday night game, then returning to Brockway. Here he would pick up his suit and tux, then drive seventy more miles to State College for a Saturday a.m. rehearsal and a Saturday p.m. ceremony. Now the bride and bridegroom had all of Saturday night and Sunday for a honeymoon. However the benevolent Brockway School

Board, "as a wedding present" presented teacher/coach Toretti with a personal day-off on Monday. Their generosity however didn't make a big difference as Toretti insisted on being back at Brockway High School Monday afternoon for football practice.

Mrs. Sever Toretti a coach's bride of less than one week learned another lesson about being the wife of a coach at Brockway's Friday night home game. Mrs. Toretti who was all of twenty-two years of age went to the game and sat among a group of Brockway teen-agers and some other fans approximately her age. At some point in the game these young people became disenchanted with the progress of the game and they began booing the coach. Well, this was more than "Mrs. Newly-wed" could take, so she lectured them, particularly one boy, about loyalty, school and team spirit etc.

As soon as she finished she said she felt badly, but "it had to be done."

After the game when she and Tor were back in their room, this was the best they could do in Brockway as there were no affordable furnished apartments, she told Tor what she had done. Tor in disbelief said, "You didn't?"

Ruth replied, "Yes I did."

Tor said, "Ruthie don't *ever* do that again, anytime they boo me in the future you just join in and boo right along with them."

At the start of W W II Coach Toretti tried to enlist and enter the Gene Tunney program, headed by the famed boxer. The program took coaches, and people involved and trained in physical fitness, gave them special training and then sent them to various bases to be in charge of improving the physical condition of the men under them. Coach Jim O'Hora served in such a capacity at Chicago Naval Pier until he became an officer and was put in command of a large landing craft with fifty men and four officers under him. Toretti however was turned down because of varicose veins.

As soon as it was known that Toretti had been turned down by the Selective Service, Steelton High School hired him as teacher and football coach feeling confident that they would have him for years. Six months later he was drafted, varicose veins not withstanding.

In 1946 upon leaving the service Toretti returned to his pre-war position of teacher and head football coach at Steelton High School. Steelton, Pennsylvania was, at the town level, what the United States was on the national level, the proverbial melting pot. Steelton was a mixed strata of residents, there were professional people, business people, state and federal government workers and a large percentage of Bethlehem Steel workers that populated this town just south of Harrisburg, Pennsylvania. There were many ethnic groups and while the Serbs had nothing but animosity for the Croats and vice versa, it was remarkable that this diverse population of Eastern Europeans, African-Americans, Caucasians etc would come together in team sports as they did, particularly in football and basketball. And as small as Steelton was, the town turned out teams that gave the Harrisburg city and surrounding schools a run for their money even though they were outnumbered in student-body size anywhere from two to one to seven to one. This desire to be the best and to be winners reflected their coach's persona and resulted in a team meeting which Tor related to the author with obvious relish.

Coach Toretti had called the meeting of the football squad to get their input relative to a movement that was afoot among a segment of the town's population and some of the school board directors. These people felt Steelton High School should, in the future, schedule schools its own size. This would allow their teams to win a higher percentage of their games by leveling the competitive field thus allowing Steelton to be league champion more often. At the football team meeting Tor explained that playing against schools their own size would enable them to be good, year-in and year-out. They wouldn't be perennial underdogs who lacked the depth and talent of the other big schools. Playing against their present competition they had to perform at the peak of their potential every game, and when a player was lost due to an injury, their ranks were weakened considerably as they didn't have the depth the big schools had. Toretti was trying to set forth the pros and cons without interjecting his opinion. He definitely didn't want his players to feel as if they were surrendering if they opted to "drop down." As he spoke he knew the players were listening to him but he couldn't get a read as to what they were thinking. When he paused briefly one of the players stood up and said, "Coach, we hear all the reasons for dropping down, but if we win every year at that level what does it prove? So we're county or state champs of the little schools; how good are we compared to the other schools? Hey if we lose to Harris or Reading by six points and they go on to become State Champs or we beat them – then we know just where we stand!" Immediately a group of three players stood up and the spokesman stated loudly and clearly while the others raised their arms, "Coach if we can't play the best, we don't want to play!"

Tor said, "Ken, you know a coach can never be prouder of his kids than I was then."

On those occasions when Toretti played golf with the author at his club in the Harrisburg area we would, upon completing our round, have a coke and a sandwich in the grille room. In those years – our club had only waiters, no waitresses, and as soon as one of the waiters spotted

Coach Toretti, there would be a procession of waiters from the dining room upstairs etc., even cooks from the kitchen coming out to say, "Hi" to Coach Toretti and to tell him what that person's brother, cousin whatever, who played for him back then, was doing or how their mother and dad were. I said more than once, "Tor, it seems like you're the member here and I'm the guest from out of town." On one occasion Tor said to me, "Ken, to this day I could probably walk through the darkest back streets of Steelton on a Saturday night and from here and there I'd hear, 'Hi, Coach.'"

But after two years at Steelton, Toretti had the opportunity to move to a much larger school, Williamsport, Pennsylvania, and as one has to do in the coaching profession in order to advance, he took the offer and moved on.

At the Friday afternoon pep rally prior to Williamsport's first game under their new coach, Coach Toretti and the entire team were on the auditorium stage in front of the assembled student body. The cheerleaders and the band had tried to rouse the student body but the students basically sat on their hands. Seeing what was transpiring, Coach Toretti went to the microphone and told the band to stop playing. He motioned to his players to stand, then he said, "There's a football game tomorrow afternoon and you're looking at the team that's going to win that game… with you or without you." He then motioned to the team and they strode off of the stage and out of the auditorium.

Saturday afternoon the crowd was there, "with bells on."

It didn't take Coach Toretti long to put his stamp on his new team. Toretti never drank or smoked and he insisted his players do likewise. While he and Ruth were taking a stroll one day, two Williamsport football players smoking cigarettes came walking toward them. As Ruth related the incident, neither boy made any attempt to hide his cigarette and they said "hello" as they passed by. She recalled that Tor mumbled something which he never verbalized but she knew what he was thinking. Monday when the two players, one a starter, reported for practice they couldn't find their equipment or their uniforms. Coach Toretti called them into his office and informed them they were off the team for the season.

Toretti's move to Williamsport may have brought his name to Joe Bedenk's attention since Bedenk was a Williamsport native. After just one year as head coach of "The Bills" or "The Millionaires" as they are known, Toretti was offered a spot on Bedenk's coaching staff. Despite the fact that he had to take a cut in pay, Toretti made the move.

Over the years Tor also passed on to me some of his Rules of Recruiting, three of which I will list,

1. Promises you don't make can't come back to haunt you.
2. Accentuate the positive – in other words tell the recruit why he *should* come to Penn State rather than why he shouldn't go to that other school.
3. This is a "Tor" original which falls in the same category as "The grass is always greener on the other side of the fence," "The prowess of the recruit increases proportionately with the distance from the recruit's home to the campus of the school recruiting him."

Tor also pointed out something I hadn't thought of previously. For years, the only Penn State game he attended was the last game on the schedule because he was always scouting the up-coming opponent.

Toretti and Defensive Coordinator Jerry Sandusky also conveyed the following gems to the author which apply to scouting opponents and recruits and helps explain Penn State's black shoes, which more and more schools have begun wearing and their generic white away uniforms that more and more recruits refer to as "those cool Penn State uniforms."

There are three optical illusions in scouting football teams and players: 1. Players wearing white shoes look like they are faster than players wearing black shoes. 2. Players look faster at night than they do in daylight. 3. Players in white uniforms look bigger than players in black or dark uniforms.

Toretti, I'm sure, over the years told me, and audiences of which I was a part, a hundred stories, episodes, incidents, etc., many humorous, but always interesting and informative. I have one story to tell on him.

Following a Lancaster Penn State Alumni Club "Sports Night" at which Tor had been the featured speaker, he motioned to Marie and me to come to the door and stand next to him as the crowd disbursed so we could talk later. His wife Ruth wasn't with him so he was more or less a one person receiving line, responding to all the people who chose to stop by to thank him for coming, or to compliment him on his presentation. Toretti knew at least half of the people by name, knew their face or something pertinent about them. Two of the very last persons to stop and pay their regards appeared to be in their seventies. Toretti didn't recognize the man, or the woman who did the speaking for both of them. The conversation went like this.

While shaking his hand the lady said, "Mr. Toretti we thoroughly enjoyed your talk, it was good, we'd really like you to come back again next year, every year."

Toretti said, "Well thank you very much. It's a pleasure to come here and talk to your group but next year you should get someone else… Rene Portland." (First name pronounced, "Ree-knee.") Rene Portland is the head coach of the Penn State Women's Basketball team.

The lady apparently didn't hear him clearly, confusing "Rene Portland" with "really important," she therefore responded, "We don't need someone really important, you'll do just fine."

A humorous moment, unfortunately the woman didn't know how really important "Tor" Toretti was to Penn State. From the time he came to Penn State in 1935 until the day he died, he represented the University in the finest manner and the highest tradition. If any person or persons warrant the title "Mr. Penn State" no one deserves it more than Sever J. "Tor" Toretti, PSU Class of 1939.

Toretti whose football number was 22 passed away on 02/20/2000. His casket was appropriately draped with his blue letterman's blanket, with the block white "S," he received in 1938.

Newly-weds Mr. & Mrs. Sever Toretti and the bride's parents.

Serviceman Sever Toretti on furlough with his wife, Ruth.

The Nittany Lion and one of State's finest "alums." (Photos on pages 217-220 courtesy of Ruth Toretti)

CHAPTER 39

The Coach Who Came to Dinner and Stayed Ten Years

When Joe Paterno came to State College, Pennsylvania, in 1950 to join Rip Engle's staff, he had a lot to learn about coaching. College football head coaches sometimes rise from the high school ranks, others start at the college level as a graduate assistant or assistant coach. Many of these pilots progress from head coach at a small college, to assistant coach, then head coach at a larger school or directly to head coach at a larger school. Some high school coaches, lacking a physical education background get on-the-job-training at the high school level and may advance to the college level but the odds aren't comforting. The author can immediately think of three high school coaches who jumped directly from high school coach to the post of college head coach; of the three, only Paul Brown, who went from Massillon High School to Ohio State, achieved great success. Seldom does a person with no physical education background and no experience get to *start* as an assistant coach with a major football program. But this was bachelor Joe Paterno's good fortune. Living with fellow assistant coach Jim O'Hora, his wife "Betts" and their family for the next ten years helped him to parlay a good break, into a ten year post-graduate course which will surely see him enshrined in the Collegiate Football Hall of Fame.

Joe roomed with Steve and Ginger Suhey during his first year at Penn State, then for the next ten years he had a room in Jim and "Betts" O'Hora's home. Jim O'Hora, "The O" to all the players, was not only well-versed in the theoretical and the practical sides of coaching having been a graduate assistant, a head coach (in high school) and as we've mentioned an assistant at Penn State, but he also had a calming influence on Paterno's more impetuous nature. O'Hora was like an uncle or almost a father figure to Paterno and they had *countless* discussions about football and all the administrative aspects of the game. From the beginning, Paterno was always looking for ways to make actual on-the-field practice time shorter, more effective, more efficient, better organized, and Coach O'Hora had a large storehouse of ideas *and* experience that Joe could sample. So Joe and his mentor spent many an evening discussing football, communications, public relations, staff management, anything and everything related to football. During those ten years O'Hora not only shaped Paterno's coaching career but on several occasions he also saved it. Joe was once quoted as saying, "Were it not for Jim O'Hora and

Rip Engle, I probably would have been fired ten times."

In Joe's earliest days he was long on ideas and short on experience, however all football coaches are extroverts and talkers, therefore Joe found an inexhaustible supply of football minds ready, willing and able to debate anything related to football. Joe's first football office when he joined Rip's staff was right next to Frank Patrick's and next to their offices were Al Michaels' and "Tor" Toretti's. Joe Bedenk's and O'Hora's offices were side-by-side next to Head Coach Engle's office on the other side of the secretary. After just a short time as head coach, Rip changed the arrangement of the football offices when the staff re-located from the track level in Rec Hall down to the second level. After this move, all of the assistant coaches were basically in one room and Coach O'Hora's desk was positioned between Joe's and Tor's. This arrangement led to a freer exchange of ideas among the assistant coaches. O'Hora said some of the discussions were quite spirited, with everyone joining in.

When the author and Coach O'Hora discussed these intra-office debates, more than forty years after they happened and thirty years after Joe became head coach, the author found it hard to imagine Joe as a rookie coach. Yet in the early fifties he was the most junior member on the staff. When J.T. White arrived in 1954, he became the newest coach on the staff but J.T. was probably seven years older than Joe and had been coaching longer, so I'm sure he felt and probably acted senior to Joe.

Approximately three years prior to actually being named head coach in 1966, Paterno was given the title of associate head coach and he assumed some administrative duties and responsibilities the other assistants didn't have. But Joe's peers certainly knew he was being groomed to be the next head coach and they were comfortable with the situation. However, prior to 1962, Joe was perceived by the other assistant coaches as just another coach and strange as it might seem to-day, many a debate or heated discussion ended with one or more assistants telling Paterno flatly, "You're wrong, Joe."

"Rip" Engle's first meeting with his coaching staff. (left to right) Frank Patrick, Joe Paterno, Al Michaels, "Tor" Toretti, "Rip", Earl Bruce and Jim O'Hora. (Photo courtesy of Coach Jim O'Hora.)

A Young Head Coach Paterno Signs Autographs for the
Author's Son and Daughter.

CHAPTER 40

Nobody Told Me

In his early assistant coaching years, Paterno was single and he was refining his Italian recruiting charms. Paterno found early-on that it's not a coincidence that college football players, if the TV cameras get up close and personal, always say, "Hi, Mom" or "Hi, gang" they never say, "Hi, Dad." So if you're doing some serious recruiting and Mom is in the kitchen, remember more recruits are literally signed, sealed and delivered out in the kitchen while tasting Mom's spaghetti sauce than while smoking a cigar or having a beer with Dad.

On this recruiting evening as Paterno related the story years later at a Nittany Lion Club Banquet, he was being as suave as he could be. He had the Brown University Ivy League look with the blazer, "rep tie" and men's hose with garters. No low socks to show skin or leg hair when you sit down, should your trousers get pulled up a bit. On this particular occasion in 1952 Paterno wasn't alone, he was accompanying Rip Engle and Jim O'Hora, and all three were in a Wilkes-Barre, Pennsylvania home, talking with the parents of Corny Salvaterra regarding their son, a standout football quarterback at Wilkes-Barre G.A.R.

In the 1950s, as well as today, high school football coaches were the conduits through whom college coaches had to work to recruit one of the coach's players. These high school coaches had their favorite colleges and their personal favorite college coaches.

As Coach O'Hora explained the facts of life to the author, if O'Hora were to approach fictitious high school head coach "Smith" about his star tailback Joe Runner, and Coach Smith was not sending any of his players to Penn State the coach would say, "Oh you can't get him, he's going to Ohio State." O'Hora might say "Well what about that big end Peiro Terminus?" The coach would shake his head, "His Dad's from Lansing, Michigan; Michigan State's got him all tied up. But we have this defensive halfback he's just a little bit undersized but he's fast as a whippet and really tough, he loves to hit." Coach O'Hora might then say, "What about that quarterback Mick O'Hern he's only a junior but we like what we've seen of him." Coach Smith would come right back with, "No, chance the whole family and the in-laws are all big Notre Dame fans and he's at the top of Notre Dame's list. But we have a good linebacker Fritz Fidler, he's only 6 foot 1, 185 pounds, but he's just a junior, too and he'll probably be 6 foot 2, 210 pounds, by the time he graduates." So the good ones were always taken, but the coach would try to get you to take the third, or fourth or fifth best player on the team. However you can't build a top notch team with third, fourth and fifth best.

But back to Corny Salvaterra. Until recently all the smart money was saying he was a "lock" for Notre Dame. Then all of a sudden Pitt was being mentioned with increased frequency.

When word of this possible change of heart on Corny's part reached Jim O'Hora he passed it on to Rip, who decided to have O'Hora approach the Salvaterras directly, to set up an appointment where Jim, Rip and Joe would all appear. Certainly the presence of two assistants and the head coach would be an indication of how interested they were in Corny and maybe one of them could say just the right thing to change the Salvaterras' minds *or* in case there was a tug of war going on, could Penn State emerge as a happy compromise? So here was Penn State's head coach, the quarterback coach and an assistant coach who grew up in neighboring Scranton all present in the home of Mr. and Mrs. Salvaterra at one time, to make their pitch for the football services of their son Corny and to emphasize everything else they wanted to do for him *off* the football field.

Rip, Joe and Jim knew it was an uphill climb but maybe there was something one of them could say, an assurance they could give like "We will take good care of your son, we have mandatory study hall for freshmen five nights a week, we're away from the big city temptations and distractions etc."

Paterno was in the kitchen where he was doing his utmost to strike that one chord that would make Mrs. Salvaterra want to send her son to Penn State. "We have academic counselors," Joe was saying, "tutors are available at no cost and while we aren't a Catholic University like Notre Dame, I'm Catholic, Jim O'Hora is Catholic as are some other coaches on the staff. And we have a very active Newman Club, which meets weekly and has its own Catholic service right on campus. So there's a lot we can do for your son."

Mrs. Salvaterra said, "You want me to call you Joe, not coach?"

Joe replied, "Definitely."

Mrs. Salvaterra then said, "Well Joe ,that all sounds quite reassuring as far as the academics and your support systems and groups and its nice to know that you have some Catholic coaches on the staff, a Newman Club etc. but that's not something that would influence *us* much - because you see we're not Catholic."

If you are interested, Corny signed with Pitt and lettered all three years 1954-56. While the author always wished he were our quarterback rather than Pitt's, in the three head–to-head meetings between Pitt and Penn State each team won one game and there was one tie. Notre Dame and Pitt played in 1954 and '56 and each team won once.

George Werley had a similar real life experience on his first trip to St. Louis, Missouri, in the 1930s. He came to St. Louis by railroad but for some reason such as an early a.m. arrival he did not see the Mississippi River as the train came into St. Louis. This was as far west as George had ever traveled and he was excited about seeing the mighty Mississippi River. After a few morning business calls the first day, he had the entire afternoon free so he returned to his hotel, had lunch and decided to set out on that walk to the river he had promised himself. After walking a few blocks George spotted a policeman so he walked over to him and inquired, "How much farther down this street is it to the Mississippi?" The policeman paused, put his cupped hand to his chin and said, "Well, it's a deuce of a long way to the Mississippi River down this way, but it's only eight blocks back that way" as he turned and pointed in the direction from which George had just come.

CHAPTER 41

California Dreamin'

The search committee that identified Charles A. "Rip" Engle as Penn State head coaching material and those that interviewed and hired him, were they good, I mean really good or were they lucky?

Rip had languished at the high school level for eleven years before being named to the Brown University staff in 1942 and two years later he had become the head coach. In his first collegiate head coaching position at Brown, Engle's teams won only 38% of their games in his first four years. Then in his last two years he reversed the numbers as those teams won 83% of their contests. Here at Penn State his first two years were barely better than break even seasons, 5-3-1 then 5-4. Questions abounded, was this grandfatherly coach going to improve on this very so-so start or was he just a "five hundred" coach; someone who would win fifty-seven percent of his games, as he had done overall at Brown? There was one thing about which there was no question – everyone liked him, the media, the administration and the townsfolk. His players at Penn State loved him, a feeling they didn't have for Paterno, since Joe pushed his players to the limit as an assistant and as a head coach. It seemed like Engle got along with everybody, and everybody got along with him – with one big exception, Syracuse coach Ben Schwartzwalder. Surprisingly, but happily, after they both retired, they became good friends.

By 1956, his seventh season at Penn State, Engle had compiled a 41-20-3 record giving him a winning percentage of .664 which meant his teams were winning virtually two of every three games they played.

Engle must have been doing a lot of other things correctly because after the 1956 season, athletic director Ernie McCoy was contacted by "Jess" Hill who had just completed his sixth season as the head coach of USC's football team. Hill's teams had won 45 games, lost only 17 and tied 1 for a winning percentage of .722 over those six seasons and he had taken the "Trojans" to two Rose Bowl games winning one and losing one. In a move which was a double-barreled surprise, Jess informed Ernie that he would be stepping up to the athletic director's post at Southern California and he wanted Ernie's permission to talk to Rip about the soon-to-be-vacant head coaching job at USC. Suddenly Penn State which had had two head coaches in thirty-one years, 1918-1948, might now have a fourth head coach in just ten years.

For Engle, being the first choice of a school with Southern California's heritage must have been very heady stuff. Not too many years ago he was the head football coach at Waynesboro High School and here he could become the fourteenth head coach at Southern California, a school that had already gone to the Rose Bowl twelve times, six times in the last thirteen years. Thirty-three Southern California Men of Troy had already been named All-Americans, while just this year Penn State had only their twelfth All-American, in the person of Sam Valentine. (Through 1998 USC had had more than one-hundred and twenty All-Americans compared to Penn State's seventy-nine.)

Southern California had just closed their season on December 1 with a win over Notre Dame and now "Jess" Hill wanted to proceed at top speed because of recruiting and other considerations. After getting McCoy's permission he talked with Engle explaining all the things they were prepared to do for him and Sunny (his wife) as far as a home, a car etc. I can only guess that the financial package was impressive since Southern California must have had a war chest far exceeding anything Penn State could muster at the time. Because of USC's location in Los Angeles, big bucks were available and since USC is a private school, the state government had no control over their purse strings. Recruiting at Southern California would be one hundred times easier than at Penn State because of USC's tradition, its schedule, its Rose Bowl and conference affiliation, its stadium, TV exposure, climate etc. So Rip was sorely tempted. Now, however, he had some hurdles of his own to leap before he accepted the offer. Like any sane person Rip did not want to switch jobs and then fall on his face, therefore when he made his list of pros and cons relative to moving-on, he apparently set one pre-requisite above all the others. He would take the job only if he felt he would succeed; and what he needed to succeed were some very competent, loyal assistant coaches like those he had on his present staff. Therefore Engle decided he had to get authorization to bring three of his assistants with him. Hill quickly gave his approval. Step number two, Engle had to get Ernie McCoy's permission to talk to the three assistant coaches he wished to take with him. McCoy, the fine gentleman he was, gave his approval. Now step number three. Rip had to talk with the three men he had chosen and see if they would be willing to pull up stakes and go with him. Which of the three men Engle spoke with first, I don't know nor do I know if a "yes" from one of the men on the list would carry more weight than another. Certainly Rip wanted all three.

Engle had one affirmative answer very quickly. Bachelor Joe Paterno was a definite yes, in fact he tried to recruit at least one of the other two, his landlord Jim O'Hora. O'Hora wasn't nearly as enthusiastic as Paterno was. Jim and Betts had started their own family, plus they had family in Dunmore, and Mahanoy City, and Los Angeles was an entire continent away. Jim also had tenure having been on the staff since 1946. Joe and Jim and Betts discussed the move on several occasions with Joe promising to drive the moving van, baby sit in California so Jim and Betts could get out more often, etc. As O'Hora recalled, Joe was willing to promise anything to get his "yes" vote.

The third coach Engle felt he had to have was "Tor" Toretti. Toretti, like O'Hora, had a family along with in-laws in State College, and relatives in Western Pennsylvania. He and O'Hora were emotionally attached to Penn State and State College going back to their college days more than twenty years ago. Toretti and O'Hora talked frequently wondering exactly what would happen if they said they wouldn't go and Rip went anyway. Understandably they simply "dragged their feet" not saying, "Absolutely no, we won't go," but never saying, Yes. However, little things they said to Engle, made it apparent they weren't gung-ho about making the move. Jess Hill finally had to give Engle a deadline of "this Thursday" at which time he had to have a definite "Yes" or he would go on to the next name on the list.

Thursday Engle called Hill and told him the answer was, "No."

What would have happened had Engle decided to take Paterno along and leave O'Hora and Toretti behind? Who would have been the new coach at Penn State? Would Engle have stubbed his toe at USC? Would he and/or Paterno have been out of a job in a few years?

Don Clark a USC letterman in 1942, '46 and '47 and assistant coach 1951-'56 got the USC job and went 1 and 9 in 1957, his 1958 team had a 4-5-1 season, and even a Man of Troy despite his 8-2-0 record in 1959, couldn't keep his job with a 13-16-1 three-year mark. In 1960 John McKay took over the reins at USC where he compiled a 127-40-8, .749 record over a period of sixteen years, including four national championships.

(Incidentally the University of Southern California dislikes being referred to as Southern Cal. USC, Southern California, Troy and Trojans are preferred names.)

Rip Engle's coaching staff and wives circa 1953 from left to right Joe Paterno, Ruth and Tor Toretti, Betts and Jim O'Hora, Sunny and Rip Engle, Dorothy and Frank Patrick, Mary and Earl Bruce.

CHAPTER 42

The Ivy League Comes Calling—Who or What Do They Want?

The smooth transference of the mantle of power from Engle's shoulders to Paterno's, when it came in 1966 had been planned well in advance so that the transition would be seamless and there would be no repeat of the 1948 scenario.

Years previously in December 1962, Athletic Director Ernie McCoy had received a telephone call from another University with considerable heritage and tradition. This time it was an East Coast university that wanted to talk to one of his coaches. The University was Yale and they wanted to talk with Paterno, not Engle.

From Paterno's standpoint the post at New Haven, Connecticut, had considerable appeal to him. He would be closer to his Mother and Brooklyn his birthplace. He also relished the thought of returning to the Ivy League and competing against Harvard, Columbia, Princeton etc. from a position of power and influence and *beating them* as he felt sure he could do. Here in 1962 Paterno had already been an assistant coach for thirteen seasons and he was anxious to move up the ladder. There was no telling how long Engle intended to continue coaching so a move to another university looked like the percentage play; after all he was now thirty-six and still earning just an assistant coach's salary.

Since Engle had coached in the Ivy League, Paterno sought his advice. When Engle responded with words to the effect, "Don't rush into such a move," Paterno probably interpreted that to be a typical Rip Engle approach, don't rush headlong into something; examine the situation from all sides. But Rip continued in a direction Paterno hadn't expected, "Be patient Joe, I've already discussed it with Sunny and I'm going to coach for only a few more years."

Joe's immediate response was, "Well do you think I can have the job when you quit?"

Rip replied, "I'll set up an appointment with Dr. Walker" (Penn State's President) "and we'll see what he has to say."

The day of "the sit down," Paterno told Dr. Walker of his offer from Yale and Engle endorsed Joe's candidacy for the Penn State head coaching position. The talk went around and around regarding Paterno's ideas, his aspirations for Penn State football, student–athletes in general, the support programs (academic and athletic), etc. As the meeting was breaking up Paterno pressed for an answer because he had a decision to make.

He asked very bluntly, "Can I get the job?" Dr. Walker said, "If Rip recommends you and you're good enough you will get the position."

Paterno replied, "I'm good enough."

CHAPTER 43

Putting the Foot Back in Football

The 1963 season would be Engle's third-last and what a season it might have been. There were back-to-back wins over Pacific Coast Conference teams, Oregon and UCLA, plus a victory over both a Southwest Conference team Rice, and a Big Ten power, Ohio State. But there were three critical losses by a total of thirteen points. A total of seven field goals in three games (Pitt, Syracuse and Army) would have turned a 7-3 season into an 10-0-0 record good enough for fourth place or better in the AP Poll rather than somewhere in the second ten. Of those three losses the 10-7 loss to Army hurt the author most. For the third year in a row, Army had beaten State and in *all* three games, 10-6, 9-6, 10-7, the deciding points were field goals and/or extra points kicked by a young Cadet, Dick Heydt, who grew up just a short distance from the author's home in Palmerton, Pennsylvania. If only Heydt had been a Nittany Lion instead of a Black Knight, State might have won those three contests. (Heydt ended up in the top ten at Army in career field goals made, field goals attempted, extra points made and attempted.) Did young Heydt have his sights set on an Army career well before he graduated from high school or would he have gone to any Division 1-A school which valued his services as a kicker enough to provide him with a quality education on a full scholarship? I don't know. Penn State, because of grant-in-aid constraints or because of a certain mind-set, did not recruit a kicking specialist until 1971. In 1971 Paterno brought in his first kicking specialist, a junior college transfer, named Alberto Vitiello. Until that time Penn State had used a position player as a kicker generally with very pedestrian results.

In the ten years 1961-1970 Penn State kickers tried 103 field goals and made 47 for only a 45.6% success ratio, less than half the hundred or so attempted. In the ten-year period starting with Vitiello, kicking specialists attempted 205 field goals, twice as many, and succeeded 129 times for a 62.9% success ratio. More important then the 17% increase in the percentage of successful kicks were the extra 246 points scored. Points that were not realized in the previous ten years. In the three years 1961-63 a grand total of thirteen field goals would have won six more games. Changing 8-3, 9-2 and 7-3 seasons into 10-1, 10-1 and 10-0 records.

With the non-specialist kickers succeeding less than 50% of the time, (and one year they were successful in only 25% of their attempts, with one player making just 3 of 14 tries), any head coach who was aware of the low percentage of successful attempts would try only the shorter ones because, generally speaking the longer the attempt the less chance it will succeed. So common sense tells us that the kicking specialists racked up their higher percentage of successful kicks from farther away. Further supporting evidence is the fact that fifteen of Penn State's all-time successful field goals measuring fifty yards or more, were registered by kicking specialists. The only field goal of 50 yards or more by a position player was recorded by Pete Mauthe back in 1912, when the football was rounder and easier to kick.

Also note the number of all-time Penn State career scoring leaders ho are place-kick specialists (indicated by *).

All-Time Career Scoring Leaders

*1.	Craig Fayak 1990-93	282 points
*2.	Brett Conway 1993-96	276 points
*3.	Travis Forney 1996-99	258 points
4.	Lydell Mitchell 1969-71	246 points
5.	Curtis Enis 1995-97	230 points
*6.	Massimo Manca '82, 84-86	206 points
7.	Ki-Jana Carter 1992-94	204 points
8.	Curt Warner 1979-82	198 points
9.	Charlie Pittman 1967-69	192 points
	(tie) Bobby Engram '91,93-95	192 points
*11.	Matt Bahr 1976-78	191 points
*12.	Nick Gancitano 1981-84	190 points

While soccer players make very good field goal and "point after" kickers, they don't enjoy the same success when employed as punters. Over the years at Penn State, Chris Bahr and V. J. Muscillo were the only soccer-style kickers who also doubled as punters, to the author's knowledge. Position players who also punt are more numerous than those that kick field goals. There are several explanations for this. Soccer kickers, except for goalies, kick the ball "on a line" they rarely try to see how high and far they can kick the ball. Another factor is the use of hands. A punter must catch the center snap in his hands (soccer players other than goalies, have to learn to resist the impulse to catch the ball) and then the punter must coordinate the drop of the ball from his hands to his foot and basically kick from a stationary position. A soccer style place kicker never needs to catch the ball and he can take a moving circuitous path to the ball prior to kicking it, also the ball's on the ground.

Over the years at Penn State the Top Ten Career punters based on average yards per kick are as follows (Specialists denoted by star, only Chris Bahr doubled as a place-kicker.):

*1.	George Reynolds	43.0	*6.	Doug Helkowski	39.0
*2.	Ralph Giacomarro	41.8	7.	Bob Parsons	38.9
*3.	John Bruno	41.7	*8.	Chris Bahr	38.6
*4.	Pat Pidgeon	41.6	9.	Joe Cologne	38.4
*5.	Chris Clauss	40.5	10.	Milt Plum	38.0

Judging punters, strictly by the average length of their kicks can be very misleading as the following examples will prove:

1. If punter A kicks the ball 65 yards measured from the line of scrimmage but the kick is "on a line," the football will get to the opponent's punt return man before the kicking team's punt coverage team has run 25 yards. Then the punt coverage team will cover 20 yards toward the punt returner while he covers 20 yards toward them and there they will meet, 45 yards from the previous line of scrimmage A net gain of 45 yards on the punt. If punter B hits a very high punt which travels 55 yards from the line of scrimmage and his punt coverage team is so close to the punt return man that he can't advance the ball, the net gain on this punt is 55 yards. That is 10 yards more than punter A's team gained, yet punter B is credited in the statistics with a 10-yard shorter punt.
2. Suppose Team A's punter delivers a punt from mid-field, which goes into the end zone. If the length of the punt from the line of scrimmage measures 50 yards, Punter A will be credited with a 50-yard punt even though the football will be brought out to the 20 yard line for a net gain of only 30 yards. If punter B hits a 40-yard punt which is downed on the other team's 10 yard line he will be credited with a 40-yard punt, 10 yards less than punter A. But punter B's team will realize a net gain of 40 yards, ten more yards on the ten yard shorter (according to the statistics) punt.

Keeping the above in mind, the author would cast his subjective votes for the five Penn State punters who impressed him the most. (The author didn't see Milt Plum, Richie Lucas or the majority of the punters in the 1940s to the early 1960s, other than Joe Cologne.)

1. Scott Fitzkee – Scott's punts were high magnificent things of beauty. In three years he never had a punt blocked and as a high school sprinter who ran a 9.6 second 100 yard dash he was *always* a threat

to run with the ball.

2. Bob Parsons - Bob's punts were also high and long. He had one punt blocked in three years and played and punted for the Chicago Bears in the NFL for years.

3. Ralph Giacomarra – An excellent punter who hit high beautiful spirals. Why he didn't last longer in the NFL is puzzling.

4. John Bruno – An excellent punter with only one punt blocked in three years. With a lesser punter, Penn State would never have won their second National Championship in 1986. Tragically John's life was ended too soon.

5. I will call it a tie among Joe Cologne who never had a punt blocked in three years, George Reynolds who was over shadowed in his first two years by Ralph Giacimarro but hung in there and averaged 42.6 yards in his last year and Pat Pidgeon who ranked #2 in the Top Ten through 1998 (with one year of eligibility remaining.)

Before we leave the subject of punting let us compare the skill involved in punting with the game of golf, two sports which would seem to be diametrically opposed. Punting involves possible severe physical contact, golf is a non-contact game. Punting might have to be performed in front of 100,000 screaming fans, golf is played in almost total silence and with no one moving within the golfer's field of vision. We could lengthen the list but now that we have shown how opposite the two are, let us show how they are actually more similar than they are dissimilar. The golfer and the punter are basically on their own. A bad snap can penalize a punter as can an on-rushing lineman, but the catch, the drop, the leg swing, his mechanics will mostly determine the punter's success. For the golfer it's his grip, his swing mechanics, etc., which will determine whether he *can* become a top notch golfer. Just like a bad snap from the center, the golfer may be victimized by a bad bounce or a change in the wind after the ball is in flight. All the rest of it for the punter and the golfer is mental. And to some degree the toughest part of the golf swing and putting stroke plays a part in the punter's art of punting the ball. That is the fact that the swing of the club and the swing of the leg all start with a conscious act. A reflex action is more natural and keeps the brain from sabotaging the player's natural ability and talent, a *conscious* action is more contrived.

Going back to the days of the Wild West it has been postulated that the success of the gunslinger was the fact that he goaded his opponent into going for his gun first, since the gunslinger wanted to act in self-defense, rather than being accused of shooting a man in cold blood before the victim could even draw his gun. Those who have done the research say conclusively that a conscious action is considerably slower than a reflex action. (This is dramatically apparent in baseball when a line drive is hit back *at* the pitcher, or just to his side.) The victim, therefore had to make a conscious effort to go for his gun, while the gunslinger repsonded reflexively, unrestrained by any conscious "thought-out" movement. Conscious efforts leave time and room for doubt, reflex reactions don't, and the gunslinger unless and until his reflexes were too slow, was usually the combatant still standing when the smoke cleared.

On a different front, when the author's son began his collegiate golf career playing at Western Maryland the author couldn't believe the times Kenn's coach had his team playing outdoors in snow, sleet, rain, frigid weather etc. Horrid conditions. I thought the coach was without a doubt, "a few bricks shy of a full load." What was to be gained by this insanity – no one could play even close to par under those conditions. However when spring intercollegiate competition began, his strategy was very clear. Although even-par, or better, would be very rare under the weather conditions that prevailed 10 to 15% of the time when Western Maryland was playing, Coach Moyer's team played *less worse* than many of the other teams because they weren't mentally defeated. No matter how bad the weather in March or April they could always say, "We've played in worse than this (in January and February)."

So does it go for the punters at Penn State. At practice, on virtually every punt, they are kic   into the wind. If the wind begins blowing the opposite way, they change ends of the field and kick the other way. They are always fighting the elements. None of this kicking a wind-aided 85-yarder enabling the punter to inflate his chest and pump his fist into the air. Instead it's all about not out-kicking your coverage with a line drive into a strong wind, and yet getting the ball up field for as much positive yardage as is possible under the conditions. And "Oh Yes," one day each week is "wet ball" practice day. Balls are immersed in buckets of water before making the cycle from the snapper to the punter to the return man and back to the bucket. All of this makes punting in a game the most fun a punter has week-in and week-out.

CHAPTER 44

Brutus Buckeye: "It'll Be a One-Sided Shutout"

T he year was 1964 and for most of the season Penn State had lacked a healthy, talented quarterback. Their best quarterback Gary Wydman hadn't lettered since '61 and early in the 1964 season he still wasn't available for duty.

Of their first five games State had lost four. Navy, UCLA, Oregon and Syracuse each scored 21 or 22 points while the Lion offense couldn't tally more than 14 points in any game. Only a 6-2 win over Army (at long last, Dick Heydt had graduated) held out a glimmer of hope for a winning season. But a person "would have to live where the busses don't run" to even *think* this Penn State team could, in up-coming successive weeks beat West Virginia, Maryland, Ohio State, Houston and Pitt, with Maryland and Pitt being the only home games.

In the 1964 season, West Virginia had already taken the measure of Syracuse (who had already beaten Penn State) and Kentucky, and they would end up playing in the Liberty Bowl game (held inside Convention Hall in Atlantic City). Pitt, while posting a losing season, would nonetheless beat Notre Dame 15-7 and Army 28-0. Ohio State tuning up for Michigan had beaten SMU (27-8), Indiana (17-9), Illinois (26-0), Southern California (17-0), Wisconsin (28-3), and Iowa (21-19) leading up to their game against Penn State, a team that had upset them last year in Columbus, 10-7.

Ohio State's fans, media, etc., instead of vowing they would not look past the Lions and underestimate them again this year, took the approach that Penn State "lucked-out" last year, playing over their heads against one of Woody's poorer teams. The '63 Ohio State team (5-3-1) had posted the third-poorest record for any Woody Hayes team to-date. But this year, Buckeye rooters were sure it would be an entirely different story. Penn State would be coming up against a 6-0 Woody Hayes team that would undoubtedly go undefeated if they could get by Michigan in Columbus. Michigan had beaten OSU in Columbus only once since Hayes became head coach in 1951.

Penn State administered a good licking to West Virginia 37-8 and squeezed by a five and five Maryland team, which had lost to #2 Oklahoma by the close score of 13-3, but couldn't beat fellow ACC foes, N.C. State, Duke or Wake Forest.

So the stage was set for some revenge and redemption in Ohio

Stadium come November 7, where and when Woody Hayes' team would treat a crowd of 84,000 plus, mostly Scarlet and Grey fans, to an offensive and defensive show that would have their mascot Brutus Buckeye cavorting all around the playing field.

A young Jim Tarman, who was in his seventh year at Penn State as the Director of Sports Information went to Columbus, Ohio on Tuesday November 3 to "advance" the upcoming Penn State-Ohio State football game. When Tarman arrived he contacted Wilbur Snypp his counterpart at OSU, who set up all the media appointments Tarman could fit in, around a scheduled appearance before the local Penn State alumni group.

Tarman was staying in downtown Columbus, as that central location made it easier to "hit" the radio and television stations as well as the newspapers. In restaurants, coffee shops and taxi cabs Tarman heard only one message – how badly Ohio State was going to beat those across-the-border, country-clods. The aversion to even speaking Penn State's name must have been a trick they picked up from Coach Hayes. Woody consistently referred to Michigan as "that team up north" or "that school up north."

There was no restraint in the voices that were predicting the final score for the game. Ohio State ranked #1 in one poll and #2 in the other, with its three All-Americans, was being picked to win the game by every Ohioan who had an opinion. The only waffling was exhibited by those who picked OSU to win by four touchdowns or less. The loudest voices were predicting victory by more than 40 points and up to 60 points, with few conceding that Penn State would even score. All Tarman heard was 40-0, 54-0, 60-0 and on and on.

By Friday Tarman was pretty well brainwashed, and even he, feared that Ohio State was going to embarrass the Lions. He departed his downtown hotel and checked into the motel where the team would be staying outside of Columbus, anxious to hear something other than Ohio State boasting.

After the team arrived and was settled in, Tarman met with Paterno and Jim O'Hora later that evening in the motel coffee shop as was their custom. Paterno, to start the conversation, asked Tarman how things went the past week. Tarman replied, "FINE. *Just fine,* except everyone says we're going to get killed. Joe, there's no diversity of opinion about who'll win and they aren't pulling any punches about the score. They're saying they'll win by 30-40 points. Can we make a game of it, we're not going to be embarrassed are we?"

"Embarrassed" Joe snorted, "Hey we might shut them out." Tarman looked quickly from Paterno to O'Hora; and O'Hora was just smiling – he said nothing.

242

Taking into account everything he had been hearing all week Tarman felt they might be pulling his leg. Jim shot back, "Come *on* Joe."

Paterno said, "Wait and see," and then turned to O'Hora and queried him, "How 'bout it Jim, didn't we just have one of the best practice weeks we've had all season, maybe in two seasons?"

O'Hora nodded his head, "The kids are fired up about playing a #1 team, they're not intimidated. They're not coming out here to take a licking, you could sense it on the plane."

Paterno went on to say that this team had gotten better every week since the quarterback position jelled. They were gaining in confidence by leaps and bounds and lately, getting better each day.

He added, "They're looking at this game as a chance to show everyone how good they really are... It's an entirely different team than the one that started the season." Paterno continued, "The way I feel about this team, I think we'll shut them out."

Tarman had expected Paterno to say Penn State had a good chance, but to say they'd probably shut out the #1 or #2 team in the country, greatly surprised him. After everything he had been hearing all week long he wasn't certain exactly what to believe. He was certain about one thing – *someone* was in for a HUGE surprise.

1960 Penn State coaching staff (left to right back row) "Tor" Toretti, Joe Paterno, Dan Radakovich, J. T. White, (seated) Jim O'Hora, Frank Patrick, Earl Bruce, Head Coach "Rip" Engle. (Photo courtesy of Penn State Sports Information)

CHAPTER 45

Upset of the Year

The Associated Press Named It the College Football Upset of 1964

P enn State with its 3 and 4 record stepped out onto the football field of Ohio Stadium in front of 84,279 mostly partisan fans. It was a sunny November day and there was a raucous crowd on hand to watch the highly favored Buckeyes give the white clad visitors a good thumping.

The game didn't go exactly as anticipated in the first quarter. The Lions were down knocking on Ohio State's goal line door threatening to score six points, not the other way around, as the crowd had expected. Then on a Tom Urbanik fullback plunge into the line from the two-yard line, the football squirted loose into the end zone but Dirk Nye beat two Ohio State defenders to the ball for a Penn State touchdown. The score at the end of the first quarter was 7-0 in favor of the visiting Lions.

While the Ohio State crowd was still into the game, some of the home-town fans were sullen. They weren't prepared to be satisfied with an Ohio State *lead* of seven points at the end of one period much less a seven point deficit.

With Gary Wydman's play-action passing and the running of speedy Don Kunit the second quarter was no better for the Buckeyes. The scoreboard at halftime showed Penn State leading 14-0.

An Ohio State lead of 41-0 was more what the partisans expected from those three numbers. The scoreboard was just a minor revelation of the way the first half had gone, as the halftime statistics showed. In the category of first downs Ohio State had none. Under the net yards rushing heading there was a negative number, minus 16 yards. Under pass completions there was another familiar number, zero. When, in anyone's recollection, had a Woody Hayes team been so completely dominated?

Throughout the stadium at the start of the second half Ohio State fans "knew" there would be a change in those statistics. Penn State fans on the other hand had their finger crossed. The first half score and the important statistics were *ALL* zero or a negative number as far as Ohio State was concerned. Could their Penn State team *possibly* continue its stellar performance?

Ohio State's defense continued to react to the "keys" as they were coached to do and their linebackers bit on virtually every play-action

Joe Paterno, Penn State and College Football - What You Never Knew

pass. Penn State scored again, to lead 21-0, in the third quarter. Ohio State finally erased one of the zeros on the game "stat" sheet when midway through the third period Ohio State got its initial first down, by way of a penalty.

Penn State scored again in the fourth quarter. By this time Ohio stadium was emptying and Brutus Buckeye couldn't be blamed if he ceased his efforts to motivate the crowd. OSU, first or second in the country was a 27-0 loser to unranked PSU.

When the Nittany Lion team exited the visitor's locker room there was a small but wildly delirious group of Penn State rooters waiting for them. One of them, Jim Tarman, went over to Joe Paterno, "Son-of-a-gun how *did* you know?"

Paterno responded," Well, I said I knew we'd play well." Now with the look of the cat who had just eaten the canary he admitted, "They might have gotten a field goal."

Number 53, Glenn Ressler for his standout performance was chosen as the AP Defensive Player of The Week (nationally). (Tarman ventured, he could also have been the Offensive Player of the Week based on his blocking from his center position.) Even in 1964 when most players played both ways, there still wasn't any such thing as a one-man team. But Ressler who made ten All-American teams at the end of the season, won the Maxwell Award as the nation's outstanding player and went on to be an All- Pro guard on the Baltimore Colts from 1965-1974 gave a performance against Ohio State on November 11, 1964, which coupled with his square jaw and studious look, when wearing his glasses, reminded one and all, of the alter-ego of a certain "mild-mannered " comic strip news reporter at "The Daily Planet."

Penn State's 1964 Lambert Trophy Team and coaching Staff. (Photo courtest of Penn State Sports Information.)

CHAPTER 46

With My Head Held High

A fter bringing the 1964 season to a hugely successful conclusion with five straight victories over West Virginia, Maryland, Ohio State, Houston and ending with a 28-0 shutout of Pitt many people thought that henceforth Penn State's football teams would appear in the Top Twenty almost every year. The Lions had appeared in four bowl games 1959-1962, and for six years starting in 1959, Penn State finished in the Top Twenty in at least one poll. The thirteen most successful programs across the country as far as number of Top Ten finishes at that time, were Alabama, Arkansas, Mississippi, Texas, LSU followed by Ohio State, Minnesota, Wisconsin, Washington, Navy, Michigan State, USC and Oklahoma.

Penn State however was not yet one of those "reloading" programs and the 1965 team wasn't able to simply continue where the 1964 team left off. Main cogs in the 1964 machine like Glenn Ressler, Gary Wydman, Ed Stuckrath, Tom Urbanik and Bill Bowes were not immediately replaceable.

As a consequence the Lions started off in 1965 just as they did in 1964 losing three of their first four games. In 1964 Engle, normally a worrier, somehow sensed that his squad was going to be all right, they just needed a quarterback and time. This year he was thinking maybe he should have retired last year.

A 44-6 Homecoming victory over West Virginia gave Penn State its second win of the year and a glimmer of hope. But the following game was the cruelest cut of all. Penn State had outplayed the University of California in Berkeley for 59 plus minutes and clung to a 17-14 lead with time left for one play. The distance was too great for a tying field goal for the Golden Bears. The only possibility was a one-in-a-thousand- chance, "Hail Mary" pass. On the previous Cal throw downfield Penn State had been in a prevent defense which made a short pass a certain completion, but connecting on several of those then, or one of them right now, would not win the game. Thus on this last play of the game the Cal quarterback dropped back to throw the football as far as he could. Three Penn State defenders were ten yards beyond the Cal receivers and leading in the race to the goal line when the Cal quarterback heaved the ball toward the end zone. By the time the ball descended, the end zone was crowded with seven players, three Cal receivers and four Penn State defenders and despite the best efforts of the four State defenders the ball somehow found its way into the arms of a Golden Bear receiver and California had unbelievably won the game 21-17.

State was now 2-4 for the season and they had to win 3 of the remaining 4 games to avoid a losing season. While Rip had chased away the end of the season bug-a-boo of a sure loss to Pitt he had won only one more Pitt contest than he had lost in fifteen games. A loss at Pitt would mean Kent State, Navy and Maryland would have to be vanquished with the season ending Maryland game being played in College Park, Maryland, in December.

As we might have predicted Penn State beat Kent State (21-6) and the Middies (14-6) and Pitt beat Penn State (30-27). It was something they would not do again for ten years. In that ten-year period Joe Paterno's teams would roll up 394 points while yielding just 135 to the Panthers.

This brought Engle's last season (Paterno would be officially named head coach in February 1966, at this time he was listed as Associate Head Coach) down to a final game at Maryland. Should the Lions lose or tie this game a record of consecutive non-losing seasons, which started in 1938, would be broken on Engle's watch. Rip's boys however came through for him winning the contest 19-7 and they triumphantly carried him off the field on their shoulders.

The 19-7 Penn State win against Maryland's Terrapins on December 4, 1965 ushered *out* Rip Engle's career as a Penn State head coach. Oddly, Penn State's new head coach would usher *in* his career as head coach on September 17, 1966 with a 15-7 win over the same Terrapins of Maryland.

Postscript: Before his final season Rip made it official that 1965 would be his last year at the helm. When asked why he was stepping down with 104 victories 48 losses and 4 ties, he simply said, "I want to go out with my head held high." And he certainly did.

It took Paterno less than thirteen seasons to top Engle's sixteen-year career total of 104 wins. But it would take Paterno years to develop the same rapport with his staff, his players and others, that Rip Engle enjoyed, from day one until the day he retired.

III

THE PATERNO ERA
THIRTY-SIX YEARS AND COUNTING

CHAPTER 47

What Do They Say?

September 17, 1966 Saturday, 1:30 P.M. Beaver Stadium

Like any rookie head coach Paterno was nervous prior to his first game. However, his first game brought some extra baggage with it. For seventeen years he had stifled his Italian curiosity. He had wanted to know what coaches said to each other when they met at mid-field at game's end but he refused to ask and thus show his lack of savvy. As we know Paterno was never a head coach even at the high school level, Therefore the dialogue that took place at the center of the field was something he could only imagine.

Paterno probably wanted to be prepared, if Penn State won, to say something gracious. If it was a close game and State won he might say to the other head coach, "It's a shame anybody had to lose this game, both teams played hard." Hard is one of those ambivalent words used in football. If both teams played poorly but one team won just because they played "less worse," you'd be a hypocrite to say to the other coach, "Tough loss but both teams played well." However it's acceptable to say "Both teams played hard." It can be a diplomatic evaluation of a sloppy game or a game between two teams that simply don't have many good athletes.

After the game ended, with Paterno notching his first win, he trotted onto the field in the direction of the Maryland bench ready to say something conciliatory to Coach Lou Saban at mid-field about Maryland's 15-7 loss to the Lions. But search as he would, he couldn't find Lou. Paterno felt sure that the short time he spent accepting congratulations from some players and coaches hadn't unduly delayed his presence at mid-field. A protracted delay might have caused Coach Saban to think, "Hey I'm not hangin' 'round here all day just to have somebody pat me on the back and commiserate with me."

Paterno probably reflected on this missed meeting a time or two on Sunday and even Monday morning. Not wanting to start his head-coaching career slighting another head coach he had Cheryl Norman put in a call to Coach Saban. And although their conversation would lack the spontaneity of an on-the-field meeting it would give him a response he could tuck away in his cerebral filing system for possible use when he would be on the losing side.

When Saban picked up the telephone at his end, Paterno opened up with words to this effect, "Hey Lou, I looked for you after the game but somehow we missed each other, I want you to know I did look for you to pay my regards." Saban responded, "Nah Joe I didn't hang around, I went right to the locker room. I thought we both stunk so I saw no reason to stand out there and embarrass each other talking about it."

Don't get the impression that Paterno wrings his hands obsessing over something he just said when it comes to his football team or anything that pertains to his management of his personnel, his play-calling, Penn State's football uniforms, etc. In a personal conversation the author mentioned to Paterno that it must be difficult to be fair, when dealing with the one hundred-plus individuals on a football squad. He replied, "Ken, we not only have to be fair, we have to appear to be fair." However the statement "we have to appear to be fair" doesn't mean Coach JoePa feels he needs to justify the use of any personnel or any position switches to anyone outside of the team and staff and that includes family, even his younger brother George, witness the following exchange:

At a recent spring Blue-White game, Paterno was in the radio booth with brother George and Penn State's legendary play-by-play announcer Fran Fisher. On this particular occasion George made an assessment of a Penn State fullback who previously had played defensive end as a true freshman. George declared, "He'd make a better defensive end because..." Joe curtly cut him off when he said, "No he wouldn't." Silence. This little bit of brotherly competition or reiteration of the pecking order created a charged atmosphere; an atmosphere which was apparent to any radio listener who was paying attention. Fortunately the two brothers were in the presence of a consummate professional radioman who took over and dissolved the tension. In a neat bit of tight-rope-walking Fran Fisher calmly said, "George, you're not always right, but this is one time you're wrong."

CHAPTER 48

Passing the Baton

With the elevation of Joe Paterno to head coach, Penn State made its last football head coaching change more than thirty-four years ago (1966). Retired athletic director, Jim Tarman remarked to the author, on the occasion of his retirement at the end of 1993, that he came to Penn State in 1958 where he served as sports information director, assistant to the athletic director, then associate director of athletics and finally director of athletics spanning a period of nearly thirty-six years. In all that time he worked with just two football head coaches, Rip Engle and Joe Paterno. In fact from its first head coach George Hoskins, who was actually a player/coach 1892-1895, through Joe Paterno, Penn State has had only *fourteen* head coaches. And for the eighty year period analyzed in the schedule on pages 256 and 257, Penn State is the hands-down leader in head coach stability with just five head coaches.

Even a school with as storied a football history as Notre Dame, second most wins of all Division I-A programs and the best won-lost percentage of all schools with at least 750 games played, has had *twenty-six* head coaches. The longest tenure of any head coach was the thirteen seasons posted by the legendary Knute Rockne, who died in an airplane crash between the 1930 and 1931 seasons. In the next seven decades there were four coaches who could qualify as mini-legends – Elmer Layden, Frank Leahy, Ara Parseghian and Lou Holtz, none of whom lasted more than eleven seasons.

Penn State's stability at the head coaching position is also reflected at the assistant coaching level. From 1950 to 1999, the Rip Engle to the present day Joe Paterno Era, the following assistants served fifteen or more years under Rip and/or Joe:

Dick Anderson	21
Tom Bradley	20
Earl Bruce	20
Fran Ganter	26
Jim O'Hora	27
Joe Paterno	16
Frank Patrick	24
Bob Phillips	21

Jerry Sandusky	31
Joe Sarra	15
J. T. White	26
Jim Williams	15
	262 years

These twelve assistant coaches have averaged nearly twenty-two years of service each; and Anderson, Bradley and Ganter can be expected to add to their totals.

As mentioned previously Penn State had five head coaches in the time frame 1920 through 1995. Of all the teams shown in the schedule on pages 256 and 257, Alabama, Georgia and Georgia Tech with nine each, had the next fewest skippers in the same seventy-six year period. At the opposite end of the spectrum Maryland had nineteen and Pitt and N. C. State had eighteen. Thus Penn State has had a disruption in its head coaching continuity once every sixteen years, Alabama, Georgia and Georgia Tech have changed head coaches approximately every eight to nine years and Maryland has had a new man at the helm oftener than once every four years. When consulting the schedule be aware that a zero in any particular decade does not mean that the school didn't have a head coach, it just indicates that a coach hired in the previous decade served through the following ten year period.

	1920s	1930s	1940s	1950s 1997	Total
Alabama	2	1	1	5	9
Army	3	3	1	8	15
Auburn	5	2	2	4	13
Colorado	1	2	5	7	15
Duke	7	1	1	8	17
Florida	4	2	2	7	15
Georgia	3	2	0	4	9
Georgia Tech	1	0	1	7	9
Iowa	2	3	3	7	15
Kentucky	4	2	2	7	15
Lehigh	5	1	3	5	14
Maryland	1	3	5	10	19
Michigan State	5	1	1	6	13
Minnesota	3	2	2	7	14
Missouri	4	2	1	7	14

Nebraska	4	1	5	4	14
NC State	4	4	1	9	18
Notre Dame	1	2	3	7	13
Ohio State	2	1	4	3	10
Penn	2	3	0	8	13
Pitt	2	1	3	12	18
Syracuse	3	2	3	3	11
Temple	3	2	2	8	15
Tennessee	3	1	1	7	12
Texas	3	2	1	5	11
Texas A & M	2	1	3	7	13
UCLA	3	1	2	7	13
USC	2	0	2	7	11
West Virginia	6	0	2	6	14
Wisconsin	4	2	1	7	14
Yale	2	2	3	3	10
PSU	1	1	1	2	5

Coaching staff stability is almost always a good thing and even the loss of one assistant coach can necessitate some adjustments. When a head coach leaves, whether he takes most of his staff with him or not, there is a disruption which affects the program from top to bottom internally and can adversely affect recruiting and relations with high school coaches externally. That's why dynasties under legends like "Bear" Bryant at Alabama, Bobby Dodd at Georgia Tech, Darrell Royal at Texas and General Robert Neyland at Tennessee showed considerable drop-offs when the legend retired.

Having built a national power from a program that sixty plus years ago didn't have a single scholarship player and couldn't register a winning season despite playing a de-emphasized schedule, Penn State fans can only hope when Paterno has run his leg that the transfer of the baton to the next man in the relay can be effected smoothly without a stumble, a break in stride, or a botched hand-off.

In Division 1-A football programs, assistant coaches hold a job for 3 to 3 ½ years on average and the average head coach lasts 4 to 6 years. If those numbers are averages there must be many assistant head coaches lasting less than three years and many head coaches lasting less than four years. Compare those averages with the following numbers at Penn State:

Current Penn State assistant coaches
Years at PSU Through 1999

Years on Staff	*Active Assistant Coaches*
21	Dick Anderson
20	Tom Bradley
26	Fran Ganter
7	Kenny Jackson
4	Larry Johnson
10	Bill Kenney
5	Jay Paterno
31	Jerry Sandusky
15	Joe Sarra
139	Total Years
15.5	Average Years per coach

Assistant coaches who retired and closed-out their assistant coaching careers at Penn State

Years on staff	
22	Joe Bedenk
24	Earl Bruce
31	Jim O'Hora
25	Frank Patrick
21	Bob Phillips
31	Jerry Sandusky
14	Sever Toretti
26	J. T. White
194	Total Years
24.3	Average years per coach

Penn State stumbled to its first losing season since 1988 following the retirement of assistant coach Jerry Sandusky at the conclusion of the 1999 season. Was his retirement a factor? The author doesn't know anyone who said it helped the situation. The loss of Courtney Brown, LaVar Arrington, Eric Cole, Chafie Fields, Brandon Short, Anthony King, David Macklin, Derek Fox, Askari Adams, David Fleischhauer, Kevin Thompson, Travis Forney and Pat Pidgeon also hurt; but the following coaching staff position changes went unnoticed by most observers:

	1999	**2000**
Dick Anderson	Quarterbacks/Passing Game	Offensive Line/ Guards and Centers
Tom Bradley	Defensive Backfield	In charge of Defense
Fran Ganter	Offensive Coordinator/RBs	Ass't Head Coach/ In charge of Offense
Larry Johnson	Defensive Line	Defensive Ends/ Special Teams
Bill Kenney	Offensive Line	Offensive Tackles and Tight Ends
Jay Paterno	Tight Ends	Quarterbacks
Jerry Sandusky	Defensive Coordinator/LBs	Retired
Al Golden		Linebackers
Joe Sarra	Defensive Line	Administration
Bob White		Defensive Line Ass't/Special Teams

Only Kenny Jackson who was in charge of wide receivers kept the same assignment.

CHAPTER 49

Notre Dame Mania, Knute Rockne and George Gipp

Notre Dame with its storied past, competed in its 1000th football game in 1996. Back in 1887 they played their first football game against a group of students from the University of Michigan, four days after Penn State concluded its inaugural season. The Michiganers came to South Bend by train, toured the campus and beat the Irish 8-0 in a Wednesday game; then after lunch they returned to Ann Arbor.

Notre Dame played Michigan twice in 1888 on April 20 and 21, both games played in South Bend and they lost both contests. They completed their season *seven months* later on December 6 when they beat Harvard Prep (of Chicago, Illinois) 20-0 for their first win. After posting a 3-3-1 record in their first four seasons, the "Fighting Irish," the term was first used at the turn of the century, went forty consecutive seasons without a losing season and that came only after Knute Rockne died in an airplane crash and was replaced as head coach by "Hunk" Anderson. In fact after 1888 only head coaches Anderson in 1933, Terry Brennan in 1956, Joe Kuharich in 1960 and '63, Gerry Faust in 1981 and 1985 and Lou Holtz in 1986, had losing seasons, through 1996. (Kuharich in his five year tenure never had a winning season.) Incidentally, exactly when the nick-name "Fighting Irish" started is not known. Some say the press coined the nick-name, another version had a Notre Dame player yelling at some of his Irish teammates while they were trailing in a game, "What's the matter with you guys- you're all Irish and you're not fighting a lick."

One can only wonder what Notre Dame's won and lost record would have been prior to 1997 had Knute Rockne coached for another twenty-five years and had the Irish not hired Joe Kuharich and Gerry Faust. However Notre Dame would not have hired Frank Leahy, Ara Parseghian and Lou Holtz, had Rockne's death and the dismal coaching records of Kuharich and Faust not dictated coaching changes when Frank Leahy, Ara Parseghian and Lou Holtz were available. Rockne, Leahy, Parseghian and Holz had won-lost records of 105-12-5, 87-11-9, 95-17-4 and 100-30-2 respectively. I suspect some avid Notre Dame rooters believe what happened was pre-ordained by a higher power for the greater good of Notre Dame. Along that line of thinking when the Penn State-Notre Dame series was announced, a good Catholic friend of the author told him there were only three reasons why the Irish *ever* lost a game. Reason number one – the Catholics hadn't prayed hard enough. Reason number two – God felt the Catholics were getting too "uppity" and he decided to remind them of their need to be more humble and reason number three – the Protestant referees cheated.

Over the years, Penn State had made numerous overtures to Notre Dame regarding a home and home series between the two schools, but even following State's move from New Beaver Field to the larger Beaver Stadium, the Nittany Lion's home field capacity in 1966 was only 46,284 while Notre Dame was playing in front of away crowds such as the following: Miami 68,077, Michigan State 80,011, USC 88,520, Illinois 71,227, Navy (at Philadelphia) 63,738, Army (in Yankee Stadium) 63,786, etc. Since State College wasn't, and still isn't a metropolis with a large Roman Catholic populace, Notre Dame's response to Penn State's proposal of a home and home series with games in South Bend and State College was a counter-offer of one game in South Bend, the other game in Cleveland, Baltimore or Philadelphia. When Penn State found this arrangement unsatisfactory, negotiations stalled until Penn State and Notre Dame met in the Gator Bowl at the end of the 1976 season. By this time Beaver Stadium's capacity had grown to 60,203, larger than Notre Dame Stadium's 59,075 capacity, and the Lions had ended up in the AP Poll Top Ten, five of the first seven years in the 1970s. Surprisingly, in the same seven years Notre Dame finished in the Top Ten only three times. However the Irish won a National Championship in 1973, a feat Penn State wouldn't accomplish for another nine years. None-the-less a home and home series with the Penn State home game being held in State College now was doable and a twelve game series was initiated in 1981. The six games at Beaver Stadium drew an average of 86,793 spectators with the largest crowd, 96,672, occurring on November 16, 1991. Meanwhile every game at South Bend was a capacity crowd of 59,075. All twelve games were on TV, seven of the last nine games were telecast nationally. So a series which was several decades in the offing finally came to pass and it was a hit in every way.

The Penn State-Notre Dame series currently stands at eight wins for each team with one tie. In the recent twelve game series, PSU won eight and Notre Dame won four. In earlier games Notre Dame won the games played in 1913, '26, '28 and 1975. The 1925 game ended in a tie.

Finances are an important part of any arrangement between two major collegiate football powers. Since football stadiums can hold crowds of 50,000 to more than 100,000 and since, at most, Top Twenty teams have six or seven home games in an eleven game season it's important for the business managers at all of these schools to maximize their income from these few games. In general, only football and men's basketball make money and all the other women's and men's sports operate in the red. At Penn State there are more than twenty such sports that cost more to operate than they generate in revenue.

Until Penn State began playing football in the Big Ten, the Lions and the Irish were two of the biggest independent names in collegiate football. Independent teams like State have contractual agreements with all the teams they will play, on a home and home basis, as well as those other teams that will come to Penn State for a game or more and not require that State reciprocate and play at their field.

Small schools, or at least schools with small stadiums, aren't able to play Notre Dame or Penn State on a home and home basis since they can't come up with the needed guarantee. In contrast some lesser schools are thrilled to play at Penn State or Notre Dame for a guarantee of $100,000 or more, since that amount plus any TV split, less travel expenses might equal their net income for the balance of their season. A net take of $80,000 to $125,000 for a small program can mean the difference between finishing in the black or ending up in the red. A negative balance sheet may result in a school dropping a pair of sports, one women's, one men's, such as softball and wrestling.

Home and home arrangements may involve modest guarantees where a Temple or a Rutgers is involved while a major football power like Nebraska or Notre Dame might command a guarantee of $400,000 plus. In reality the amount of the guarantee in a home and home arrangement between major football powers is immaterial. In a Penn State – Notre Dame arrangement for example, if State guarantees Notre Dame $400,000 and Notre Dame guarantees State $400,000 all that has been done in effect is to shuffle the same $400,000 back and forth. Were it not for the budgetary problems that would arise every other year when one team would have travel expenses and no offsetting income, each team could keep all of the gross income from their home game, no money would need to change hands and both schools would be equally well off.

The mere mention of Notre Dame brings to mind many football games and football stories, however two names and one story will always be linked to Notre Dame and Notre Dame football only. The setting for the story is a hospital room were a dying George Gipp makes a death bed request of his coach Knute Rockne. This dramatic tale bears retelling, for the moving story it is and to set the record straight.

In the movie film *Knute Rockne – All American*, which had its world premiere in South Bend on October 4, 1940, we have the moving story of two Notre Dame football legends who died at the height of their careers. Notre Dame coach Knute Rockne and Notre Dame football player George Gipp, were portrayed in the movie by Pat O'Brien, and Ronald Reagan respectively. George Gipp who never played high school football, his first love was baseball, died at the age of twenty-five, two weeks after being selected to Walter Camp's 1920 Football All-American team. On his deathbed Gipp made a last request of his coach Knute Rockne saying, "I've got to go 'Rock' and it's O.K., I'm not afraid. But some time when the team is up against it, when things are wrong and the breaks are beating the boys – tell them to go in there with all they've got and win just one for "the Gipper." I don't know where I'll be then 'Rock,' but I'll know about it and I'll be happy."

Rockne waited eight years before mentioning the "Gipper's" request. According to Frances Wallace of the *New York News*, after losing two of its first six games, an injury- riddled Notre Dame team traveled to Yankee Stadium on October 10, 1928 to face unbeaten Army. In his pre-game speech Rockne said this to his underdog team, "The day before he died, George Gipp asked me to wait until the situation seemed hopeless – then ask a Notre Dame team to go out and beat Army for him. *This* is the *day* AND *you* are the team." Notre Dame won the game 12-6 on a pair of second half touchdowns. Jack Chevigny scored the first TD and after reaching the end zone he touched the ball down and said, "That's one for the Gipper."

Contrary to Hollywood and the words Pat O'Brien spoke in his splendid portrayal of Coach Rockne, Knute didn't tell a Notre Dame football team, to go out there and "Win one for the 'Gipper.'"

Notre Dame's All-American halfback George Gipp.

Author's autographed picture of legendary Notre Dame Head Coach Frank Leahy, 1942.

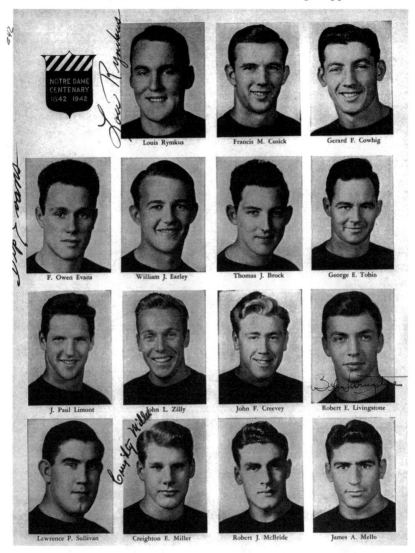

Louis Rymkus Francis M. Cusick Gerard F. Cowhig

F. Owen Evans William J. Earley Thomas J. Brock George E. Tobin

J. Paul Limont John L. Zilly John F. Creevey Robert E. Livingstone

Lawrence P. Sullivan Creighton E. Miller Robert J. McBride James A. Mello

Autographed program October 31, 1942 Navy-Notre Dame game.

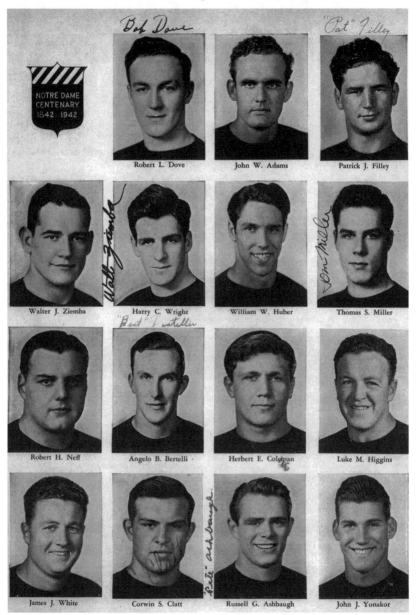

Autographed program October 31, 1942 Navy-Notre Dame game.

CHAPTER 50

Paterno Breaks the Wishbone and Gets His Wish

Most readers of this book and all good Penn State fans who became Nittany Lion fans in the 1960s or earlier are well aware of the composition of the 1967-1969 squads – familiar names like Ebersole, Reid, Smear, Onkotz, Kates, the Smith and Johnson boys, Jackson, Kwalick, Sherman, Burkhart, Campbell etc. By 1970 the Penn State depth chart showed some new names (Franco Harris, Lydell Mitchell, Gary Gray, Dave Joyner, etc.) and just a few carry-over familiar names like George Landis, Charlie Zapiec (Zay-peck) and Jack Ham.

A year later in 1971 the pre-season outlook showed the following lettermen and non-lettermen who would make names for themselves in future years (one, at another school).

1971 Team

	Veterans	Newcomers
Offense		
Wide-outs	Scotty Skarzynski*	Chuck Herd Jimmy Scott
Tackles	Dave Joyner*	Charlie Getty
Guards	Carl Schaukowitch*	Mark Markovich
		Phil LaPorta
Center	Mike Botts*	Rick Brown
Tight End	Bob Parsons**	
Quarterback	John Hufnagel*	Steve Joachim
Backs	Lydell Mitchell**	John Cappelletti
		Carl Cayette
	Franco Harris**	Tom Donchez
		Kenny Andrews
Defense		
Ends	Bruce Bannon	
Tackles	Frank Ahrenhold**	Randy Crowder
	Jim Heller*	
Linebackers	Charlie Zapiec**	Jim Laslavic
	Doug Allen*	
	Gary Gray**	John Skorupan*
D-Backs	Greg Ducatte*	Bob Nagle Ed O'Neil

* Number of letters earned through 1970 season.

With John Hufnagel back for his final season as quarterback, (John because of his lack of size 6'1" and 187 lbs. didn't make it in the NFL but played for many years in the Canadian Football League), State drubbed Navy, Army, Iowa, TCU, Maryland, N.C. State, Syracuse and Pitt. The margins of victory in those games ranged from a low of 30 points in the Iowa game to 53 points in the season opening Navy game.

With a close 16-14 win over Air Force, Penn State pulled off a trifecta; beating all three service academies in one season. The Air Force win was the second of a three game sweep against the Falcons. The victory over Army was the seventh win in nineteen games against the Black Knights of the Hudson, who would not beat Penn State again in the Twentieth Century, and it was the sixteenth win verses sixteen losses and two ties against Navy. State would win two of the last three games played with the Naval Academy in the century, to move ahead of the Midshipmen with eighteen wins and two ties in thirty-seven games. Recalling the above three teams will give the reader three-fifths of the answer to a trivia question. What five Division I football teams *do not* have the word University in their name? Answer at the end of the Chapter.

Mitchell and Harris who last year rushed for 751 yards and 6 TDs and 675 yards and 8 TDs respectively, burst right out of the starting gate in 1971 with Mitchell scoring four TDs against Navy, while Harris returned the favor with four TDs against Iowa in the next game. The tailback/fullback tandem rushed for 211 yards and 145 yards respectively in the Iowa game. Through the 1998 season on 30 occasions two Penn State backs have rushed for 100 or more yards in the same game. (Actually two of those thirty games saw *three* backs rush for 100 yards each; in 1965 Bill Rettig (109), Dave McNaughton (105) and Mike Irwin (100) against Maryland and in 1969 Harris (136), Mitchell (120) and Charlie Pittman (106) against Boston College.) Mitchell and/or Harris were involved in four more two-back 100-yard games. On five occasions Steve Guise was a part of two 100-yard performances in a game, teaming up with Mike Guman twice, Bob Torrey twice and Matt Suhey once.

As the season progressed Tom Donchez saw more and more playing time and he finally started some games when Franco Harris was banged-up. (Meanwhile John Cappelletti and Ed O'Neil were playing defensive halfback.) Donchez also started the Cotton Bowl game in place of Harris, in Harris' last game in a PSU uniform. Reports came out of Dallas that Harris had been late for a meeting or practice and Paterno said in front of the team words to the effect, "you do that again and you won't start in the Bowl Game." Whether he felt compelled to exhibit his manhood or whether it just happened Harris *was* late again and this left Paterno with no choice but to not start Harris. Otherwise he would send a message to the squad that rules don't apply to starters/ stars, etc. Under the heading of *he must be doing something right* Paterno not only didn't alienate Harris with his action, in fact Franco has been one of Paterno and Penn State's most hard-working and giving supporters.

A win over N.C. State, now being coached by Al Michaels, the ex-Penn State assistant coach, just one year before he was replaced by Lou Holtz, and a 55-18 spanking of Pitt, where the Lions rolled up 538 yards of total offense, second only to the 632 yards tallied against TCU, brought Penn State to the last game of the regular season in hostile Knoxville, Tennessee. Here, the Lions undefeated season came crashing down basically because of turnovers and a special-team breakdown. The Volunteers scored on a 76-yard fumble return, a 44-yard punt return and a 43-yard pass interception. State had 23 first downs to Tennessee's 14, and 117 yards more total offense but Penn State threw four passes that were intercepted and lost two fumbles. The longest Tennessee touchdown drive was 15 yards but Tennessee prevailed 31-11. Lydell Mitchell set three NCAA season records in 1971 – most touchdowns (29), most touchdowns rushing (26) and most points scored (174).

Despite beating Iowa, Air Force, TCU and N.C. State the Tennessee loss gave the nay-sayers another opportunity to proclaim that Penn State couldn't beat any good intersectional opponent. With the losses to #18 Colorado 41-13, unranked Wisconsin and Syracuse in 1970 and the 31-11 loss to #11 Tennessee in 1971 Penn State hadn't beaten a Top twenty team since January 1970. Thus the Cotton Bowl game against #12 Texas and its state-of-the-art wishbone attack, was much like the pivotal game against N.C. State game in 1967. Paterno verbalized what every Penn State rooter felt when he said, "I don't think we've ever had a game that we had to win more than this one."

The first half of play did little to make Paterno and Penn State fans feel comfortable as the teams went to their locker rooms with Texas holding a two field goals to one, 6-3 lead. Texas began the game by moving the ball easily with its vaunted Wishbone attack. But State's defense seemed to stiffen as the second quarter wore on. As the teams left the field Paterno was deep in thought wondering what he might say to his "troops" at half time. Just then Co-captains Charlie Zapiec and Dave Joyner jogged up along side him and simply said as they continued on by, "Don't worry, we've got them, you can feel it, they're beginning to crack." Paterno's half-time speech was just three short phrases he said very matter of factly, "We're got them, they're beginning to crack, let's go finish the job." The Lions started the second half with a Zapiec fumble recovery, a Hufnagel to Parsons pass and two Mitchell runs for twenty yards and a touchdown. On their next possession Hufnagel hit Scotty Skarzynski for a 65-yard touchdown. A Hufnagel run and two more Alberto Vitiello field goals made the final score 30-6 as the Lions held Texas without a touchdown for the first time in their last eighty games.

In a bit of sweet revenge State ended up the year #5 in the AP Poll ahead of #9 Tennessee.

Answer to Trivia question — The Naval Academy, Air Force Academy, United States Military Academy, Boston College and Georgia Institute of Technology (Georgia Tech).

Coach Joe Paterno and co-captains Charlie Zapiec and Dave Joyner look ahead to the up-coming season.

CHAPTER 51

There Goes Your No-Hitter

While attending a baseball game, sandlot to major leagues, in the 1930s and '40s it was the cool thing to do, when the first batter in the top or bottom of the first inning got a hit, to yell in the pitcher's direction "There goes your no-hitter."

Penn State lost for the first time in 1971 in its eleventh game of the season. But here in 1972 Penn State lost its "no-hitter" when Tennessee spoiled State's undefeated season in the very first game. It was a tough opening-game for the Lions, playing on the road in front of 71,647 mostly hostile fans in Knoxville, Tennessee. Especially when the Vols, coming into the game, had a 28-3 victory under their belt by virtue of moving their Georgia Tech game scheduled for October to September 9. As Joe has consistently said, since he first became a head coach, "A team should improve more between their first and second games of the season than between any other two games." Predictably Penn State played a jittery first half and they went to the locker room at the end of the second quarter trailing 21-0.

After half-time State scored twice to narrow the margin to 21-14. Tennessee tacked on seven points in the fourth quarter, to go ahead 28-14 but Penn State responded in kind, to make the score 28-21 and now Tennessee wasn't looking so confident. In the waning minutes Penn State began a sustained drive which ended with the Lions completing a pass from John Hufnagel to Jimmy Scott for a first down on the Tennessee 16-yard line; but before the chains could be moved and State could get off a play the gun sounded. Again, Penn State had the better of the statistics, 17 first downs to 15 and 367 yards total offense to 225 for Tennessee. But the only numbers that really count showed Tennessee with the larger number, 28, to Penn State's 21.

The Penn State depth chart for 1972 showed the following lettered veteran returnees, some back-ups who had already won a letter and others who had great futures ahead of them.

1972 Team

Offense

Veterans		Newcomers
Wideouts	Scott Skarzynski**	Gary Hayman Joe Jackson
	Chuck Herd*	Jim Eaise
	Jimmy Scott*	
Tackles	Charlie Getty*	Jeff Bleamer
	Mark Markovich*	
Guards	Carl Schaukowitch**	
	Phil Laporta*	
	Bob Rickenbach**	
Center	Rick Brown*	Jack Baiorunos
Tight Ends	Gary Debes*	Dan Natale John Reihner
Quarterbacks	John Hufnagel**	Tom Shuman
Backs	John Cappelletti*	
	Kenny Andrews*	Walt Addie Carl Cayette
	Tom Donchez *	Bob Nagle

Defense

Ends	Bruce Bannon**	Dave Graf Greg Murphy
	Gary Hager*	
Tackles	Jim Heller**	Mike Hartenstine
	Randy Crowder*	John Nessel
Linebackers	John Skorupan**	Jim Rosecrans Tom Hull*
	Jim Laslavic**	
	Ed O'Neil*	Larry Ludwig*
	Doug Allen*	Buddy Tesner
		Chris Devlin
D-Backs	Buddy Ellis*	Jim Bradley
	Mike Orsini*	
	Greg Ducatte**	Steve Stilley*

The Lions' quarterback was senior John Hufnagel but behind him, the veterans Lydell Mitchell and Franco Harris were missing and Mitchell's tailback replacement, John Cappelletti had no varsity experience on offense as he was a defensive halfback last year. Initially, many on the coaching staff saw him more as a linebacker than a ball carrier. A sprained ankle near the end of spring practice meant some missed practice time which left his roster position a bit in limbo. Paterno was also indicating his concern about the health status of Tom Donchez when he said, "Tom is an excellent blocker and a hard runner but his status is questionable because of his injuries." The only other backfield letter winner was Kenny Andrews. Andrews a six-foot 215 lb. speedster possessed an uncommon mixture of weight and speed. In the early '70s State's real speed merchants were players like Jimmy Scott who weighed 160 lbs. But somehow Paterno and Andrews never seemed to be on the same page. In his first two years he had a total of twenty-two rushes and one catch and in his senior year he rushed the ball twenty-three times for ninety yards, averaging four yards per carry. He helped State come from behind and beat West Virginia at Morgantown when he took a screen pass 67 yards for a TD. However when John Cappelletti went down with the flu and was bed-ridden the night of the Sugar Bowl meeting between #5 Penn State and #2 Oklahoma, Paterno used Walt Addie, who hadn't practiced all week because of a badly bruised foot, and it showed with a botched hand-off or two, and Gary Hayman, a wide receiver who got four carries which went for eleven yards. Andrews carried the ball only once even though his one carry gained nine yards. Andrews also had two receptions for twenty-five yards which was third highest behind Scott (3 for 64 yards) and Dave Bland (3 for 39 yards) and more yards than Addie, Chuck Herd and Hayman totaled on their combined four catches. In a bit of irony, Carl Cayette who quit the squad during the season because of a "lack of playing time," would have had the tailback spotlight all to himself with Cappy and Addie sidelined. The Lions who had ridden on Cappelletti's shoulders all season long could manage just 40 yards on seven Walt Addie and ten Bob Nagle attempts and State couldn't dent the Sooner goal line, losing 14-0. Oklahoma had to forfeit several Big Eight games that year for using ineligible players but when they offered to forfeit the Sugar Bowl game to Penn State, Paterno declined saying, "We all know who won that game." How much did John Cappelletti mean to the Lion's running game and point production? Try 233 carries, 1117 net yards gained and 13 touchdowns in eleven games. Cappelletti scored in every game except the Tennessee, West Virginia and Pitt contests (where Penn State was ahead 42-0 in the third quarter and Paterno played all his reserves) while racking up five 100-yard games. He averaged 21 carries per game and set a record with 34 rushes against West Virginia.

Penn State ended up 10th in the AP Poll when the sportswriters voted Nebraska 4th and Tennessee 8th, however State finished 8th in the UPI, where the coaches had Nebraska 9th and Tennessee not in the Top Ten.

As we will see in the next chapter, while Penn State lost their Sugar

Bowl game on December 31, 1972, they recorded, less than a week later, a victory which would affect many seasons to come not just the past one.

Postscript — A Reading, Pennsylvania minister, obviously a Penn State fan, did an encore prior to the 1972 Sugar Bowl on his church's outdoor bulletin board when he posted the following message: "Now Is the Time for All Good Christians to Root for the Lions – Go Penn State." His message the previous year was, "God is Impartial but Some Ministers Are Not, Go Penn State."

John Cappelletti, All-American halfback and 1973 Heisman Trophy winner. (Photo courtesy of the author.)

CHAPTER 52

Sleeping with a Millionaire

Into the wee hours of the morning, two men in their forties and their wives sat around a kitchen table in a modest State College home, discussing a deal which would make one couple instant millionaires. The other couple might accompany their closest friends in their new venture or they might stay at Penn State and always wonder whether they made the right choice. For both couples it was the old game show, door one or door two?

The two couples had talked for hours about the pros and cons, the opportunities, the calculated risks, life in Pennsylvania, and State College, in particular; and life in Massachusetts, specifically Foxboro and suburban Boston, the public and private school systems, college for their children, family life, where they might reside, the daily commute and now it was time to call for the question.

Would Joseph Vincent Paterno accept the offer of Billy Sullivan, owner of the New England Patriots NFL football team to become their new head coach and part owner? Paterno had been invited by Weeb Ewbank, a number of years ago, to become an assistant coach with the Baltimore Colts, at the time Ewbank was the head coach, but Paterno gave this offer short shrift. (Ewbank had ties to Rip Engle going back to Brown University.) Paterno was later courted by Art Rooney to become head coach of the Pittsburgh Steelers but Paterno, despite being fond of Rooney, backed away from the deal when he wasn't certain he would have the final say regarding trades, certain draft picks and the power to keep or "cut" any player. (Also, Paterno felt that his wife, Sue, was not ready to leave State College for Pittsburgh.) The Patriots' offer went *much* farther. Paterno could bring Jim Tarman along and there would also be a coaching position for Joe's brother, George. Also in Boston, he would be a part owner, General Manager and head coach and Sullivan assured him he would have the final say on personnel and related issues, and now Sue was more amenable to a move.

Finally Joe broke the silence of the moment saying he would take the job if Sue agreed, and when she did the die was cast. Jim and Louise Tarman offered their congratulations and they drank a toast (maybe coffee, maybe wine). The discussion at the Paterno residence ended after 1 a.m., and it was now time for Jim and Louise to go home and decide what they were going to do.

For Joe and Sue their life would fast forward through a short night's sleep (which Joe later reminded Sue was the first time she slept with a millionaire) and to-morrow, first thing he would have to break the news to his assistant coaches, the team, President Oswald and Athletic Director Ed Czekaj. He wanted all of them to hear the news from him, not second hand or through the rumor mill.

A last minute confirmation of Joe's acceptance would have Billy Sullivan's personal jet winging to State College, Pennsylvania to bring Joe and Sue to the Plaza Hotel in New York City where the Patriots retained a suite. There, Sullivan would announce at an afternoon press conference that Joe Paterno would be the new General Manager in-charge-of-Player Relations, a part owner and the head coach of the New England Patriots. Upon signing the agreed upon contract Brooklyn-born Joe Paterno would be an instant millionaire and part owner of an NFL team.

CHAPTER 53

How Can You Sleep?

Had Joe and Sue decided to remain at Penn State, Jim and Louise could have gone home, gone to bed and when the alarm went off in the morning Jim would arise, head off to the office and another day on the job. But Joe and Sue's decision changed all that.

Now Jim and Louise held their own meeting at *their* kitchen table. There seemed to be only two choices. Two widely divergent choices. One was to hitch their star to Joe Paterno's blossoming career and leave Penn State for New England; the other was to stay at Penn State where Tarman was Associate Director of Athletics and Assistant to Robert Scannell the Dean of The College of Health, Physical Education and Recreation. Staying would mean a parting of the ways with Joe (and Sue).

Jim and Louise re-hashed many of the subjects, that had been discussed and mulled over with Sue and Joe, but this time they had to discuss what was best for them and their family. At 2:00 a.m. Jim and Louise had made their decision. They would leave Penn State and seek their future with Joe and the New England Patriots.

****

At daybreak Louise rushed upstairs and roused Jim, "It's Joe, he wants to speak with you before you speak with anyone else, he said it's important!"

Still groggy Jim put the telephone to his ear and questioning the caller uttered, "Joe what's up?"

Joe retorted, "What are you doing sleeping when I can't sleep?"

Jim's considered reply was, "What's the problem , have you been up all night working on the player draft?" (In those years the NFL draft was held much earlier in the calendar year.)

Joe answered, "No, I'm *not* going." He continued, "We can talk about this in more detail in the future but just *forget everything* we discussed and said last night, it never happened. I'm going to call Billy Sullivan and tell him to cancel the jet and the press conference, I've decided to stay here at Penn State. I hope you and Louise didn't lose too much sleep deciding what you were going to do. I tossed and turned all night. I got up and made a list of the reasons I should take the job and other than the challenge to prove I could win at that level, and I'm sure I could, all the other reasons were tied to money. So I told Sue as soon as she was awake of my change of heart and she didn't seem at all disappointed."

Jim gave a chuckle and responded, "Well it looks like today will be just another day on the job. I'm glad I don't have to tell "Billy" how close he came" (to getting the head coach he had his heart set on).

CHAPTER 54

A Good Place to Live
Too Good a Place to Leave

With Penn State President John Oswald at his side on January 6, 1973, Joe Paterno addressed a news conference and made a statement which included the following: "…I talked to Mr. Sullivan and told him I decided to stay at Penn State. I've been in Pennsylvania now 23 years and the Pennsylvania people have been great.….As you know I've said many times I've had a dream that Penn State could be the greatest in everything. The challenge of that is what kept me. I suppose if I summed it up, I just feel Penn State's too good a place to leave."

For their June 16, 1973 commencement, the student committee asked Joe Paterno to be their guest speaker.

The following are excerpts from his Commencement Day text "I was thrilled (to be asked). However I wasn't sure I should do it…could I contribute something which would make this commencement a more meaningful experience to you? …There has been generous praise…for my decision to remain at Penn State (which) made me wonder (about) our commitment to materialism and made me think that perhaps I could say something to you which would put things in perspective. However, I assure you that in stepping outside of my role as a football coach I do it with great trepidation and humility.

"One of the tragedies of Watergate is bright young men…prostituted their honor and decency…to get ahead. I warn you, don't underestimate the world, it can corrupt quickly and completely. …Realize…that money alone will not make you happy, success without honor is an unseasoned dish, it will satisfy your hunger but it won't taste good…You will become victims of this system if you fail to execute your responsibilities to yourself and to your fellow human beings." Paterno then quoted W. H. Auden when he said, "Everyday there die among us those who were doing us some good and knew it was never enough, but hoped to improve a little by living."

Returning to football he spoke, "I cannot describe to you the love that permeates a good football team – a love of one another. Perhaps as one of my players said, 'we grow together in love – hating the coach.'"

"I enjoy coaching at Penn State...we set high goals for our people. Then interjecting one of his favorite quotes Paterno continued, "my squad even has to listen to me quote Browning who said, 'A man's reach should exceed his grasp or what's a heaven for?' We strive to be No. 1. We work hard to achieve our goals and when Saturday comes...we tighten up our belts, we say, come on let's play. Let's see how good you are. We aren't afraid to lose. If we win, great, wonderful, and the alumni are happy for another week. But win or lose it is the competition which gives us pleasure.

"To be in a locker-room before a big game, grown men...reaching out to be a part of...something bigger than they are – this is what living is all about."

While he made a strong statement about his commitment to Penn State on January 6, did the rumors of Paterno's departure at the end of 1972 have an adverse effect on Penn State's recruiting that year which even Joe's protestation couldn't negate? There is no way to prove the point one way or the other however, the 1973 incoming freshman would be the seniors of the 1976 team which had the worst record of any Joe Paterno team from 1967 (Joe second year) through the 1983 season.

But Joe was at Penn State to stay.

CHAPTER 55

Four Year Cycles

As the 1973 season approached, observers got their first glimpse of a recurring pattern. Paterno's last outstanding season was 1969. Here four years later Penn State was "loaded for bear." A look at the following depth chart shows many returning players who, going into their senior years, had already earned the maximum number of letters possible. Freshmen were not eligible to play varsity football in the 1950s, '60s and early '70s.

1973
Offense

	Veteran	Newcomers
Wideouts	Gary Hayman*	Jim Eaise
	Jimmy Scott**	
	Chuck Herd**	
	Dave Bland**	
Tackles	Charlie Getty**	Tom Rafferty Jeff Bleamer
	Phil LaPorta**	
Guards	Mark Markovich**	John Nessel
	Paul Gabel**	
Center	Jack Baiorunos*	
Tight End	Dan Natale*	John Reihner* Gary Debes*
Quarterback	Tom Shuman	Dick Barvinchak
Backs	John Cappelletti**	Woody Petchel
	Walt Addie*	
	Bob Nagle*	Tom Donchez*

	Defense	
Ends	Gary Hager**	Greg Murphy
	Dave Graf*	Buddy Tesner*
Tackles	Randy Crowder**	John Quinn
	Mike Hartenstine*	
Linebackers	Ed O'Neil**	Jim Rosecrans Greg Buttle
	Doug Allen**	Tom Hull**
D-Backs	Buddy Ellis**	Jim Bradley Tom Odell
	Jack Koniszewski*	Jeff Hite

The depth chart on offense showed experience at every position except quarterback and the defense seemed strong except for the secondary which was short on experienced players. There were four co-captains John Cappelletti (TB), Randy Crowder (DT), Mark Markovich (OL) and Ed O'Neil (LB) among a total of thirteen players who had already earned two letters. And Tom Donchez who missed the 1972 season was back. Donchez and fellow fullback Bob Nagle would contribute 640 yards to go along with tailbacks Walt Addie and Woody Petchel's 450 yards, which combined, equaled roughly two-thirds of John Cappelletti's Heisman Trophy-winning 1722 yards gained on 286 carries.

The schedule had the Nittany Lions opening on the West Coast against Stanford. This would be the seventh PAC-8 opponent to meet Penn State on the gridiron. State would later play Arizona State in 1977 and the University of Arizona in 1999 both of whom joined the PAC-8 in 1978 to make it the PAC-10. Thus the only PAC-10 team Penn State has never played, through the 2000 football season, is Oregon State.

Cappelletti began the year with 26 carries for 86 yards and one touchdown in a 20-6 win over the Stanford Cardinal. A national TV audience saw the Penn State defense hold Stanford scoreless into the fourth quarter and to minus eight yards rushing and only eight first downs. (Stanford, in 1972 had changed its nickname from the Indians back to the Cardinal. The latter being their official school color since 1891 and their school nickname from 1891-1930.)

Game two found Joe Paterno going head-to-head against one of his former assistants, George Welsh, who was in his first year as head coach at his alma mater. "Cappy", playing just half of the game, gained 104 yards as State led 37-0 at the end of three periods. Navy registered only five first downs and 78 yards rushing in a 39-0 loss.

Next, Iowa's Hawkeyes came to State College, as the Lion's Homecoming opponent, and they found nothing in Beaver Stadium to brighten a sunless, rainy day. Down 21-0 at the end of the first quarter, the Iowans finished the game with 4 yards rushing in a 27-8 loss. Cappelletti carried 22 times for 92 yards, giving him 71 carries, 282 yards and 3 touchdowns in three games.

At Air Force, Cappelletti scored two touchdowns on 34 carries for 188 yards, in a 19-9 Lion victory. Ben Martin, U. S. Naval Academy football player now Air Force's head coach said, "Cappelletti didn't look tired at all. He could have played for another hour and a half." Air Force gained just 71 yards rushing against the Lion defense of Crowder, Hartenstine, Hager, Graf, O'Neil, Hull, Rosecrans, Buttle, Bradley, etc.

Four and zero Penn State, hosted Army the next week and my, how the times had changed. The Lions, winners in just four of their first sixteen meetings with the Cadets had now won four in a row and the margin of victory increased each year. Here in 1973, Army gained just 53 yards rushing and had only 10 first downs. Cappelletti rushed for 151 yards on 17 carries prior to leaving the game in the third quarter with a shoulder injury. Army registered only a 46-yard field goal while giving up 607 yards total offense in a 54-3 loss.

The following Saturday was a cloudy, windy, chilly day in Syracuse, N.Y. and even those of us who flew up for the game and stayed at the hotel with the team were caught completely by surprise when Penn State on their first possession sent Cappelletti, the I-back in motion wide to the left and ran a play up the middle. Second down and third down were carbon copies of the first-down play and on fourth down State punted. Cappelletti never returned to the field and only then did people realize that his shoulder injury in the Army game was more than a "ding." A player who has one of the following; a sore ankle, a dislocated finger, a sore or bruised knee, shoulder, foot or hand is said to be "dinged-up." Football players must learn to play with a certain amount of pain or discomfort. No player who starts and plays most of each game goes through a season unscathed. Different players however have different thresholds of pain which perplexes head coaches no end. As team doctors put it, a player can play hurt, but he won't be allowed to play if he is injured. This can be a fine-line distinction occasionally, and no one can tell for sure just looking at a player, whether his "hurt" is moderately painful or more than even a stoic can tolerate. Mike Reid whose toughness was legendary, had a serious knee injury but he said the worst pain he ever played through in a game was a severe headache. Bob Campbell, in a game, came off the field, his head hurting so much he went behind the bench and threw-up. A few plays later he was right back in the game. Even without Cappelletti the Lions dumped the Orangemen 49-6 with Syracuse completing only 6 of 24 passes for 75 yards, to go along with 94 yards rushing.

On Saturday October 27, a sunny, picture-perfect day, Bobby Bowden, in his 4th year as head coach at West Virginia, brought his 3 and 3 Mountaineers into Beaver Stadium. All-American wide receiver Danny Buggs went 96 yards with a pass reception for a WVU touchdown and Artie Owens a Pennsylvania All-State running back ran a kickoff back 95 yards for another Mountaineer touchdown. Unfortunately for the "Eers" Cappelletti scored two touchdowns before Buggs' touchdown and one before and after Owens' run. Those four touchdowns along with a 76-yard Shuman to Herd pass, a Bob Nagle 53-yard run and touchdowns by "Rusty" Boyle, Mike Pirogowicz and Greg Buttle left Bowden's team on the losing end of a 62-14 score. West Virginia recorded just 7 first downs and zero yards rushing.

Saturday November 3, in College Park, Maryland, was another beautiful sunny day; perfect for fans in the stands but a bit warm for the players. In front of the third-largest Byrd Stadium crowd ever, the Lions jumped out to a two touchdown, twelve-point lead and the game had the appearance of another PSU runaway. But Maryland which last year had its first winning season since 1962 sandwiched two pass-reception touchdowns around a Steve Mike-Mayer (pronounced Mick-Meyer) field goal to take a 16-12 lead. A Shuman to Natale pass, a Bahr field goal and a 83 yard punt return by Bob Smith for Maryland made the score 22-22 at halftime and neither the Penn State fans nor the Penn State team looked comfortable or confident as the team left the field. Because of the heat the double-door to the Penn State locker room, next to Cole Field house, was propped wide open and the Lion players could be observed sitting on trunks and on the floor taking liquids and toweling off, they looked frazzled.

The second half however was like a "whole 'nother ball game." Although he didn't score a touchdown the whole game, Cappelletti carried the ball a school record 37 times for 202 yards and the defense blanked the Terrapins, while Shuman hit Jimmy Scott and Dan Natale for touchdowns and Bahr booted two field goals for a 42-22 win.

Quarterback Tom Shuman, fullback Tom Donchez and tailback Walt Addie, line up behind center Jack Baiorunos. (Photo courtesy of the author.)

CHAPTER 56

Iron Man Irony

The State College Quarterback Club luncheon prior to the N.C. State game was proceeding smoothly, Mickey Bergstein had interviewed Ed O'Neil and the other player guest, Paterno had spoken and he was now fielding some questions.

One of the attendees had asked Paterno a question about linebacker play and Joe had just concluded a good comparison between playing linebacker and driving a car. He explained that inexperienced drivers have to be careful to stay in their lane, they may have to feel around a little bit with their feet to be absolutely sure of the clutch, brake and accelerator positions, they must remember to look ahead for merging and cross-traffic, stop signs etc. Once you are an experienced driver it isn't necessary to make a conscious effort to stay in your lane, you know where all the pedals are without the need for repeated confirmation and additionally you're aware of traffic flow in front of you, to the side, approaching intersections etc. It's exactly like that playing inside linebacker, he had explained, in that an experienced linebacker has a feel and a sense for everything that is going on about him, without having to turn and look in each direction. Many of the best players say after you have enough experience it's almost as though what is happening around you, is going on in slow motion.

In keeping with the subject, linebacker play, another person in the crowd asked Paterno about the technique used by an offensive lineman attempting to block a linebacker and conversely how would a linebacker play off the blocker while staying "square to the line of scrimmage," a phrase Paterno had just used.

Moving away from the microphone, Paterno volunteered, "O'Neil, come over here, and we'll show you." Pulling the 6' 4" 235 lb. O'Neil by the sleeve of his blue blazer to an open area in the room, Paterno directed O'Neil, "You're the linebacker and I'm the big bad tight end coming at you." Like a director on a movie set, Joe said, "Ed show them how you would handle me," Having said that Paterno "broke down" into the stance and posture a blocker would assume when trying to block a linebacker and he expected O'Neil to go along with the demonstration by breaking down into his attacking or defending posture and pretending a big bad tight end *was* coming at him.

O'Neil stood there looking kind of sheepish, he glanced quickly at the other player as though he would be embarrassed to go along with this charade with a teammate watching. Then as quickly as the blink of an eye, O'Neil's facial and body language seemed to turn mischievous.

Paterno took a step toward O'Neil and said, "Show them how you'd handle me." Standing stiff and without the movement of any other of his major muscles, O'Neil slightly raised his left and right forearms waist high, palms down and then he flicked his fingers toward Paterno as though he were shooing a bug or a fly away from him. The demonstration never went any further, as an obviously embarrassed Joe Paterno, with a wry smile on his face, wordlessly returned to the microphone. And you wonder why some football players who are good young men have run-ins with coaches and other authority figures, and in some cases have been known to pelt Santa Claus with snowballs.

The author is reminded of a similar true incident when his brother, Carl, ambushed his fifth-grade geography teacher with this question, "Mrs. Sellers how do you pronounce the capital of Kentucky, Louie – ville or Louis – ville?"

Mrs. Sellers without a second's hesitation said, "Louie – ville".

Carl replied, "That's funny, I always thought it was Frankfort."

Ed O'Neil might have had a harder than normal practice that afternoon, or the rest of that week. Carl Werley, did not fare well in Mrs. Sellers' geography class for the remainder of fifth and sixth grades.

Lou Holtz brought a 6 and 2 Wolfpack team to State College, Pennsylvania on a cold, twenty-nine degree, blustery November Saturday. The 'Pack's only two losses had come at the hands of Vince Dooley's Peach Bowl-bound Georgia Bulldogs, 31-12 and the Nebraska Cornhuskers, in their first year under Tom Osborne, by the similar score of 31-14. (Bob Devaney had retired at Nebraska the previous year having won 101 games in just eleven seasons. Devaney said that all the time he was head coach, the alumni called him "sweet old Bob," as long as they were winning; but they just used the initials when the 'Huskers lost.)

A betting football fan, a smart one; had he had advance information that the PSU—NCSU game would be played on a windy, 29° day would have bet the farm that Penn State would cover a 13-point spread easily, with the boys from down South turning the ball over several times on fumbles due to cold, stiff, numb, fingers. What transpired was a game reminiscent of the 1967 nail-biter, as the Lions preserved their victory only when Cappelletti registered his third touchdown of the game and State's defense stopped the 'Pack on State's 40 yard line in the last minute of play. Again Cappelletti was the difference. In a "six-bagger game" he set a school record with 41 carries – good for 220 yards, fourth best all-time through 1973. N.C. State did not have a passing touchdown. Oh yes, the fumbles; Penn State had two, N.C. State had none. (A "six-bagger" game means that after the game "Cappy" had six bags of ice taped to various parts of his anatomy to minimize swelling from the "hits" he took in the game.)

The Lions' next opponent, on Band Day, was Ohio University. You knew it was Ohio University not Ohio State because there's no way there would have been almost 500 seats available for high school band musicians if the Buckeyes, not the Bobcats were the foe. Cappelletti again tap-danced a number of tunes on the prostrate bodies of the Ohio University Bobcat players, as he racked up Penn State's first four touchdowns of the day and gained 204 yards in a 49-10 stomping.

The last of three straight home games brought Johnny Majors and his initial Pittsburgh team to University Park. When he arrived at Pitt, Majors was greeted by 36 lettermen returnees, including 18 of 22 starters. (The author heard a story about a Sports Information Director who supposedly made this editorial comment in the school's football media guide "Last year's team lost every game - and the bad news is everybody's back.") Well, last year Pitt won 1 lost 10 and almost everybody would be back.

As the first meeting between Paterno and Majors unfolded, the first half proved most surprising. After a 40-yard Chris Bahr field goal got State on the board in the first quarter, it looked like there was "a new sheriff in town" as Pitt blanked State the rest of the first half, while the Panther offense tallied thirteen points to lead 13-3 at the intermission. However the second half was the "same old same old' as Pitt was held to minus fifteen yards *total* offense in the third quarter and State scored 32 unanswered points in the second half, for a 35-13 victory.

And now it was on to the Orange Bowl. The bowl game would be Penn State's third in six seasons, for another very-little-to-gain and a-lot-to-lose game against a strong LSU Tiger squad that was not a Top Five team that year. Number One Alabama would square off in the Sugar Bowl against #3 Notre Dame while Oklahoma was playing in the Cotton Bowl and 10-0-1 Ohio State would meet USC in the Rose Bowl. Eleven and zero Penn State would be odd-man-out, again, finishing fifth behind Notre Dame, Ohio State, Oklahoma and Sugar Bowl loser Alabama in the final 1973 AP Football Poll.

Joe Paterno has, in spoken word and deed, decried the used of the option offense saying that late in a crucial game or somewhere in the season, the quarterback you have built your whole offense around will take one hit too many and your offense will be in a rudderless boat. However when it came to Cappelletti, Paterno virtually put his whole offense on Cappy's shoulders for two full seasons. Two seasons, both of which came to the final game with Paterno's squad having a shot at a Top Two finish, and in both games "Cappy" was hor's de combat.

In the 1972 and '73 seasons "Cappy" set regular season records for most carries in a game (41) and in a season (286). The Penn State record for carries in a career is 649, held by Curt Warner 1979-82. This figures to an average of 162.25 carries per year. Cappelletti, as mentioned previously, played offense for *only two* seasons during which time he carried the ball 519 times, an average of 259.5 carries per year. At that rate, "Cappy" would have had 778 carries in just *three* years compared to Warner's 649 in *four* years. Additionally Cappelletti had three games in one season where he gained more than 200 yards. In fact the 200-yard games came in three consecutive games. (In Penn State history, through 1998, only four other backs have had *two* 200 yard games in their entire career, Ki-Jana Carter, Curtis Enis, Lydell Mitchell and Curt Warner. Of these four, only Carter, Mitchell and Warner had both of them in the same season.)

Now as the day of the game approached, actually a night game, Paterno was politicking hard for his team to be given equal consideration for #1, if they could beat Charlie McClendon's Louisiana State team. Normally an LSU head coach is not a very familiar figure in Pennsylvania but McClendon's face was familiar to a number of Pennsylvanians, in the 1970s. Recently, McClendon had seemingly become more attached to a relative of his in the Scranton/Wilkes-Barre area, than had been the case for many years, with Charlie flying up to Northeastern Pennsylvania frequently to see this "long lost kin." What occasioned this sudden renewed interest? One could only wonder if it just might be the fact that the hottest high school senior in the east was a Pittston, Pennsylvania scatback by the name of Jimmy Cefalo. Cefalo, was being courted by every big-time football program in the country but the two odds-on favorites, according to those who thought they knew, were Notre Dame and Penn State. However, would it be possible for a team from the Deep South to make the long distance effort and again turn the head of a Pittston, Pennsylvania tailback? Knowledgeable football fans agreed that Cefalo was the fastest, most elusive running back in the area since Charlie Trippi, who left Pittston in the early 1940s to play for the legendary Wally Butts at the University of Georgia. Trippi a three year letterman (1942, '45, '46) was the captain of the 11-0-0, 1946, SEC Championship team and is one of four University of Georgia players whose uniform number has been retired. Interestingly, another of the four was also a tailback who was born in Pennsylvania, Frank Sinkwich. Charlie Trippi, who later played professional football for the Chicago Cardinals of the NFL and professional baseball with the Atlanta Crackers is still widely regarded to have been the greatest all-around athlete to play for the Bulldogs. He was a unanimous All-American in football in 1946, he won the Maxwell Award and was runner-up to Army's Glenn Davis for the Heisman Trophy and was an All-American in baseball. He set single game SEC records for most yards *passing* (323) and total offense (384) in one game, against Georgia Tech, and in the same season, against Florida, he set the SEC record for most yards *rushing* in one game (239). Trippi's uniform number at Georgia was a very unlikely one for a scatback and a passer, #62.

But here in Florida less than 48 hours before the LSU—PSU showdown, the author was talking with linebacker coach Jerry Sandusky at the hotel where the team was staying. Nearby, John Cappelletti was talking in his distinctive manner to Frank Patrick and Bob Phillips. Despite my interest in my conversation with Jerry, I heard Cappy say, "Well I can stand on it, but I can't change direction very well." With that, Jerry moved to include us in the conversation and it was quickly clear to me that the workhorse on whose shoulders the upcoming game would ride, was far from 100%. Despite his ankle being tightly taped, Cappelletti was still reticent to put his full weight on that leg. When the discussion ended I felt rather special that the whole conversation went on to completion with me there, and when Jerry and I walked away nobody felt it necessary to ask me to keep what I had heard to myself. I now held some information that any gambler would pay dearly for or that I could have used to lay money on LSU to beat the point spread, but I never considered doing either as I felt that saying anything would be betraying the confidence the coaches obviously had in me. I recall that on the bus ride to the Orange Bowl I sat next to or directly behind Gordon White who covered Penn State football for the *New York Times*. Gordon turned to me and mentioned something about Cappelletti but I wasn't sure whether he knew of "Cappy's" injury and was trying to tip me off or whether he had heard rumors and was trying to get confirmation from me, but I didn't volunteer anything. Later Marie asked me what Gordon was talking about. When we were in our seats I told her what I had heard and seen.

In a scenario similar to the one in the Sugar Bowl the year before, Penn State was like a prize fighter with one useless arm. Cappelletti carried the ball 26 times for just 50 yards. Bob Nagle had seven rushes for 29 yards, while Donchez had four carries for seven yards. With yards lost on sacks etc., State had 43 rushing plays for 28 yards. *But*, Paterno did what he does so masterfully – he seldom loses a game he shouldn't lose. Some coaches spring great upsets, but they turn around and lose to a team that has no business beating them. From 1966 to the end of 1975,

Joe lost to Navy twice when he should not have. The 1967 defeat can be rationalized because the injury to Mike Reid was a catastrophic loss for a head coach in just the first game of his second season. The 1974 Navy loss should not have happened but a driving rain storm was a huge factor. Also few people probably remember that Paterno had a reliable PAT kicker in Chris Bahr but he eschewed the almost certain 7-7 tie for a long shot 2 point play for a win, which failed as did almost everything in the sloppy weather that day and State lost 7-6.

The 1970 loss to Syracuse could *possibly* have been headed-off but Paterno was facing a problem he never confronted before. He had his first black quarterback and Mike Cooper just wasn't cutting the mustard. But fate wasn't very kind to Paterno in his predicament. When Cooper threw an interception or two, he'd pull Cooper out and put Bob Parsons who was white in, but Parsons was not the answer either, so Paterno reverted back to Cooper as his quarterback. Like Paterno supposedly said to a coach regarding his dilemma "It doesn't matter what I do – if I continue to play him (Cooper) it's because he's black, if I bench him it's because he's black."

In the pivotal fifth-game of the season Homecoming loss to Syracuse, Penn State threw five interceptions and scored only 7 points on a Syracuse defense that had given up 100 points in three previous defeats. The eleven interceptions and the mid-season record of two wins and three losses finally enabled Paterno to "bench" Cooper *and* Parsons and go with sophomore John Hufnagle since the move not only "was fair," but by now "it appeared to be fair" to all concerned.

Following the 1970 Syracuse loss, through the end of the 1975 season, Penn State lost only seven more games. The two Tennessee games, the Oklahoma and Alabama bowl games and the 1974 N.C. State game could *not* be classified as games Paterno lost that he should have won. Loss #6 a 17-9 Ohio State victory was a case of a confident Ohio State team with a two-time Heisman Trophy-winning tailback in Archie Griffin and an unstoppable 270 lb. fullback, Pete Johnson. The Buckeye converted six consecutive third-down plays in a time-consuming fourth quarter drive that pounded the Lions into submission. Griffin, 128 yards on 24 carries, and Johnson, 112 yards on 23 carries, combined for 240 yards.

The remaining game was the 1975 N.C. State game. Coaches like to say that in almost every game there are three to six plays which will decide the outcome of the game; you lose, if you don't make them or if the other team does. Having been at the game in question I can say that one play in the fourth quarter won the game for Lou Holtz and the Wolfpack. The N.C. State game was a back and forth contest even though

Penn State got the first two scores; one in the first period and one in the second to lead 14-0. But Ted Brown, who would rack up 148 yards on 31 ball-controlling carries, scored for N.C. State just before half time. The 'Pack however missed the "point after," for a 14-6 Penn State lead at halftime. Brown scored again in the 3rd quarter, while N.C. State had the wind, a gusty one, at their back. On the third play of the fourth quarter place-kicker Jay Sherill who had missed the point-after-touchdown kick after N.C. State's first touchdown (they tried a two-point conversion after the second touchdown, it too failed) now made a slightly longer 24 yard field goal *into* the wind, to give the Wolfpack their first lead 15-14.

The contest now became a game of field position and with the wind at its back, Penn State, continued to push N.C. State back ever closer to their own goal line at the north end of the stadium. Anyone with any feel for the game of football could sense Penn State was grabbing the momentum and it seemed to be only a matter of time until they scored and recaptured the lead. Following another change of possession the 'Pack was deep inside their own 15 yard line. After two plays they were faced with 3rd down and more than 15 yards for a first down. I "knew", as did the Penn State coaching staff and the Penn State players on the sidelines, that if our defense could just keep them from getting a first down we were going to win the game. Failing to make a first down almost certainly meant we would get possession inside N.C. State's 40 yard line, following the Wolfpack's fourth down punt. It only made sense. Into the wind, with maximum punt protection by the kicking team, to prevent a blocked punt, meant a decent return; even a great return, if the punter kicked the ball low and out-kicked his coverage. Or if he got the ball too high into the wind the punt wouldn't travel as far as mid-field. Penn State would then be in business, well into Wolfpack territory. All we had to do was keep N.C. State from converting this third down play and we'd have the lead back very quickly.

N.C. State still had the Buckey twins, David at quarterback, Don at wide receiver and, with them in the game they ran more of an option and roll-out passing game. But the Wolfpack had another quarterback Johnny Evans, a much bigger and taller drop-back quarterback who got a good number of "snaps" in obvious passing situations, since he had a stronger arm. Therefore on third down Evans was in the game in the shotgun formation. Penn State knew they must not let him complete a pass out beyond the thirty-yard line, thus giving the 'Pack better field position before they had to punt the ball away. Evans took the snap and immediately made a quarter turn to his right and to the surprise of 59,536 fans in the stands, and the entire Penn State team and coaching staff, yelling frantically on the west side line, he quick-kicked a line drive over the head of the Penn State safety man who was still trying to determine which of the receivers coming down field he would be defensing. The ball took an end-over-end bounce beyond mid-field; and now low and "out of the wind", it began bumpity, bump, bump bouncing toward the Penn State 35 yard line, over the 30, down to the 20, over the twenty, down inside the ten yard line and when the ball stopped rolling and was touched "dead" by the N.C. State receivers, John Evans' third-down quick-kick was officially measured at 81 yards. Penn State never recovered from this 180° change in field position and a final-play 48-yard field goal attempt by Chris Bahr, even with the wind at his back, was unsuccessful. Wily Lou Holtz had out-foxed the diminutive Italian. You could say Joe didn't lose it; Holtz won it. Sometimes you just have to doff your cap and say, "Maybe someday I'll pull that rabbit out of my hat and my adversary that day will be scratching his head thinking, 'Why didn't *I* see that coming?'"

The LSU game began in a slight drizzle and the Bengals from the Bayous marched right down the field like it was a scrimmage between LSU's first team offense and State's third string defense. LSU 7 PSU 0. The Lions got three points when Chris Bahr kicked a PSU field goal later in the first quarter but the Lions weren't looking impressive. In the second quarter, with a misty rain continuing to fall, Chuck Herd outraced the LSU defensive back trying to cover him and fully extending his left hand in front of him like an outfielder catching a baseball in his glove he snagged the football one-handed and raced the remaining twenty yards into the end zone to complete a 72-yard pass play.

Instant replays proved that Herd caught another pass in the end zone for a touchdown (an official ruled he was out of the end zone) and Gary Hayman ran a punt back for a touchdown, but again an official ruled no touchdown, saying Hayman's knee touched the ground when he fielded the punt. Instant replay clearly showed Hayman's knee was a good six inches off of the ground and even fans in the stands saw that his knee was not "down." The Lions did get another touchdown and gave up a safety, when punter Brian Massela downed a bad snap in the end zone for a safety, to win 16-9 Again Paterno won a game he should have won; Penn State had superior personnel. BUT if Joe expected to be voted #1 with a 16-9 win over LSU when Notre Dame beat Alabama by a point and Ohio State dumped USC 42-21 he was dreaming. The extra two scores State should have had could have made the score 30-9 but even that probably wouldn't have moved State all the way to #1.

Throughout the game the coaches in the press box noted how the whole LSU defense went wherever Cappy went and he just didn't have the ability to cut or drive off of his bad leg with the result that he averaged *less* than 2 yards per attempt. Seeing this the coaches continually called for a reverse or counteraction and misdirection plays but Paterno who was handling the play selection never sent those plays in. He continued to give the ball to Cappelletti for 2 yard gains with the result that the Lion offense managed only *nine* first downs in the game (LSU had eighteen) and State had 28 yards rushing to LSU's 205 yards. Paterno had played it safe and won the game, but to be #1 that season under that set of circumstances, he needed a dominating win – one where his 12-0 upperclassmen were sitting on the bench in the fourth quarter, not on the field protecting a one touchdown lead.

Besides the Penn State records he set, Cappelletti should be in the NCAA record book for most yards gained rushing per game in 1973. However due to a statistical technicality John Cappelletti didn't win the NCAA rushing title. "Cappy" had 1522 yards gained during the regular season. Cappelletti amassed his yardage in just ten games as he never carried the ball in the Syracuse game, being in the game just as a decoy for three plays. His 1522 yards divided by 10 games averaged 152.2 yards per game, tops in the country. However the fact that he took the field in the Syracuse game, even though he never came close to touching the ball, meant he had participated in eleven games. (Bowl games don't count toward NCAA records since only a small percentage of teams get to play in a bowl game which can give those players the advantage of an extra game.) "Cappy's" 1522 yards divided by 11 games gave him an average of 138.4 yards per game which put him in second place.

John Cappelletti did win the Heisman Trophy and in one of the most moving speeches ever made anywhere, he dedicated the trophy to his younger brother Joey who was dying of cancer. (The story of Joey Cappelletti and his famous brother was made into a fine movie entitled *Something for Joey*.)

When Cappelletti finished his acceptance and dedication speech at the Downtown Athletic Club there wasn't a dry eye in the room and Bishop Fulton Sheen who was supposed to give the benediction said words to the effect "You don't need a benediction tonight, God has blessed you with John Cappelletti."

CHAPTER 57

Freshmen Eligibility Costs Penn State an All-American Tailback?

In the upcoming 1974 season Penn State would be playing the exact same schedule they played in 1973 except that Wake Forest had replaced Air Force in the middle of the 1974 schedule.

Stanford, West Virginia and Maryland looked as though they might be improved as did N.C. State. Since Lou Holtz took over as head coach from the ex-Penn Stater, Al Michaels, in 1972, he had put together back-to-back 8-3-1 and 9-3 seasons, the latter good enough to win an ACC championship. And the 1974 season would again feature the identical-twin Buckey brothers, Dave (QB) and Don (WR). The twins broke in as freshman in 1972, even appearing on the cover of the October 30 issue of *Sports Illustrated*. In their senior year, 1975, their fourth year as lettermen, they would become the first brother combination ever named first-team all ACC.

1974

Offense

	Veterans	Newcomers
Wide Outs	Jim Eaise*	Jerry Jeram Dick Barvinchak*(QB)
Tackles	Jeff Bleamer*	Rich Caravella Brad Benson
Guards	Tom Rafferty*	Ron Coder Greg Kubas
	John Nessel*	George Reihner
Center	Jack Baiorunos**	Rick Knechtel
Tight End	Dan Natale**	Brian Masella**
Quarterback	Tom Shuman*	John Andress
Backs	Walt Addie**	Woody Petchel
	Tom Donchez**	Duane Taylor Larry Suhey

Defense

	Veterans	Newcomers
Ends	Dave Graf**	Dennis Zmudzin
	Greg Murphy**	

Tackles	Mike Hartenstine**	Dave Stutts	
	John Quinn*		
Linebackers	Jim Rosecrans*	Buddy Tesner**	Kurt Allerman
	Greg Buttle*		
	Chris Devlin**	Ron Hostetter	Ron Crosby
	Joe Jackson*		
D-Backs	Jeff Hite*	Tom Odell	
	Jim Bradley*		

As the Penn State 1974 depth chart shows, State looked strong at linebacker, where they had depth, and on the defensive line, but there they were thin. There wasn't much depth in the secondary either. The offense had lost "Cappy," and the only tailback in the East who could have replaced him was wearing blue and gold, not blue and white.

At the conclusion of the 1972 football season, the most sought after player in Pennsylvania, a 5-10 whippet-fast 165 lb. tailback from Hopewell High School, stood on a locker room bench, and holding aloft the game ball he had been awarded, said, "And on to Penn State." Penn State thought they had Tony Dorsett and the word that was out said he was a lock for State. Then Pitt hired Johnny Majors away from Iowa State. The avid Pitt football alumni were "fed-up" losing year after year to Penn State (Pitt had won only twice since 1960). Those disenchanted folks would have felt blessed if they had compared their situation with the Penn State fans who didn't see a Lion win over the Pitt Panthers from 1919 to 1939. The consecutive Pitt losses would mount to ten in-a-row before the Panthers, with Tony Dorsett carrying the ball 38 times for 224 yards and two touchdowns in 1976, ended the streak as Pitt won its first football national championship in forty years.

In the 1960s the Pitt football boosters who wanted to restore Pitt to its glory days of the '30s, thought they had the rock-hard Windber, Pennsylvania ex-marine Frank Kush for their new coach. Kush who played his football at Michigan State, 1950-'52, could whip a squad into condition, to play almost anybody in the country. Even though Kush had been the head coach at Arizona State for sixteen years he was always considered a western Pennsylvania lad because of his Windber roots and thus was a top choice for Pitt. However at the last minute the deal fell through and the Panthers had to look farther afield. Some rumors had it that Kush had been assured that some of his recruits would not be required to take a foreign language, a requirement for all students in order to graduate from the University of Pittsburgh and the board reneged when it came contract time. Another rumor said that Kush at the last minute wanted to be able to bring in a handful of players in any given year "no questions asked" meaning they wouldn't have to meet any rigid entrance requirement. This proposal, *if* it was made, was turned down. But Johnny Majors, when he was hired, implemented a tactic reputedly used at his alma mater, Tennessee, which involved bringing in many more freshmen then needed, then "cutting" the weak and "the faint of heart" via a rigorous pre-season camp. In order to accomplish this, the University of Pittsburgh withdrew from the Big Four (Penn State, Pitt, Syracuse, West Virginia) in 1973. Majors supposedly recruited more than 85 freshmen and junior college transfers, his first year at Pitt. One quarterback, who thought he was just one of two or three quarterbacks recruited, left camp the first day when he found out he was one of seven quarterbacks on the depth chart. Tony Dorsett wouldn't have to worry about that happening to him.

While Penn State maintained a low key approach in their recruiting of Tony Dorsett, Majors having nothing to lose courted, wooed and showered attention on Dorsett telling him he could come to Pitt and play immediately whereas at State he'd have to wait his turn behind John Cappelletti. In the end Dorsett switched to Pitt and after viewing the Big 33 game in Hershey, Pennsylvania in July, Majors knew he had the real deal. Fresh from watching Dorsett turn the corner repeatedly with his jet-like speed, Majors could barely contain himself from the time he left the stands until he got back to his motel room, at which point he jumped as high in the air as he ever did in his life and yelled "Wow" at the top of his voice.

After high school Tony Dorsett changed the pronunciation of his last name from Door' sit to Door-set'. Following four years at the University of Pittsburgh where he set game, season and career rushing and scoring records, Dorsett played thirteen seasons in the NFL, all but two years with the Dallas Cowboys.

The following are two "name stories" that have Tony Dorsett as a common denominator. One involves his college coach Johnny Majors, whose father was a well known coach in Tennessee, and Johnny's mother. Mr. & Mrs. Majors' first names were Johnny and Shirley, but beyond the borders of Tennessee most people don't know that Johnny Majors' father's name was Shirley and his mother's name was Johnny. The other "name story" involved a Dallas Cowboy wide receiver named Golden Richards. When asked by a sport reporter were he got the name "Golden," Richards replied, "My parents gave it to me."

CHAPTER 58

"He's Better, No, He Isn't; Well, He Will Be, No, He Won't"

There were clues in the inaugural game of the 1974 season that this year's team wasn't the equal of the dominating 1973 group. Last year's team gained 2994 yards rushing and 1552 yards passing for a total offense net yardage of 4546 yards. Meanwhile the opposition eked out only 848 yards rushing and a creditable 1405 yards passing for 2253 yards of total offense. Less than half State's 4546 yards. Here in the 1974 opener State had to drive 80 yards, with 2:19 left to play, to defeat Stanford 24-20. It was the only touchdown the Lions scored in the entire second half. There were also other indicators for the attentive observer that this would be a bit of a down year as the first year in a new four year cycle – 1969, 1973, 1977, 1981, 1985. "The start of the four year cycle was actually set back one year to 1974 making the cycle 1978, 1982, 1986." As a consequence State had one of it's greatest teams and should have won a National Championship in 1978, that *was* a game Paterno should have won and he didn't. He "had the horses" but critical mistakes, play-calling on the Crimson Tide goal line and a twelfth man on the field for State when the Alabama punter "shanked" a punt out of bounds which gave 'Bama a first down, enabled the Tide to hang on and win, 14-7. Four years later in 1982 State did win its first National Championship and they won their second, four years later in 1986. (Eight years later, in 1994, PSU had their 12-0 Rose Bowl team which certainly deserved to be at least co-National Champions that year.)

In the 1974 Stanford game, the Cardinal quarterback Mike Cordova threw for 301 yards and two touchdowns. State's leading rusher in this game, and the Navy game to follow, was fullback Tom Donchez with two 100-yard games. Senior tailback Walt Addie had 27 carries for a total of 57 yards in the two games combined, an average of roughly 2 yards per carry. Anytime Penn State's fullback is the leading rusher in back-to-back games and the first string tailback averages two yards per carry all is not right in Happy Valley.

The following week State was at home again. The game was played in a driving rain storm, but this time the fourth quarter touchdown drive by the Lions did *not* snatch victory from the jaws of defeat. In the second quarter Navy had its only drive of more than 31 yards and they put seven points on the board. Penn State spent three quarters trying to score a touchdown or even a field goal; the Blue and White lost *five* fumbles, four inside Navy's 10-yard line, missed on four field goal attempts, and the two point conversion, after getting their only touchdown in the fourth period. Final score Navy 7, Penn State 6.

Understandably Joe Paterno was not in the best of humor at the Wednesday Quarterback Club luncheon following the Navy upset. His teams in the last three years had lost only two regular season games out of thirty-three. So far this year he had come dangerously close to losing two out of the first two. Nonetheless, Paterno was present, along with the two player guests, and the master of ceremonies who brings the whole show together, Mickey Bergstein (pronounced Berg'steen). After Mickey interviewed the players and Paterno commented on each of them, the two players left to get to their next class and Paterno and Bergstein shared the podium for the balance of the meeting. Mickey got "the ball rolling" by asking some questions that he thought might be on the minds of some of the Quarterback Club members, and others that he felt might bring forth some interesting comments from Paterno. During this question and answer session Paterno chose to explain to the audience that the fans needed to be patient with the squad as the team had lost the four co-captains – offensive lineman, Mark Markovich, defensive tackle Randy Crowder, linebacker Ed O'Neil and Heisman Trophy winner John Cappelletti. Other departed lettermen who would be sorely missed were offensive tackle Charlie Getty who could handle almost anyone who lined up opposite him (including Maryland's Randy White), guard Phil LaPorta plus wide receivers, Chuck Herd, Jimmy Scott, Dave Bland and Gary Hayman. Other contributors not mentioned by Paterno included Doug Allen, Gary Hager, Tom Hull, Jack Koniszewski (pronounced Kohna-shev-ski), Bob Nagle, Paul Gabel, Scott Mitchell, Gary Debes, Mike Orsini etc.

Whether he meant to make Paterno feel better, or for whatever rea-son an attendee in the back of the room, when acknowledged by Bergstein or Paterno, spoke out, "Joe, I understand you have a young linebacker, Greg Buttle, who's better than Ed O'Neil."

Paterno replied snappily, "No he's not."

The man now waffled a bit and qualified his remark by saying, "Well, he will be."

Paterno replied, "No he won't." Having cut the man off at the knees Paterno did explain briefly, "He's not as big as O'Neil, he can't run a sub, four-six, forty like O'Neil can; and he doesn't have O'Neil's awareness on the field."

There was no-way to debate the point with Paterno, since he had all the facts and figures. Plus, he certainly was a better judge of players than anyone in that audience. However, even head coaches can underestimate a young player. Had our statement maker compiled the statistics below he might have asked Paterno years later if he had ever revised his opinion.

Defensive Tackle Leaders

Year	Total Tackles	Solo Tackles	Assists	Player
1972	126	72	54	Ed O'Neil
1973	104	57	47	Hartenstine
1974	165	86	79	Greg Buttle
1975	140	76	64	Greg Buttle

Career Tackle Leaders
(including 1999 season)

Years	Total Tackles	Player	Ranking
1973 – 1975*	343	Greg Buttle	First
1991 - 1994	315	Brian Gelzheiser	Second
1967 – 1969*	287	Dennis Onkotz	Third
1970-1972*	274	John Skorupan	Fourth
1983-1986	274	Shane Conlan	Fourth
1996-1999	273	Brandon Short	Sixth
1971 – 1973*	196	Ed O'Neil	Twenty-third

* Only three years of eligibility in these years.

However Paterno could still have prevailed if he were to say that State used a different defensive scheme when Buttle played, which funneled more plays to "The Backer," or that Buttle had a better defensive line in front of him, or that State's defensive philosophy changed after O'Neil left. And of course Buttle played more in his sophomore year than O'Neil did in his. In fact Buttle started two games as a sophomore when O'Neil was injured. Regardless both #87, O'Neil and #67, Buttle were team captains, All-Americans and had substantial Pro careers; O'Neil seven years, Buttle nine.

Postscript: Sub, four-six, forty in layman's terms means the player can run forty-yards in less than 4.6 seconds.

CHAPTER 59

Return to the Surface from Davy Jones' Locker

Game #3 was against Iowa in Iowa City and the beginning of a new winning streak as the 1974 squad recorded a shut-out while outgaining the Hawkeyes 278 yards to 100. There were two unfamiliar names in the Penn State scoring summary. Dave Stutts, normally a tight end was moved to the backfield in short yardage goal line plays and scored two touchdowns and John Reihner kicked two field goals and all three extra points when Chris Bahr didn't make the trip due to a soccer injury incurred the previous day. In the Iowa game, Jimmy Cefalo, not yet eighteen years old, carried the ball three times for 31 yards playing as a true freshmen. For years Paterno declined to play true freshmen, although they were eligible, saying young men just out of high school needed a year on campus to mature and to get their "academic house in order." But Paterno finally had to relent since other schools were using that stance against Penn State when recruiting head-to-head for the best players in the country. These players were good and they knew it and they didn't relish playing four games of unnoticed freshmen football when their contemporaries were playing high-visibility varsity football and making headlines. Additionally all of Penn State's traditional foes had dropped freshman football and the only opponents available were prep schools. Now ironically one of the first freshmen, if not the first, to play for Paterno turned out to be a *seventeen* year old.

The Army game at West Point had an eerie resemblance to the earlier Navy game. State fumbled twice in the first quarter and was down 14-0. But the defense rose-up and blanked the Cadets the rest of the way to win 21-14.

Homecoming opponent Wake Forest was no match for the Lions who rolled up 532 yards total offense as Cefalo and Duane Taylor scored twice, along with four other players who recorded touchdowns – Jim Eaise, Dick Barvinchak, Tom Donchez and Neil Hutton.

State had trouble with both Syracuse and West Virginia winning 30-14 and 21-12 respectively. Syracuse scored on the first play of the game and led 14-10 at halftime. West Virginia was down only eight points at halftime but six turnovers gave the Lions all the help they needed, aided by Ron Coder's recovery of a West Virginia fumble in their end zone, after a Penn State field goal attempt was blocked.

A look at the year's to-date rushing statistics showed immediately the Lions did not have a tailback capable of carrying the team. Fullback Tom Donchez had rushed for 588 yards so far and was on his way to a regular season total of 880 yards; four tailbacks – Woody Petchel, Rusty Boyle, Walt Addie and Neil Hutton would amass only a combined 826 yards for the entire season.

Tom Shuman threw only 183 passes, but completed 97 for a .530 completion percentage which still remains the tenth-best season completion percentage at Penn State, including the 1998 season. Shuman's career passing yardage is still the tenth-best among Penn State passers and he is fifth-best all-time for career yards per attempt through the 1999 season. These statistics should put to rest the good-natured kidding Shuman took from some of his teammates who every so often would resurrect the old line, "Shuman could throw a football through a mountain – if he could hit it."

The next game on the schedule was Maryland, and the Terrapins were on the threshold of their best seven year record since they went 60-9-2 under head coach Jim Tatum, 1949-1955. (Not many people are aware that Paul "Bear" Bryant coached one year, 1945, at Maryland posting a 6-2-1 record.)

But this was 1974 and "Here's... Randy."

CHAPTER 60

The Murph
"Answer Me This, Coach."

A lthough the Penn State – Maryland series is top-heavy with Penn State wins (35) and of course an equal number of Maryland losses, there have been some very close games and Maryland has had its share of outstanding players. Of Maryland's fifteen first-team All-Americans, Randy White (Defensive Tackle) may have been the best player ever to wear a Terrapin uniform. An All-American in 1973 and '74, White won the Outland and Lombardi Trophies in 1974, spent 16 years with the Dallas Cowboys, where he was an annual All-Pro selection and was inducted into the College and NFL Halls of Fame. White lettered in 1972, '73 and '74, and while the PSU- Maryland games in 1972 and '73 were not very close contests, the 1974 game as it drew near, looked to be a different story, and it was.

Maryland started the year ranked #14 in the nation, and despite losing two very close games to start off the season (16-21 to #3 Alabama and 10-17 to Florida in Florida), the Terps came to State College in November very confident. In addition to this being Randy White's senior year, Coach Jerry Claiborne had the overall "strongest" team Maryland had had in recent years, and possibly all-time.

When Coach Claiborne arrived at Maryland in 1972, he was appalled at the lack of strength among Maryland's "up front" people. He immediately put an all-out emphasis on strength training, emphasizing free-weight lifting and bench- pressing, in an effort to make his team more competitive. Randy White led the rest of the players in the weight room, setting strength records, some of which may stand to this day. His efforts were emulated by his fellow linemen to the best of their ability and as the months and seasons passed, rumors and press releases were publicizing the amazing weight room exploits of White and his cohorts. Starting with the third game of the 1974 season, a 24-12 win over North Carolina, Maryland found new confidence and suddenly began overwhelming teams with their strength and physical play, beating-up on the likes of Syracuse, Clemson and Wake Forest 31-0, 41-0, and 47-0 respectively. The author doesn't mean to infer that in a matter of weeks, the Maryland players became strong. That was not the case but over the years here's what did happen.

After three years under Roy Lester's tutelage during which time the

Terps went 3-7, 2-9 and 2-9, Jerry Claiborne came on the scene and made a quick turn around, followed by consistent success.

Starting in 1972 the Terrapins won 5, lost 5 and tied 1. In the years 1973 through 1978 Maryland won at least eight games each year. After finishing sixth, seventh or eighth in the ACC in the four of the five years prior to his arrival, Claiborne directed the Terps to four second-place ACC finishes, plus first place finishes, in 1974, '75 and '76.

Coming into State College in 1974, their third year under Claiborne, and sporting a 5 and 2 record the Randy White-led Terrapins were now thinking very positively about themselves. The "Terps" were ranked #15 in the country and they had played #3 Alabama tough. This squad wasn't traveling to University Park to take their annual beating. They weren't just hoping for a win, they were believing they *would* win.

The Penn State staff did not want a repeat of the Navy upset which occurred earlier in the season, thus they were pushing all the buttons hoping they could get the Lions completely focused on this game. They had had a close call just last week in West Virginia. Thinking ahead to a Bowl game this week and/or expecting to beat Maryland 42-22 as they did last year, just by stepping out on the field would be fatal. Having rallied in the past to beat a particular team or having beaten a team twelve straight times, as State had done to Maryland, can lead to over-confidence, when playing that team. Also several come-from-behind victories in a season, can make a team believe they are unbeatable, and able to snatch victory from the jaws of defeat whenever they decide to turn on the power.

Therefore, at their weekly team meeting, Paterno was followed to the microphone by one of the staff who was trying to jump start the team, emphasizing the improvement in this Maryland team over last year's. After giving Randy White his due, the coach went on to discuss each lineman, detailing how much each player could lift or bench press and how many "reps" (repetitions) he could do. As the talk progressed, one could sense the mood among the players getting much more somber, and it seemed that Paterno's idea to counteract any complacency might be missing the mark. The silence might mean the players weren't "buying " the sermon being delivered *or* their self-confidence was "taking a hit" and the lecturer had taken his audience from, full of confidence, to developing a healthy respect for the opposition, and beyond that to a point where they might be questioning their ability to handle these "Incredible Hulks."

At this pivotal point there was movement, mumbling and coughing at the rear of the 120-seat amphitheater. When everyone turned his head, there stood a large African-American team member. It was Greg Murphy, a big defensive end and a heck of a football player. "The Murph" was noted for two things. One was his physical style of play; he loved to mix it up on the line of scrimmage - nothing dirty, just let's have at it, and see who says "ouch" first. Secondly, "The Murph" was the team's fashion plate. Patent leather shoes to match his outfits were commonplace. The players expected "Murph" to make his last appearance after the final bowl game with a walking stick and a purse. Maybe because he was from Flatbush (Brooklyn), Murphy seemed to get a kind of special treatment from Paterno.

However, right now none of the other players wished to be in Murphy's patent leather shoes, regardless of the particular color "Murph" was wearing, because Joe doesn't take kindly to disruptions during a team meeting. But with the same disregard he would show for a 200 pound blocker trying to stop his pass rush, "Murph" just broke in, as he addressed the speaker in his distinctive voice, "Yo Coach! I hear all this about how much this guy can lift and how much this other guy can press and how many reps he can do…answer me this coach, out there on Saturday are we gonna lift weights or are we gonna play 'fuhball'? Some Penn State 'fuhball' huh?"

Paterno, ever the master of capturing the moment, reportedly ended the "weight-lifting lecture" and challenged the team to really play some "Penn State football" on Saturday.

In an exciting game Maryland was driving for a first period score when defensive back Jeff Hite intercepted a pass and ran it back 79 yards for a touchdown and a 7-0 Penn State lead.

In the second period, quarterback Bob Avellini threw a thirty-four yard touchdown pass to Walter White to tie the score. Later in the quarter, *three* touchdowns were recorded in just *twenty-five seconds*. First, a Tom Shuman to Dick Barvinchak touchdown pass made the score 14-7 in favor of State. On the ensuing kick-off Maryland tried a trick play where the kick return man ran behind his wall of blockers near the west sideline. He then threw a backwardly directed "lateral pass" to the east sideline where there was supposed to be just one Maryland player; the play was expected to go for big yardage. Fortunately for Penn State Jeff Hite had "stayed home" and he cut in front of the intended receiver to intercept the lateral pass and Hite ran it in for a touchdown to give Penn State a 21-7 lead. On the next kick-off Maryland did not try any trickery, running the ball out to the thirty-four yard line. On the first play from scrimmage quarterback Avellini hit his big tight end Walter White on a streak up the middle, which went for 66 yards and a touchdown, making the score 21-14. All in just twenty-five ticks of the game clock.

The second half was a defensive war with each team managing only a 4th quarter field goal for a 24-17 final score. Randy White and his defensive cohorts had given up only 10 points in the whole game, but they lost, on Jeff Hite's two big defensive touchdowns.

CHAPTER 61

They Also Serve

Again Johnny Evans' punting was a factor in an N.C. State Wolfpack win over Penn State; a Penn State team that couldn't score until the last minute of the game. For the fourth time in nine games, fullback Tom Donchez was State's leading ground-gainer, but with a mere 61 yards. Now Lou Holtz had gotten the monkey off his back and he had the first of two consecutive losses he would pin on Joe Paterno. The final score was NCSU 12 PSU 7. JoePa's team rebounded and climbed all over Ohio University in the final home game of the 1974 season, with Donchez notching three touchdowns to stake his team to a 35-0 lead. Ohio rallied for 16 fourth-quarter points to make the final margin 35-16.

Prior to the start of the game, the Penn State crowd said good-bye to a number of players who were household names in the homes of Nittany Lion fans, such as, Walt Addie, Jack Baiorunos, Jim Bradley, Chris Devlin, Tom Donchez, Jim Eaise, Dave Graf, Mike Hartenstine, Greg Murphy, Dan Natale, Tom Shuman and Buddy Tesner.

There were some other players who ran out of the tunnel on to the Beaver Stadium turf that day, some like center Ralph Perri who in the 1974 media guide no longer even had a number assigned to him, and he was nowhere to be found among the player pictures and biographical sketches which occupied pages 34-49 of the press guide. Perri and others might never have dressed for a game until this game, might never have been on the field for a meaningful play in their entire four year career. And yet some, like Ralph Perri, who according to some teammates, never missed a practice or a meeting due to injury or sickness in four years, displayed a devotion, a discipline that defied explanation by admiring teammates. As someone said, "It can't even be the love of the game, when you never-ever get to play." Football at Penn State is demanding, but if you star, if you help your team win on the playing field, if you at least get to play, *that* can make it worthwhile. As one of the co-captains put it, regarding those who don't get to play, "I have the highest respect for someone who is able to stay with the program, never play, but whose dedication is a tremendous example to those who are more fortunate to play."

While such players labor in obscurity, I have been told Joe Paterno never forgets those who only practice and never play, when it comes graduation time. At that time a letter of recommendation or a telephone call from Paterno can open doors that are otherwise closed.

CHAPTER 62

The Sphinx Speaks

Penn State had lost two regular season games, and in each game the Lions were held to a single touchdown. This brought the Lions to their Thanksgiving night game with the Pitt Panthers at Three Rivers Stadium, sporting an 8 and 2 record.

Since Three Rivers Stadium was a neutral site, each team was allowed approximately an hour in the afternoon to work out on the field. The teams would use this time to test the artificial turf, try shoes with various cleat lengths and patterns, check out the wind currents at field level compared to the wind direction indicated by the flags around the top of the stadium and also evaluate the background and the glare of the lights, when looking into them while fielding punts and kickoffs, and catching passes.

Penn State was just completing their workout and leaving the field when the Pitt players came out of their locker room. Penn State (looking typically Penn State-ish) was wearing plain gray sweat pants and sweat shirts. The Panthers appeared in beautiful blue and gold shiny nylon warm-ups with each player's name on the back of his warm-up top. Several of the Pitt squad snickered, scoffed and outright commented derogatorily upon seeing State's mundane, off-the-rack warm-ups. Hearing and sensing the nature of the comments left many Lion players just below the boiling point; and game time was still hours away.

The Lions retired to their hotel, to be off of their feet for a few hours then returned to Three Rivers to go through their normal pre-game routine. With the pre-game warm-up completed, both teams returned to their locker rooms prior to the start of this ABC nationally-televised Thanksgiving Night game.

Just prior to *leaving* the locker room for the opening kick-off it is customary for the coaches and trainers to vacate the locker room temporarily while the captains address the squad. Normally at this time only the captains speak. However this was the last game of the season, and traditionally at Penn State, any senior player who won't be back next year is allowed to be heard.

Amazingly one of the first to speak was Mike Hartenstine (pronounced Harten steen). The assembled squad probably wouldn't have been anymore surprised if Knute Rockne had come through the door and launched into a pep talk. To fully understand the effect of Hartenstine addressing the group the reader has to be aware that Hartenstine could go through an entire practice, saying not one word more than was necessary. Even Paterno couldn't get a rise out of #79, Hartenstine just went about doing his job and what a job he did at defensive tackle, letting his actions do the talking on the field. Jack Baiorunos who was as good a center as Penn State had during the Paterno era, said if an offensive player could get a good block on Hartenstine two times out of five he was fortunate.

But here in the locker room, before his final regular season game, it was as though Mike had saved-up four years of emotion and it was all pouring out now. Stunned players, some of whom said Hartenstine hadn't started a conversation with them all the time they were at State, sat stunned, looking at Mike, and each other in disbelief. Was this someone else in Hartenstine's uniform? Was this shouting voice really Mike Hartenstine's? Who could be sure? Hartenstine was particularly incensed at the slurs made by the Pitt players, and whether correct or not he took absolute umbrage at Tony Dorsett's involvement and he vowed what would happen to him, Dorsett, and several other Pitt players if they came anywhere within his reach. Now, fullback Tom Donchez took the floor. Blonde-haired, with a fair to pale complexion, Donchez looked like the main Russian character in a CIA-KBG spy-thriller; a character, whose age could only be guessed-at. Donchez, a teammate of Hartenstine's dating back to Liberty High School in Bethlehem, Pennsylvania, was highly aroused by his friend's emotional speech and at a point in his own fiery diatribe threw his helmet down on the floor as though he were trying to spilt the helmet in two.

The upshot of Donchez's action (and it was an "upshot") falls into the familiar good news/bad news category. The good news was, the Riddell Company, whose helmets Penn State used at that time, were so sturdily constructed that even when subjected to the force that Donchez's helmet was, the helmet did not shatter or split. The bad news was that the helmets made by Riddell Company were so sturdily constructed that even when subjected to the force that Donchez's helmet was, the helmet did not shatter or split.

If the helmet did not shatter or split it doesn't take a rocket scientist to calculate that the helmet rebounded off of the floor with nearly all of the force with which it hit the floor and the *really* bad news was, that on it way to hitting the ceiling, it first made contact with Greg Buttle's chin and forehead and Buttle flopped back out-cold on the table on which he had previously been perched, while listening to Hartenstine's and Donchez's "take no prisoners" speeches.

As we stated Buttle was "out-cold." Now the Penn State team which prides itself on playing with poise rather than emotion found out why emotion is described as a "two-edged sword." These players who moments ago were ready to take on the Pittsburgh Panthers *and* the Pittsburgh Steelers combined, had gone from that emotional high to an even lower emotional low, wondering what they would do without their best linebacker, who was also one of their defensive leaders. The speeches were over, Bradley and Baiorunos never did get to speak to the team.

Quickly five of the biggest players were stationed in front of Buttle's prone body to hide him from Paterno, and the locker room door was opened to re-admit the coaches. Bradley and Baiorunos made a beeline for Chuck Medlar the head trainer and quietly told Chuck there had been an accident. Pointed in the right direction, Chuck quickly skirted the line of behemoths which was now seven across and two deep. When Chuck saw Greg lying there he lurched for Buttle's helmet and began pushing it down onto his head saying, to another player, "If we don't get his helmet on before his forehead swells, we'll never get it on." So there was Chuck, with the help of another player jamming Buttle's helmet down over his head with blood running down Buttle's face, blood dripping from the split in his chin and Greg too woozy to talk, help or fight back. On the way out of the room Bradley and Baiorunos grabbed assistant trainers Jim Hochberg and Jerry Slagle, pulled them over to opposite sides of the room and told them to stay behind and help Chuck after the team vacated the room. The curtain of flesh had done its job and they brought up the rear as the team departed without their backer/caller and best linebacker. All of the players where solemn and subdued. The double-edged sword of emotion had struck again.

Regarding Three Rivers Stadium, the name is a misnomer. This is a case of two rivers (the Allegheny and the Monongahela) joining to form the Ohio River. At no time are there *three* rivers. It's the same as combining two small tasks you have to do, into one larger task. You do not have three tasks to perform, you have one larger task made up of two smaller ones.

CHAPTER 63

Dial (the) "O" for Assistance

As head coach Joe Paterno, the players and the other assistant coaches ran out onto Three River's artificial turf, Buddy Tesner hung back and sought out his defensive coordinator Jim O'Hora. A senior, Tesner had been a three year back-up player at defensive end and at linebacker behind the likes of Ed O'Neil and now Greg Buttle. Players like Buttle and O'Neil, game after game, make the calls and make the plays until the outcome is no longer in doubt. Accordingly, there is precious little playing time for their back-ups. As the back-up to Buttle, Buddy had been going through week after week of memorizing the calls for the coming week's game, and week after week he didn't get into the game to use the calls. Consequently he probably had not been too attentive this past week, since it was always the same old drill. Each week, learn the calls for the week, don't get to use them; the next week, the same thing, learn the new calls, don't get to use them, and on and on.

Tesner, a gutsy player, hid all external signs of panic as he sidled up to Coach O'Hora. Holding on to O'Hora's sleeve he said, "Quickly 'O', lets go over some of the calls." Tesner was matching O'Hora stride for stride but this was a different Buddy Tesner than the one who, fortified with almost a full four years of experience, just went through the motions during practice this past week. Now, he was all ears. Like a droplet of water would be soaked up by the desert sand, Tesner was eager to absorb any morsel "The O" would throw his way. But "The O" figured he had more important things to think about than reviewing the calls for the week with his back-up backer who would be standing just a foot or two from him, while his first team All-American backer, Greg Buttle would be on the field taking the real calls.

Tesner quickly realized his veiled call for assistance had not rung in the "O's" brain. A direct, straight-on frontal approach was needed so he said in measured tones," 'O', Buttle's not going to be able to start, he's hurt."

O'Hora looked at Tesner incredulously, "What do you mean he's hurt, I just saw him ten minutes ago and he was fine."

Tesner said, "Well 'O' he got hurt, and he won't be out until he's had a few stitches."

Coach O'Hora replied, "Lordy, now we lose a player before the game starts."

Tesner said assuringly, "He'll be O.K., the Docs just need a few minutes." So Coach O'Hora ran through the calls quickly with Buddy, before the kick-off coverage team came off the field and it was time for State to send on the defensive team.

Number 30 (Tesner) had barely begun to run onto the field to huddle up with the other ten Penn State defenders when Paterno came charging over, "Jim, what the devil is Tesner doing in there?"

O'Hora replied, "Buttle's hurt."

Paterno countered, "Buttle's hurt? Why didn't I hear about that?"

O'Hora said, "I just found out myself."

Paterno asked, "How did it happen?"

O'Hora said, "I don't know, it happened in the locker room."

Paterno said in disbelief, "In the locker room?" Mumbling as he walked away Joe continued, "We can't get through a meeting and a team prayer without someone getting hurt!"

While signaling to Tesner, and checking his clipboard and the field, Coach O'Hora began to get some feed-back. Indeed it was Number 67, Buttle, who was hurt, but other than some sketchy information about Buttle getting hit with a helmet and needing stitches, details were lacking and O'Hora really didn't have time to hear more now.

Later in the first quarter, Number 67 walked up to the Penn State bench, and Buddy Tesner and the other Penn State players and fans emitted a huge sigh of relief. Many of the fans seeing the bulky gauze pads taped to Buttle's chin probably wondered when and how he got hurt. As the game progressed, the more observant ones may also have wondered why he never took his helmet off. When Buttle walked up to Coach O'Hora, "The O" asked if he was O.K. to go in. Buttle assured him he was, so O'Hora sent him in with the defensive call for first down, when the defense went back onto the field. On second down the Penn State defense went to a defensive set they had never shown before based on "down and distance" and field position and Pitt lost yardage on the play. Again, Paterno came charging over to Coach O'Hora and asked, "Jim, what the devil was that?"

O'Hora responded, "I don't know, its not what we signaled in. Tesner get in there for Buttle we'll signal you a play."

As it turned out the concussion Buttle had suffered was giving him trouble seeing the signals. Until his sight improved, State went to shuffling players in and out, carrying the calls.

The entire first half was a bit of a sleepwalk for the Lion offense. The defense played admirably with and without Buttle, allowing only a single touchdown on a two-yard Tony Dorsett run. But Penn State registered only two Chris Bahr field goals. Mike Hartenstine was playing like the consummate professional player he would be for thirteen years with the Chicago Bears and Minnesota Vikings. For sixty minutes with a little help from his friends, Hartenstine would limit Tony Dorsett to 65 yards on 17 carries and the one first-half touchdown.

By the second half Buttle was 80-85% of his usual self, which was better than some player's best on their best day. And Buddy Tesner and Mike Hartenstine could not have been happier when Penn State scored 25 points in the second half to Pitt's three for a 31-10 victory.

Mike Hartenstine made virtually every 1974 All-American team and was chosen as the Chevrolet Defensive Player of the Year. Jack Baiorunos was chosen for the NCAA Top Five Student Athlete Award, an NCAA Post Graduate Scholarship and National Football Foundation and Hall of Fame Scholar-Athlete Awards. Tom Donchez a finance major went on to become a C.P.A. and both Tesner and Jim Bradley became orthopedic surgeons.

The 1974 season ended January 1, 1975 with a 41-20 win over Baylor in the Cotton Bowl. State came into the game ranked #10 and finished the year at #7 after turning in a near duplication of their 1971 Cotton Bowl victory over Texas. In that game Penn State roared back from a 6-3 halftime deficit to win 30-6.

Down 7-3, in the 1975 Cotton Bowl game at half-time, State scored early in the second half and following a 35 yard retaliatory score by Baylor, the Lions recorded the next four scores, two by Jimmy Cefalo to put State up 34-14.

Baylor did score once more with just 19 seconds remaining in the contest but on the ensuing on-side kick-off State's Joe Jackson recovered the kick and went 50 yards for a Lion touchdown making the final score 41-20. The 41 points was a Cotton Bowl record.

CHAPTER 64

You Need to Have an Attitude

As our friends Greg Murphy, Mike Hartenstine, and Tom Donchez exhibited in previous chapters, good football players need to have more than a modicum of "attitude."

When someone at a cocktail party said in the presence of Duffy Daugherty, then head coach at Michigan State, that football was a contact sport, Duffy retorted, "Dancing is a contact sport, football is a collision sport."

A passive player will find himself always on the receiving end of the "collisions" on the football field and he will not help his team nor will he last long. A player must give as well as take, but within the rules. A "cheap shot artist", someone who hits "after the whistle" or when a opponent is already out-of-bonds, will also not help but will actually hurt his team. Coaches covet players who cannot he intimidated on the field, who play under control and refuse to say "ouch" first. Off the playing and practice field coaches would like those same players to be good citizens, mannerly, law abiding, scholarly, young men. Possibly the reader can sense the conundrum coaches face in dealing with young men with the assertive qualities you want on the gridiron but hoping they don't run afoul of the establishment on and off campus.

To have a competitive and fair contest, football officials have to control the game they are officiating, trying to watch the actions of all twenty-two of these aggressive "Type A" players while performing other duties. The worst thing that can happen to a crew of officials is that they let the game get out of control. Therefore while doing their best to be impartial and to make the right calls they are constantly alert for "late hits," retaliatory actions and verbal taunting. These actions if allowed to go unchecked can escalate, leading to punches being thrown which can erupt into a brawl, or even a riot.

The following true story came to the author regarding an officiating crew working a high school football game between Scranton Prep and a northeastern Pennsylvania public school. The game was a showdown between two talented teams. The contest was being played hard, but cleanly, with a shove or push here and there, but the tension and the ferocity of the play, with Prep leading by just an extra point, was building as the second quarter wound down. It was at this point that the Prep quarterback got into a good rhythm and feeding off his success he was moving his team toward another score. Twice he had gotten a pass off at the last second and completed it. He had also taken the best shot the opponent's blitzing middle linebacker could cleanly deliver. As he got to his feet the quarterback pumped his fist in the air saying "Completion, yeh, completion movin' right down the field." His comments were subdued but the linebacker knew for whom they were meant. On the next play, a called roll-out, every receiver was covered, so the quarterback threw the ball away just before he went out-of-bounds and the same linebacker who seemed to be shadowing the quarterback had to exercise all the restraint he could muster to keep from giving the quarterback a good shove in the back, out of frustration. But he managed a few words directed at the QB who had chosen to run out of bounds.

Then Prep caught their opponents with their pants down on a double reverse. Twenty yards downfield the quarterback put a darn good block, for a quarterback, on the linebacker who was close to making the tackle. The linebacker rolled with the block and bounced to his feet and was ready to return the favor but the whistle blew. So the linebacker settled for some more choice words and the two players bumped chests like a pair of male birds in a ritual mating feud. The field judge intervened cautioning both of them, "Take it easy '17', and you too, '50', there's a lot of game left. You don't want to cost your team a dumb penalty."By the middle of the third period Prep had increased their lead and linebacker #50 had unloaded on the quarterback a few more times. The quarterback wanted to show he couldn't be intimidated by the linebacker's "hits" so he tried to bounce right back on his feet after each tackle. But the bigger linebacker occasionally managed to sprawl over the quarterback keeping him down for a few seconds. On such an occasion as they got to their feet, each player tried to get in the last push or shove along with the last epithet "Wuss," "Meathead," "Sorehead." Finally, "having had it," the referee threw a flag in the air and penalized both teams fifteen yards for unsportsmanlike conduct. After picking up his flag and signaling the penalty, the "ref" called both boys together and said, "All right fellas this stops right here. The next shove, late hit, whatever, and I'm throwing both of you out of the game!" The quarterback, who had probably gotten a bit the worse of the one-on-one feud said, "Hey, Mr. Official it's O.K., we always play like this, he's my brother!"

CHAPTER 65

"Just Put a Stamp on Him...."

Going into Paterno's tenth year as head coach, Joe was sporting a career won-lost-tied record of 85-15-1 for an .847 winning percentage. And Beaver Stadium ("The House that Joe Built") now had a seating capacity of 57,723 up from 46,284 when Paterno assumed the helm. Three crowds last year, Maryland, Ohio U. and Stanford had exceeded capacity with the Maryland crowd drawing 60,125 spectators. By July 1, 1975 all tickets for the Kentucky, West Virginia and N.C. State home games and the September 20th game at Ohio State had been sold, as Penn State football was a "hit" on the field and at the ticket office. But the '75 squad was minus a lot of talent and leadership. There were at least seven giant pairs of shoes to be filled and none of them would be filled completely. Gone were center Jack Baiorunos, fullback Tom Donchez, defensive tackle Mike Hartenstine, defensive end Greg Murphy, quarterback Tom Shuman, offensive tackle Jeff Bleamer and safety Jim Bradley.

The three incoming co-captains, offensive lineman, Tom Rafferty, defensive lineman John Quinn, and linebacker Greg Buttle would have very productive years, but several members of this team were under-sized for their position or were still a year or two away from their zenith. Ron Crosby who played in the NFL for seven years and had five great years with the New York Jets was forced to play on the defensive line at 212 pounds, defensive tackle John Quinn weighed 226 pounds and defensive halfback Tom Odell who was listed at 178 pounds, but certainly weighed less than 168 pounds, all were at a size disadvantage.

The 1975 squad was lacking any pre-season All-American candidates except offensive guard Tom Rafferty and linebacker Greg Buttle. Going into the season the defensive depth chart showed ten seniors and one junior as starters.

Defense

First string			Back-ups
Dennis Zmudzin	Sr.	Defensive End	Kurt Allerman
John Quinn	Sr.	Defensive Tackle	John Dunn
Ron Coder	Sr.	Defensive Tackle	
Ron Crosby	Jr.	Defensive End	Bill Banks
Jeff Hite	Sr.	Linebacker	Ron Hostetter
Rick Kriston	Sr.	Linebacker	
Greg Buttle	Sr.	Linebacker	Tom DePaso
Jim Rosecrans	Sr.	Linebacker	Randy Sidler
Mike Johnson	Sr.	Defensive Halfback	
Tom Giotto	Sr.	Safety	Gary Petercuskie
Tom Odell	Sr.	Defensive Halfback	

By the final game of the 1975 season only seven of the ten pre-season senior starters were still starting and they - Buttle, Coder, Johnson, Quinn, Rosecrans, Odell, Zmudzin would leave a number of big voids in the 1976 squad.

In sharp contrast to the defensive unit's senior look. The offensive side of the ball had a very junior look, with just four seniors expected to start.

Offense

First string			Back-ups
Dave Stutts	Jr.	Tight End	Mickey Shuler
Brad Benson	Jr.	Tackle	Craig Brown
George Reihner	Jr.	Tackle	
Tom Rafferty	Sr.	Guard	Greg Kubas
Mark Thomas	Sr.	Guard	
Rich Knechtel	Sr.	Center	
John Andress	Jr.	Quarterback	
Woody Petchel	Sr.	Tailback	Rusty Boyle
			Steve Geise
Larry Suhey	Jr.	Fullback	Duane Taylor
Jimmy Cefalo	So.	Wide receiver	Rich Mauti
Buddy Ellis	Jr.	Split end	Dick Barvinchak

At the conclusion of the 1975 there would be four senior starters lost to graduation. They were Rafferty, Thomas, Petchel and *Barvinchak*. This 1975 squad was in the midst of a four (or five) year cycle between the 5th ranked 1973 and the 4th ranked 1978 teams, which certainly were among Paterno's ten best teams through 1999. As we discovered in some previous mid-cycle teams, State's less successful and less talented teams usually lacked a "go to" Cappelletti or Curt Warner – type tailback. The 1975 leading ground gainer was 190 pound tailback Woody Petchel who had suffered a serious knee injury in his sophomore year costing him his breakaway speed. He gained 621 yards, fullback Duane Taylor notched 556 yards on 25 fewer carries, sophomore Steve Geise contributed 252 and typical of a Paterno team that struggles, flanker, Tom Donovan, was fourth in yards-gained rushing. The Lions' starting quarterback threw for more than 82 yards in only three games, two of which were lop-sided wins, and garnered a season total of 991 yards for a grand total of 2656 yards total offense. In comparison the 1973 team had four backs who rushed for 2475 yards and quarterback Tom Shuman threw for 1375 yards, a total of 3850 yards. The 1978 squad had four ball carriers who garnered 2010 yards and Chuck Fusina threw for 1859 yards for a total of 3869 yards.

Yet the 1975 team won 9 and lost only 3. How? By holding every opponent, but one, to less than eighteen points. Those eleven foes averaged less than 8.3 points per game. Taking away two fantastic plays that opponents made against State that year, the Lions could have been 11-1. In fairness, one could also look at two games State won by a single point and a third game – a two point victory and point out they were also that close to being 6-6.

The 1975 schedule appeared a bit more robust; gone were Navy, Ohio University and Wake Forest and in their place State had added a brand new opponent, Kentucky, also Ohio State reappeared for the first time since the two big wins the Lions engineered in 1963 and '64. And in the season, opener, the third new team, Temple, re-emerged as a Penn State opponent after a twenty-three year hiatus. In the wake of ten years with George Makris at the helm and a 45-44-4 log, the Temple Owls had hired Wayne Hardin in 1970 and he promptly produced five consecutive winning seasons with an overall 35-12-1 record. However, many Penn State fans judged Temple's schedules to be suspect since they included the followings opponents: Bucknell, Connecticut, Xavier, Rhode Island, Drake, Delaware, Boston University, Buffalo and Holy Cross. Therefore, from the viewpoint of Nittany rooters, the 1975 meeting was little more than a showcase for the Philadelphia alumni and a tune-up for the Stanford game the following week. In actuality the game would prove to be a rather accurate barometer of the up and down season that was in store.

The Temple game was to be played on Saturday night of the Labor

Day Weekend, at a neutral site. A site where Penn State teams had played forty-seven times over the years – Franklin Field. Despite a ten minute delay the game began with thousands of fans still backed up on the Schuylkill Expressway, some of them still on the Pennsylvania Turnpike behind a horrific fiery accident involving some eastbound Penn State fans who were rear-ended trying to exit the Turnpike on to the expressway. West bound travelers fared no better trying to get back into Philadelphia from the New Jersey Shore and hundreds of cars, filled with fans, were so maddeningly close to the field they could hear the crowd, but were unable to find anyplace to park their vehicle. Inside Franklin Field, this game, which was supposed to get Penn State ready for next week's intersectional battle with Stanford, got off to a dramatic but unfavorable start for PSU. On the first play from scrimmage Temple halfback Bob Harris went 76 yards to put Temple ahead 7-0; with five to ten thousand fans still not in their seats. Field goals by Chris Bahr and Temple kicker Don Bitterlich were followed by a 100-yard kick-off return by Rich Mauti and another Bahr field goal, this one a 55-yarder. But, Bitterlich hit a 40-yard field goal and State was trailing again, 13-12 at half time.

Penn State took back the lead on a Duane Taylor touchdown in the third period but an Owl field goal and a 77 yard drive put Temple ahead 23-18 with just 7:47 remaining in the game. (Penn State had twice failed on two point conversion attempts.) On Temple's next possession the Owls had to punt and State's Woody Petchel ran the punt back 66 yards to put the Lions in position to resume the lead. Taylor scored his second touchdown and quarterback John Andress connected with sophomore tight end Mickey Shuler on a two point conversion attempt to put State up 26-23. This gave Penn State a chance to repeat their game-saving intentional safety strategy, employed so successfully against N.C. State in 1967. This time, quarterback John Andress ran out of Penn State's end zone with just eleven seconds remaining in the game to preserve a 26-25 Penn State win.

The Stanford contest played at Beaver Stadium in front of the largest home crowd in Penn State history (61,325) proved to be much less of a test than the Temple game, as the Lions rushed for over 300 yards and the defense caused six turnovers as Stanford failed to score a point in the entire second half. In their next game the Stanford Cardinal would play Michigan to a 19-19 stalemate.

Now it was on to Columbus, Ohio, where a deep and talented team, that had opened their season with a 21-0 win over Michigan State on their way to eleven consecutive wins and a Big Ten championship, lay in wait. This Ohio State Buckeye team was led by the incomparable

Archie Griffin, the only player ever to win two Heisman Trophies, a bruising 250 pound fullback, Pete Johnson, quarterback Cornelius Greene, Tim Fox and Bob Brudizinski (all All-Big Ten picks) and Brian Baschnagel. Griffin ran with power for his size and he had great balance and deceptive moves. Johnson on the other hand, didn't need deceptive moves. At 250 pounds Johnson out weighed every defensive player on the Penn State squad and all but two offensive linemen. During the week prior to the Ohio State game the author was speaking to one of the Penn State players about Johnson, to which the player half-jokingly replied, "If Odell has to make a solo tackle on him (Johnson), Odell won't have to catch the flight back we'll just put a stamp on him and mail him home."

As a spectator at the 1975 PSU-OSU game the author can subjectively, but impartially, say the outcome of that game turned around on one play. In the second half with the score 10-9 in favor of Ohio State, Duane Taylor, Penn State's fullback but judged by some to be faster than all but one of Paterno's stable of tailbacks, broke into the clear and headed down the left sideline for what seemed to be a sure touchdown; a Penn State lead, and a *huge* swing in the momentum of the game. There was no one between Taylor and the Buckeye goal-line. One defender, OSU's Tim Fox was near the center of the field and seemed to be on the same yard stripe as Taylor at the time the author identified him. Now, Fox was a safety and everyone one knows you put your two fastest secondary men at the two defensive halfback spots. Your free safety doesn't have to be as fast, especially in pass defense, since he "plays deeper" and thus can make up in reaction time what he lacks in foot speed. Fox was definitely a safety, not a defensive halfback and I thought Taylor would surely score, but Fox hot-footed it across the field refusing to be beaten and stopped Taylor around the OSU eighteen yard line. How Fox made up the amount of ground he did, I don't know, but the Lions never scored, and that in a nutshell was the ball game. Had Taylor scored, I think Penn State would have won, The final touchdown by the Buckeyes to made the score 17-9 was just "icing on the cake", the coup de grace by a team that had proven it's dominance.

The Penn State and the Michigan games that year would be the two "closest calls," (single digit margins of victory) for OSU, prior to their appearance in the Rose Bowl. Iowa, Wisconsin, Purdue, Illinois and Minnesota were soundly defeated 49-0, 56-0, 35-6, 40-3 and 38-6 respectively. Also the Buckeyes traveled to the West Coast where they thumped the UCLA Bruins 41-20. However a chance at a National Championship went down the drain when UCLA, in a return match, in the Rose Bowl, beat Woody Hayes' boys 23-10 and Ohio State wound up #4. Woody's OSU teams in 1972, '73, '74, '75 and '76 finished #9, #2, #4, #4, and #6. Meanwhile Penn State in those same years was #10, #5, #7, #10 and unranked. But comparing Top Ten AP Poll rankings, Penn State would end-up higher in the rankings, than the Buckeyes, five of the next six years (1977, '78, '80, '81 and '82) and to the surprise of a number of trivia buffs Penn State, during Joe Paterno's reign (1966-1998) finished ahead of Ohio State in Top Ten AP Poll rankings 14 times to 12 despite Ohio State having jumped out to a seven to three lead, 1967 through 1976. (Neither team was ranked in the Top Ten in 1966).

The Lions next traveled to Iowa City to face the Iowa Hawkeyes. In this the sixth meeting between the two schools State was ahead 17-3 after three quarters. Iowa cut the lead to 17-10 in the fourth stanza but a 70-yard touchdown reception by Rich Mauti and a Hawkeye turn-over translated to 13 points in the last ten minutes and a 30-10 Nittany Lion victory. This was only the second time Penn State had ever played two Big Ten Teams back to back.

Having held an opponent (Iowa) to no pass completions in an entire game for the first time in Joe's career, the Lions extended their stingy defense to the four opponents that followed Iowa on the schedule; permitting only one touchdown and a total of ten points in the combined Kentucky, West Virginia, Syracuse and Army scores.

In the next two games, ACC opponents Maryland and N.C. State fell behind the Lions 12-0 and 14-0 respectively. Maryland rallied to just trail State 15-13. But a 42 yard field goal attempt by the Terrapins with 15 seconds remaining in the game was unsuccessful, leaving State a two point victor.

The N.C. State game was discussed in Chapter 56. In this game with only eight seconds on the clock a 46-yard Chris Bahr attempt failed for Penn State, leaving the Wolfpack one-point winners.

In the final regular season game our 5'9" 160 pound defensive half-back Tom Odell made a play that won the Pitt game for the Lions; not by intercepting a pass, not by making a Tim Fox game-saving tackle, not by coming on a "corner blitz" to sack the quarterback, not even coming off the corner to block a punt. Our diminutive defensive back pulled a LaVar Arrington, "LaVar Leap" two and a half years before Arrington was even born. How could this 5'9" defensive back duplicate the feat of the 6'3" Arrington who used his forty-inch vertical leap to block not one but two field goal attempts by Penn State opponents in the 1999 season?

Odell's play was seen on National television but it would never have happened were it not for some film-watching by assistant coach J.T. White, a football center himself. John T. White, who everyone knew as "J. T." had a voice as gruff as George C. Scott but J.T.'s voice was at least an octavo lower than Scott's. An excellent coach with a personal magnetism and winning smile he enjoyed the respect and the friendship of the staff and his players. In his rolling manner of conversation he occasionally mouthed a word which was slightly different from the one he was thinking, which was guaranteed to "break up" his audience. According to another assistant just such an occasion occurred at practice one day when three players left the field in very short order with an assortment of minor injuries. One of the players standing next to J.T. made a comment about the rapidly thinning ranks of healthy players at that position, to which J.T. was reported to grumble, "Aw, it's just normal nutrition."

J.T. had a storied career. Born in Georgia, he grew up in River Rouge, Michigan, however World War II intervened and J.T. ended up playing football at Ohio State his freshman and sophomore years under the Buckeye's new mentor Paul Brown who was in his first two years as head coach. After a 6-1-1 freshman season, the Buckeyes, with J.T. playing end as a sophomore, won the Big Ten Championship out-right, for the fifth time and won their first National Championship. In their traditional meeting, J. T. played against his brother Paul, who was a star halfback for the Michigan Wolverines, and the Buckeyes took the measure of the Wolverines 21-7.

After three years in the service J.T., now a center, and his brother Paul a co-captain of the Michigan squad teamed-up and played together on the 1946 Michigan team which beat Ohio State 58-6. In 1947 one year after his brother graduated, J.T. played his senior year at Michigan and again was on the winning side as the Wolverines beat the Buckeyes 21-0. (J.T. White's record in Michigan – Ohio State head- to-head battle was 3-0-1. The two teams tied 20-20 in J. T.'s freshman year.) The 1947 Michigan team ended up #2 in the country and the 1948 team won a National Championship. J.T. came that close to playing on two National Championship teams for two different universities.

As an ex-center, J.T. White, when looking at the Pitt scouting films, noted a flaw in the technique of the Pitt center who snapped for punts, field goals and point after touchdown attempts. *Just* prior to snapping the football the center had a habit of moving his shoulders as the prelude to him actually snapping the ball. In addition to that he invariably kept his head down, visually following the flight of the ball back to the holder. If the Lions could exploit this "double flaw" they held a "wild card" they could use at a crucial time in the game, should the outcome hinge on one play where Pitt would be kicking the ball.

To take advantage of this "chink in the Golden Panthers armor" the staff decided that a small, adroit player had the best chance of taking advantage of this golden opportunity. If the player could get a running head start and time his approach so that he would hit the line of scrimmage "straight on" the instant after the center "hitched" his shoulders and if the center cooperated by keeping his head down and not raising-up, a player like Tom Odell could leap right over the center and have an unimpeded path to the ball and the kicker, Carson Long, who happened to be a straight-on, not a soccer style, kicker. If timed properly, Odell was certain to get to the ball and block the kick.

Pitt scored first in the second period and the Penn State coaching staff wisely decided to play its wild card right then and there. Odell timed the center snap perfectly, cued by the center's shoulder hitch, the center also cooperated by keeping his head down and Odell was right in Carson Long's face and he smothered the flight of the ball before it was three feet off the ground. Pitt had a 6-0 lead. The second and third periods were scoreless and finally Steve Geise scored for State on a 28 yard run with 6:42 remaining in the game.

Calmly Chris Bahr kicked the crucial extra point for a 7-6 Nittany Lion victory. Long, the usually reliable Pitt kicker who ranks second to only Tony Dorsett on the Pitt All-time leading scorers list, was probably unnerved by the blocked kick as he missed game-winning field goal opportunities from 51, 45 and 23 yards.

The Bowl scenario at the end of the 1975 season was as wacky as it had ever been. As mentioned previously Ohio State, the #1 team in the country had to reconcile itself to a return match with a team it had previously beaten by twenty-one points and then lost the rematch. Nebraska which was #2 right behind the Buckeyes had the Orange Bowl invitation in its hip-pocket with a 10-0 record coming into their final regular season game in Norman, Oklahoma, but the Sooners turned out to be rude hosts and shocked the Cornhuskers 35-10. The 'Huskers then went to the Fiesta Bowl where they lost to #7 Arizona State, and Nebraska stumbled to the finish line closing out at #9.

Once beaten Oklahoma ended up in the Orange Bowl where they met a Michigan team that had lost to Ohio State and was tied by Stanford (a 34-14 loser to Penn State) and Baylor. Southern California in its last year under the tutelage of John McKay was cruising along at #3 in the country and on October 25th beat Notre Dame at South Bend 24-17, to solidify its #3 ranking. The Trojans had three unranked teams remaining on their schedule before their season-ending traditional show-down with UCLA. The Bruins in their last year with Dick Vermeil at the helm, had squeezed by #10 Tennessee 35-28, and the next week were tied 20-20 by unranked Air Force. They then lost to Ohio State to drop out of the Top Twenty in the AP Poll. After clawing their way back to #13 by beating Stanford, California and Washington State, the Bruins lost to the Washington Huskies and "dropped off the radar scope" again. Meanwhile USC lost three straight to un-ranked California, Stanford and Washington and came into the UCLA game unranked. The Trojans lost this showdown 25-22 and were relegated to the Liberty Bowl game where they waxed Southwestern Conference Tri- Champions (10-1) Texas A & M, 20-0.

Undefeated Ohio State was comfortably in the lead for National honors going into the bowl game while the pretenders to the throne were Oklahoma (10-1), Nebraska (10-1), and Alabama (10-1). 'Bama lost its season opener to Missouri 20-7 but rose from the ashes to beat Clemson, Vanderbilt, Mississippi, University of Washington, Tennessee and Texas Christian University by a combined score of 255-20. There were two dark horses, Arizona State and Arkansas who would meet Nebraska and Georgia in the Fiesta and Cotton Bowls respectively. Although UCLA, Texas, Michigan, Nebraska and Penn State would end up ranked #5, 6, 8,9 and 10, they were not in the running for #1 at the end of the regular season.

"Bear" Bryant's Crimson Tide didn't lose an SEC game and finished the regular season as SEC champions. "Bear" hadn't won a bowl game since 1966 despite being in a bowl game every year (he had a 20-20 tie with Oklahoma in 1970.) Now the most challenging match-up for the Tide would be the Oklahoma Sooners. The author however had heard unconfirmed scuttle butt that coach Bryant wasn't as all forgiving as Coach Paterno had been regarding Oklahoma's use of ineligible players and Bear was adamant about not playing the Sooners. Again unconfirmed reports had "Coach Bryant" calling Joe Paterno asking for an assurance from Paterno that his Lions would beat Pitt in their final regular season game. No surprise to Penn State fans, Paterno told Bryant that his team would deliver a victory and Coach Bryant delivered a Sugar Bowl bid for Paterno's Lions. Bryant's influence was acknowledged by some to run second only to the Governor of Alabama. Since the Governor came up for election at the end of every term and "Bear's" term at Alabama ran for 25 years, and only ended then because Coach Bryant chose not to run, many people felt whoever was Governor at the time, was actually several rungs down the ladder from "Coach Bear." A true story, which can give the reader an idea of Coach Bryant's influence came to light on Alabama's first trip to Penn State. The Alabama team landed in Harrisburg and bussed to State College on a typical Penn State football Friday afternoon. The 'Bama team busses were slowed to a crawl at all the bottlenecks that typically foil, frustrate and delay Penn State fans going to State College. Upon their arrival someone in the Alabama contingent asked why Paterno didn't do what Coach Bryant would do – have the State Police stop all oncoming traffic until the team got where they were going.

Penn State made a respectable showing in their Sugar Bowl match-up with the Crimson Tide in this the first Sugar Bowl game played in the Louisiana Superdome. State outgained Alabama on the ground 157 yards on 41 carries to 106 yards on 49 attempts but Coach Bryant unleashed a secret weapon, quarterback Richard Todd. During the regular season Todd had thrown for a paltry average of 60 yards per game but in this game Todd hit on 10-12 attempts for 210 yards. Our defensive back Tom Odell was an important factor in this contest but again in a way you might not guess.

With the game tied at 3-3 in the third quarter and Odell out of the game, having been injured in the first half, the Tide struck decisively on a 55-yard Todd to tight end Ozzie Newsome pass, a play on which Odell's freshman replacement "bit" on the "run fake," letting Newsome get behind him. Newsome didn't score but Mike Stock did subsequently on a 14 yard run. Bahr and Bama's kicker Danny Ridgeway exchanged field goals and Alabama ran out the clock after stopping State on fourth and one with 1:19 left in the game. Oklahoma ended up #1, followed by Arizona State, and Alabama.

In a year-end evaluation Paterno said of his 1975 squad, "This wasn't a great team, but it might have played closer to its potential than any (other) team we had, it was a great group in that way."

Postscript: Chris Bahr was the leading scorer on the team tallying 73 points including two 55-yard field goals, Woody Petchel was second with thirty points. Three players, Buttle, Bahr and Rafferty were selected to All-American teams. Buttle led the team with 140 tackles, including 24 in one game (West Virginia). Both Buttle and Rafferty had very successful pro careers with just one team each. Buttle played nine years with the N.Y. Jets and Rafferty fourteen years with the Dallas Cowboys. Penn State posted its 37th straight non-losing season and Penn State University fielded its last freshman team.

Duane Taylor and Tom Odell pose with a young fan (Kenny Werley) at a Letterman's Banquet. (Photo courtesy of the author.)

CHAPTER 66

Joe's Rule Number One, Joe Rules

Earlier in this book we mentioned that virtually everybody loved Rip Engle. The fact that we haven't used the word "love" when referring to Joe Paterno except in Chapter 54 where he, partially tongue-in cheek, quoted a player as saying, "We grow together in love-hating the coach," might cause the reader to infer that Joe has a personality which makes people dislike him. It would be difficult for a person to be more wrong.

Paterno can be as likeable as anyone you've ever met. He "wows" mothers, fathers, siblings, recruits, teachers, high school administrators, high school coaches etc., with his personality, his genuineness, his ability to poke fun at himself to counter any perception that he is egotistical. And he does it all with CLASS. But when it comes to demanding, and getting the most and the best from his players, it isn't Paterno's intention to try to win a popularity contest. He is taking approximately thirty young men (incoming freshmen) into his program each fall and if they think that all they need to do, to be on "Joe's good side" is to "star" on the football field, they have made a serious miscalculation. These young men will learn that they have to go to class, do well academically, faithfully live by Joe's rules, and then, they may get to play some football – Penn State Football!

Some of the rules these young men will learn, and they must hold them inviolate as long as they are on Joe's team are:

Rule #1 – Unless you are five to ten minutes early for all meetings, practice and departures – You Are LATE! And you will pay a price for that transgression. One sentence can put it all in perspective - If you're early, you're on time, if you're on time, you're late and if you're late, you're history.

Rule #2 – Every player will eat breakfast every morning during the prescribed hours of 6:30 a.m. to 8:30 a.m. Attendance will be taken every morning by one of the student managers or monitors. What and how much the player eats will be recorded and reported. (Some player are under orders to gain weight, some are supposed to lose weight and some players are being monitored in order that they don't gain or lose additional weight.)

Rule #3 – Players will not skip classes. Attendance will be taken each class period by a monitor or student manger who will poke his or her head into the classroom to confirm the player's presence. Any excuse offered by a player, such as, "They missed me because I was sitting at the back of the room" will not be accepted. It is each player's responsibility to make arrangements with the course professor to have a designated seat in the *front* row for the whole semester. There will be no sprawling, sleeping or day dreaming in the back of the room.

Paterno justifies all of these rules and more, with the following brief dissertation: "I'm not concerned whether or not they love me right now. What I never want to occur, is for a former player to come back years later and say to me, 'You know Joe, I could have done so much more, I could have been someone special, a success in my life after football if you had only pushed me a little harder. I had the potential to be much better.'"

Paterno is taking these incoming freshman who were big fish in a small pond, giving them discipline and some rules they must live-by, now that they are small fish in a big pond. In high school these kids stood out because of their size, and their athletic ability. They may have received preferential treatment from teachers, administrators and/or coaches. But things change in college. Now, not only are people not doing things *for* them and giving them preferential treatment, but they are being told, it's your responsibility to keep your academic "house in order", as well as being on time, and "on the right page" for anything and everything related to football. Mother and Dad will not be here to remind you and to "bug you" about appointments and things you need to do. This can be a bit disconcerting to the town hero who previously had not been required to dress appropriately, be clean shaven, be on time, get up before noon etc.

Most teenagers wouldn't love anyone (even their own parents) if they were told by Mom, "Jeff it's 8:00. If you're re not done eating what I prepared for you by 8:30, and shaved and dressed by 9 A.M., you'll be running laps." Or if Dad were to say, "Son, you had the car, with the stipulation that you were supposed to pick me up at work at 4:30. Since you weren't there by 4:25 you'll be helping me paint the porch and the garage this week-end and...give me the keys to the car."

So it's also understandable why years ago at the annual Quarterback Club Awards Dinner, a graduating senior (naturally), stood up and in mock seriousness told the audience about a dream he had had recently. His story went roughly as follows:

"Last week I dreamed that I died and found myself at the Gates of Heaven. Standing between me and the entrance was St.

Peter. As I approached he said, "I need to have some information about you, son. You will then have to go to Purgatory for forty days and nights and then we'll determine whether you qualify for admission to Heaven. St. Peter then continued, asking my name, how old I was and what I did on earth. I replied that I was a football player at Penn State. St. Peter then questioned me 'Who was your coach?' My response was, 'Joe Paterno.' St. Peter exclaimed, you played *for Joe Paterno?* I nodded and he continued, 'Well come with me, you can go directly into Heaven. Anyone who has played for Joe Paterno...has already been through Hell."

Ten years later, players, some of whom had unfortunate run-ins with Paterno, almost to a man have "seen the light" and profess that Joe Paterno instilled values in them that have played a big part in their success in the one game that is bigger than football –the Game of Life!

CHAPTER 67

Another Quarterback Club Luncheon

The author, if he wished to, could honestly state that during the football season he had luncheon with Joe Paterno any Wednesday he chose to, over the past thirty years. Of course he wasn't alone with Joe at these State College Quarterback Club affairs. There was Mickey Bergstein, probably two football players from that year's squad, and, *oh yes*, over the years an audience of anywhere from seventy-five to two hundred people were also present.

Thirty years ago while the format was roughly the same as today the full meeting for the real football aficionados lasted almost two hours (today they last an hour) since "Tor" Toretti who scouted each upcoming opponent brought the film of the previous game which he showed after the regular meeting adjourned. In those days before ESPN and before most homes had VCRs, this was your only chance to see action you missed if you were at the game and often it was your only chance to see any of the action from an away game. "Tor's" insightful comments were especially treasured as he re-ran certain segments of the film to explain why a play did or didn't work. To-day most hard-core fans tape every game they can and virtually every Penn State contest is on TV. Therefore looking at the game film after the luncheon is no longer done. Currently the meeting springs into action as head turning and applause signify that Paterno and this week's two feature players have arrived. On cue Mickey Bergstein, the master of ceremonies, gets up on the raised stage and the two football players join him. If the players are anything other than wide-outs or defensive backs they tower over Mickey who is all of 5'7", making the players on the raised stage look like giants. (Many of the linemen weigh 300 pounds and are a foot, or more, taller than Bergstein.) Mickey plays this disparity in size for all its worth, when he holds his "mike" up to the player's mouth to get his answer or comments. As far as interviewing the players, Mickey is a professional and he does a professional and entertaining job. Mickey then directs questions from the floor to the players. Most of the players do a credible job considering their age but you can tell that many of them are more nervous in front of these two hundred people than they are in the fourth quarter of a close football game performing for 97,000 fans. Once these questions end the players leave to get to their next class. What follows is thirty to forty minutes of "off –the-cuff" questions from Mickey and the audience and Paterno's replies and return comments. Each week Mickey strives to cover certain areas – maybe there was a key turnover or a questionable penalty, possibly a Penn State player was injured and he might inquire of Paterno as to his status for this week's game or for the rest of the season. But from that point on there is no script. Some meetings are better than others but the very best sessions are free and easy, give and take sessions, where one good rejoiner leads to another, with Joe generally "trumping" the "high card" played by the audience. Sometimes the dialogue like the following interview of Mike McQueary when he was State's starting quarterback gives Mickey a chance to impart some excellent advice to a young person (and as is often the case the young inexperienced person doesn't avail himself of the offer.)

Over the years the author tucked away a number of little sayings which he used to counsel his children such as – "Good judgment is the result of experience but experience is gained mostly through bad judgment." Mike McQueary gained some experience via some not so good judgment but fortunately as the author hoped for his children, the bad judgment wasn't fatal or even of a serious nature. During Mickey's interview of McQueary he asked the big red-headed young man, aptly nicknamed "Big Red" to tell the audience some of his experiences when he was being recruited by colleges during his senior year in high school. Bergstein thought McQueary could present a different slant on recruiting since he lived in State College and played for State College High School, right in the shadows of University Park. McQueary allowed that the one night Coach Paterno saw him play he didn't have a very good night and his team was trounced. After that showing he figured his prospects were very poor. When Bergstein asked him what he would have done if Penn State hadn't offered him a scholarship, McQueary replied, "Well I probably shouldn't say this…." Before McQueary could say another word, Bergstein shot his hand over the microphone between McQueary's lips and the "mike." Bergstein now dispensed his sage advice, "Mike, if I've learned one thing in my life, it's that when someone says, 'I probably shouldn't say this' he REALLY shouldn't say it." The audience broke out in a hearty laugh, but McQueary blithely ignored the proffered advice and continued on, "You know I never really liked Penn State; I was always a Notre Dame fan." For one of the few times in Quarterback Club history a Penn State player was roundly booed. Actually the booing was probably aimed more at Notre Dame than "Big Red"; but McQueary "took a hit" he didn't have to. Bergstein smoothed things over nicely and by the time McQueary stepped off the stage the audience forgot and forgave and gave him a rousing send-off.

Now Paterno joined Bergstein on the stage and Joe proceeded to dispense some recruiting advice to the assembled group. In defense of his quarterback he remarked that McQueary was too modest, explaining that you often can tell more about a player when he's not having his best day. Paterno stated that a quarterback throwing for multiple touchdowns etc. against a weaker opponent doesn't tell you nearly as much as what he saw in McQueary on a dreadful rainy night against a superior opponent. A night when the football was difficult to grip and his receivers dropped the passes he happened to get right on target. Since football is so much a game of overcoming adversity; your opponent, the weather, the non-round ball, which takes unpredictable bounces and is harder to catch than a baseball or basketball, it is understandable that Paterno would be attracted to a player who didn't fold in the face of the inclement weather conditions and a superior opponent. That's why you will never see a dome over Beaver Stadium as long as Joe has a say. *If* Joe were to ask his team the day before a game, with possible rain and/or snow in the forecast, "Team what kind of weather do we want for tomorrow?" The answer he'd want to hear would be, "Joe, we don't care what the weather is, we play our best in all kinds of weather."

While the following question has never come up at a Quarterback luncheon, the author has heard many people speculate as to why Paterno wears so much tan and brown when Penn State's colors are blue and white. The answer is not that Paterno is still Brown University deep down inside, that is 100% wrong. The author was told by someone who should know (not family); that he is blue-black color blind, so he plays safe and stays away from those colors so he doesn't end up with blue socks and black trousers. (MAYBE that's another explanation for the white socks on game day!)

The author in his Penn State Room. (Photo courtesy of Journal Publication, Inc., Harrisburg, PA)

CHAPTER 68

Great Men Great Traits

When the author initially began attending the State College Quarterback Club Wednesday luncheons, Joe Paterno was in his first years as head football coach at Penn State. At that time the club was quite small and attendance was less than one hundred on a typical Wednesday. Although parking was a problem for attendees who couldn't walk to the Nittany Lion Inn, the location was ideal for Joe and his staff as their offices were "right next door" in Rec Hall. In fact when Joe entered the Inn, he customarily got in line with the attendees and the time spent in the buffet line went very quickly as Joe answered questions, joked and engaged in verbal by-play with anyone within earshot. While he told many stories then, and during the luncheon, I can say that I have never heard him tell an off-color or dirty story in the thirty-plus years I have known him. Joe has a quick wit and his memory for names, people etc., is excellent, however if I could steal or clone one virtue of h

is it would be his ability to say right on the spot what I normally think of the next day, and wish I had said the previous day.

Another asset of Paterno's is his ability to continually look ahead, not back. These Wednesday luncheon meetings "showcased" that asset and year after year my admiration grew for his "one-way vision." To this day I still think it is a great trait, however when I began interviewing players and coaches I realized that the fans, especially those that come to the Wednesday luncheons live in the past from one Saturday game through the next Thursday. The Wednesday luncheon attendees want to know what went wrong down on the goal line on third down, did the official "blow" the pass interference call and what about that roughing-the-kicker penalty. There are very few questions about the tactics State will use to stop this week's 260 pound fullback or the upcoming opponent's scrambling quarterback. Of course everyone knows Paterno isn't going to tell even these die-hard Nittany Lion fans what he's *really* going to do. So the fans who comprise the audience, are living in the past each week, Saturday night to Thursday, whereas the staff and the players have Saturday night to bask in the glory of their victory or to despair over a loss. Then bright and early Sunday morning (7 a.m.) the staff is already at work "breaking down" the tapes of yesterday's game to see what worked and what didn't. John Palmgren and his crew have been working all night to break the game tapes into separate packages for the various position coaches and an overall view for Paterno, since he has the final word on the overall game plan. Before the coaches leave Sunday evening, regardless of the hour, the game plan for this week's game is in place. The plan makes the best use of Penn State's strengths, knowing the opponents strengths and weaknesses, and the changes State will make to lessen the ability of this opponent to exploit any Penn State overall weaknesses or unfavorable match-ups, such as a fast 6'4" wide receiver who will have to be covered by a fast 5'9" defensive back or a slower 6'1" defensive back.

Monday, the different team components (linebackers, defensive line, receivers etc.,) meet with their position coaches to go over the new game plan and to be introduced to the coming opponent.

Tuesday is a hard practice in full pads against the offensive and defensive scout teams. This practice will often last two hours and is referred to as "Bloody Tuesday" as it is usually the most physical practice of the week. Why Tuesday? Because it is the one day that gives the players the most time to recover from the aftereffects of Saturday's game (three days), but more importantly is four days prior to this Saturday's game to make sure the squad isn't "banged-up" before Saturday's game even starts.

Wednesday's practice is not as hard or as long, probably an hour and fifty minutes in duration.

Thursday is even lighter and shorter (an hour and fifteen minutes). And the Lions don't practice on Friday even if they "are home" and are not traveling to an away game.

One aspect of practice, which Paterno conveniently never mentions when he talks to the Quarterback Club, the media and on his "talk shows," is the fact that you can add one hour of time invested in meetings, getting taped, stretching before each practice etc., to the on-the-field time he mentions when he says, "We practiced an hour and a half today and we'll probably go an hour, an hour and a quarter, tomorrow.

So you can see that come Wednesday, Paterno, his staff and his players must be completely focused on the up-coming game; the practice week is already winding down. In fact any formations, coverages, and/or plays that have not been mastered by Wednesday are dropped and *nothing new* is introduced on Thursday. Thus when seen from this viewpoint one can fully understand why any "blown" calls from last Saturday had better be "history" when Paterno talks to the Quarterback Club on Wednesday, if there's a game that Saturday.

As fans, if we keep the above information in mind we will better understand why a team that has sprung a big upset or won a crucial game and lets those emotions cloud their mind when preparing for the coming week's game might themselves be upset by a lesser opponent that week. Also the despair of a game lost on a "Hail Mary" pass in the final minutes of one game (PSU's 24-23 loss to Minnesota in 1999) can lead to a loss the following week, which can lead to a loss the next week.

Following a loss, armchair quarterbacks often speculate about the new wrinkles the coaching staff will be putting in for this week's game. In actuality Paterno may be taking things out, rather than adding plays or formations. His reasoning being you are better off if you have five plays you can execute flawlessly than you are running ten plays where the execution is inconsistent, resulting in procedure penalties, missed assignments or hand-offs, wrong routes being run, etc.

To return to the Paterno trait the author most covets we need to revisit a Quarterback Luncheon which took place circa 1974 and then fast-forward several years.

In the mid and late seventies, the author's father accompanied him to one or two Quarterback luncheons each year. Recalling the past as we strolled around campus on a beautiful fall afternoon after the luncheon was a nostalgic treat for both of us. On one occasion I suddenly had a thought which I put to Dad as a question, "Would you like to stop by Rec Hall and see the Heisman Trophy that John Cappelletti won – it's on display in the Coaches' Lounge?" Dad's reply was an immediate and unqualified "Yes."

A 180° change in direction and a five minute walk found us in Rec Hall entering Room 234. As always, we were greeted by Paterno's Administrative Assistant (in those days- personal secretary) Cheryl Norman, in that charming, friendly manner from which she never seemed to deviate; a ray of sunshine even on a cloudy day, which this day wasn't. Over the years Cheryl had come to know me, so without hesitation she welcomed me and asked if she could be of any assistance. I replied, "Cheryl, this is my father. I just wanted to show him the Heisman Trophy and look around a bit."

Cheryl offered, "By all means, look around; the two Orange Bowl Trophies are in those two corners of the room and if I can help you with anything just let me know."

Cheryl seated herself again at her desk, and as we approached the Heisman Trophy, which was directly in the center of the room, Dad and I could see into a side room, directly to our right, where Coach Paterno was seated at a movie projector, running some game or scouting film back and forth; backward and forward, over and over. (This was at a time when game films were still black and white 16mm movie films. Since the late '70s, early '80s, game films have been replaced by VCR tape but coaches and players still talk about "looking at film" although no one uses 16mm movie projection film anymore.) With twenty-two players on the field at all times and probably fifteen of the twenty-two crammed into an area roughly five yards by seven yards, coaches and players have to run the film backward and forward repeatedly in order to zero-in on the actions of each individual, to find out why the play worked or didn't work and what each player contributed to the outcome of the play.

Since Joe had just come from the Quarterback Cub luncheon I judged he was trying to make up for lost time prior to that afternoon's practice. Silently I motioned to Dad and pointed to Paterno sitting with his back to us. Dad realized what my gestures meant and who the man at the projector was.

In subdued tones, Dad and I, with our backs to Paterno's office looked at and made comments about the various trophies and the huge pictures of All-Americans, several from Dad's day, that hung high up on the four surrounding walls. Since we were being rather surreptitious I was taken completely by surprise to hear a distinct voice behind me say, "Hey Doc, how are you doing?" Turning quickly I focused on Joe Paterno standing just a few feet away. I responded to Joe's question and quickly mouthed a statement which I could not have expressed better had I written it out in advance. Gesturing to my father I said, "Joe I'd like my father to meet you." I didn't overdo the emphasis or the inflection, but I conveyed the thought I wished to convey, that it would be an honor for my father to meet him, Joe Paterno. Without a moment's hesitation Paterno grasped my meaning and in a reflex response he said, "Ken, I'd like to meet your father."

We talked for just a few minutes during which time my father pointed to some of the pictures, Charlie Way, Joe Bedenk etc. and identified them as classmates of his that he had seen play in some memorable games. Paterno then graciously excused himself and we continued to investigate the contents of the room before exiting and returning to our walk around campus.

Our story now fast-forwards to a Saturday several years later. My wife Marie, her sister Jane and husband Vince and I were among more than 1500 people present at a Testimonial dinner in honor of Joe Paterno, on a day officially proclaimed by the Governor and the Legislature as Joe Paterno Day in Pennsylvania. There were speeches, congratulatory telegrams from Pennsylvania's U.S. Senators, the President of the United States, etc. When the affair finally ended, probably three or more hours after it started, people began to file out of the ballroom while Joe sat at the head table and signed a few autographs for people who had lined up opposite him.

When we arose Vince grabbed his camera and asked me, "Ken do you think Joe would pose for a picture with me?" I replied, "I don't see why not, if we get up there before he leaves." By the time, we worked our way up to the head table where Joe was seated, the line had shrunk to less than six people so I stood behind those people holding Vince's camera. When the line was reduced to just two people, Joe said (to no one in particular), I've gotta get out of here, they're waiting for me upstairs." I said to him, "Joe can I get a picture of you with my brother-in-law, Vince?" Joe replied, "Sure" as he finished writing his last autograph, "Vince come around here," motioning to Vince to go to the end of the table and come back to where Joe was, so they could stand side by side. Joe and I stood there for a second, when pointing to the camera, Joe, with a typical grin, said, "You're sure you know how to operate that, Doc?" Before I could answer Joe continued, "How's your Dad, Ken?" I said "Great. He'll be thrilled to know you asked about him."

In a tone of voice that left no doubt as to his intent he said, "Well, you be *sure* and tell him I asked."

With all that happened that evening, for Joe Paterno to remember my father, a man he met once, years ago – that is a trait of a great man.

While recounting his admirable traits let's touch on his self-confidence as revealed in the following tale.

Joe Paterno had just become the head coach at Penn State in 1966, and after thirteen games he had won six while losing seven. Not since Bob Higgins raised his record above the .500 mark, twenty-six years previously, had a Penn State head coach been saddled with a losing record after coaching a dozen or more games. In fact only one other head football coach in the history of Penn State football had a losing record after twelve games and that was Dr. Samuel Newton whose teams won twelve games and lost fourteen in three seasons, 1896-1898. One would expect that the possessor of such a rare losing record would not be making outlandish predictions or doing anything to draw attention to his track record to that point. But not Joe Paterno.

Our cast for the following story consists of just three people, Coach Paterno and a husband and wife; the latter two, loyal Penn Staters and generous contributors to the Penn State football program. The couple was apologetically telling their friend, Joe Paterno, that they would be missing the up-coming Penn State game, something they rarely did, but there were extenuating circumstances. In 1965, '66 and '67 Notre Dame ended up ranked #8, #1 and #4 in the country, and in 1965 and

'66 Michigan State was ranked #1 and #2; and this fortunate couple had been given two choice seats for this year's Notre Dame vs. Michigan State game. A match-up that had been sold out as soon as the tickets were put on sale. This contest would be on National TV and it was being ballyhooed as *the* Game of the Year. The woman, in an attempt to justify their decision to attend this game rather than the Penn State game, said words to the effect that tickets such as these were virtually impossible to come by and the game might very well decide the National Championship.

Coach Paterno listened very patiently before pronouncing his blessing on their "defection" saying, "John and Ginger (not their real names) you go to the game, and enjoy yourself, it should be a great game. But mark my words the day will come, and not too far off, when you will *never* drive past State College to see any other game in the Country."

And he's been proven right. True Nittany Lion fans wouldn't think of passing up a Penn State home game for any other game, anywhere.

Joe Paterno, with the author (on the right), and a dental colleague, at a Nittany Lion Club function. (Photo courtesy of the author.)

George Werley, in later years when he was known as "Mr. Zinc" for his patents and his expertise on the subject of zinc alloys. (Photo courtesy of the author.)

CHAPTER 69

Conversations with a Two-Time All-American and Hall of Famer

In our journey through this evolution of college football (which, if you didn't know, began in 1869 with Rutgers playing Princeton) we have seen the size, the physical prowess, the athletic ability and the speed of the participants increase dramatically. Linemen who are 6'7" and weigh more than 300 pounds are commonplace. Players who can run 40 yards in less than 4.4 seconds and ones with a vertical leap of 36 to 40 inches are not unique. There are high school players who can bench-press almost 400 pounds before they enter college and a Division I weight room. And yet a football game is not an individual track and field event, it is the ultimate team sport. Remember what Greg Murphy pointed out in Chapter 60 when he asked, "Are we going to lift weights or are we going to play football?"

Individual prowess and athletic ability can produce spectacular plays but a player abdicating his assignment in order to attempt something dramatic may cost his team dearly. Reverses and counter action plays almost never result in touchdowns or big gainers unless one or more defensive players " takes the bait." (Remember Dennis Onkotz in Chapter 3.)

Speaking with Onkotz, a number of points came up for discussion during our several interviews. However, they were general in nature and didn't pertain to any particular game or season, so they have not been used to this point, but I think they are interesting enough that they should be included here.

In talking about a linebacker's keys, he mentioned that when playing Syracuse if you just keyed on Larry Csonka you'd end up where the ball was more than 75% of the time. Csonka a bruising fullback who later starred for the Miami Dolphins, 1968-79, as of 1997 still held Syracuse records for most carries in a game (43) and was tied for most carries in a season (261) with Joe Morris. If "Zonk" wasn't carrying the ball from his fullback position you could pretty well bet that he was blocking for the ball-carrier. Relating this to the author jogged something in Dennis' memory and he said, "You know we played against another fullback who, if he didn't fasten all four snaps from his chin strap to his helmet it meant he wasn't going to carry the ball or block for the ball carrier. You could forget about him for the next play. Later in our conversation I asked Dennis if he ever looked at the offensive linemen to see if they might tip off what they were going to do. (A lineman with his weight forward on his hand when he is in his three-point stance is probably going to drive forward and run block while the same lineman with his weight back off of his hand is probably going to "pull" or back up and pass block.) Dennis confessed he was too busy with other things to look for those "telltale signs," although he thought the defensive linemen might. A further question about changing the defensive formation just before the ball was snapped prompted me to ask what he said to tell his players when to shift. Dennis' answer shouldn't have surprised me, but it did. He said simply, "Shift." Some how I thought it would be anything but such a plain vanilla call, but it's typical Penn State and Dennis Onkotz. I had heard that some defenses yelled "Now" hoping to confuse the offense if their start signal was "Go." At the very least I expected "Roar" or "Geronimo."

When our conversation continued I asked if he sometimes waited until the last second to say "Shift" hoping to confuse the offense. Onkotz's reply was, "Well you don't want to confuse or "spook" your own players." Probing, I asked, "How about the quarterback, did he sometimes come up to the line and go on a quick count before you had time to shift?" Now Dennis dispensed some more inside football information. I assumed with all the "X" and "O" strategy on the coaches' blackboard, the defense would have an automatic call if Dennis sensed this might happen. But in this game of 300 pound linemen who can bench press 490 pounds and a LaVar Arrington who can leap completely over an offensive line, etc., Dennis then made it clear that underneath all the formations, blitzes, and men-in-motion, some things come down to fundamental things we all learned by the time we were in elementary school when he said, "You know what they say – fool me once shame on you, fool me twice shame on me."

Dennis Onkotz as a Penn State Player (1968) and 1995. (Photo courtesy of Dennis Onkotz)

CHAPTER 70

A Jack Ham Story with a Different Ending

Ninety miles from State College, Pennsylvania, and its contiguous neighbor University Park, lies Camp Hill, a West Shore suburb of Harrisburg.

Over the years, suburban Harrisburg high schools such as Cedar Cliff, Central Dauphin, Cumberland Valley, East Pennsboro, Mechanicsburg and Steelton-Highsprie, have sent players to play and star at Penn State; Mickey Shuler, "Bud" Kohlhaas, Don Caum, Kyle Brady, Troy Drayton and Askari Adams to name just a few. But no one from Camp Hill High School had ever lettered at State as of 1987.

Following the 1987 football season, fans of both the Camp Hill Lions and Penn State's Nittany Lions were optimistic that this drought might finally end. The Camp Hill Lions had a fullback/linebacker, Eric Johnson, who had been impressing the local football fans, coaches and recruiters for some time. And when he announced in his junior year that he wanted to play for Penn State, fans of both Lion teams could not have been happier.

In 1987 as a junior, Johnson had already demonstrated his ability to take a game, which on paper appeared to be a toss-up, and break it wide open, with just a little help from his teammates. The 1987 game with Susquehanna Township High School was an excellent example of the impact Johnson could have on the outcome of a game. Few players are capable of virtually deciding the outcome of a crucial game so quickly, based solely on touching the ball four times, offensively.

Susquehanna Township with a slightly larger student body than Camp Hill, had a heritage of good athletes, male and female. This year was no different; two seniors on the Township team would play Division 1-A football after graduating in the spring. Ricky Turner would letter at Pitt 1988-1990, while Doug Lawrence would win his letters at Maryland, 1990-1992. In this game between "Township", and Camp Hill, Susquehanna kicked-off to Camp Hill and on the first play from scrimmage, fullback Johnson burst up the middle and went sixty yards for a touchdown. On Susquehanna's first possession, Johnson recovered a fumble and after a first down carry, he went forty yards for a touchdown. On Susquehanna's second possession, Camp Hill intercepted an Indian forward pass and on just his fourth carry of the game Johnson went all the way for his third touchdown of the night. The score was 21-0 and Susquehanna was never able to get back into the ball game. To put the icing on the cake, consider that most recruiters thought Johnson, good as he was at fullback, was better as a linebacker (which is the position he played in college)!

In his senior year, 1988, Johnson led his team to Pennsylvania's first Class A State Football Championship. (In 1999 Camp Hill would capture Pennsylvania's first Class A State *Baseball* Championship, two firsts.) At the conclusion of the 1988 season Johnson was chosen the Player of the Year for Class A and AA schools. He was also first team All State and was selected for the Pennsylvania Big 33 team, which would play a Maryland All-Star team the following summer, before the players went off to college.

The Pennsylvania All-Stars won the game 29-19 with Johnson scoring the games first touchdown. One sports writer said, "Johnson proved that size isn't everything for a fullback. He showed why he was considered the best running fullback in the state."

Like Dennis Onkotz, Johnson was a quick, tough, instinctive player with an excellent academic record. (Johnson graduated third in his class of ninety-seven students.) Entering his sophomore year at Penn State in 1967, Onkotz weighed 205 pounds and stood 6'2". Johnson probably was 6', and weighed 210 pounds when he graduated from high school. Had he not wrestled in his senior year, this chapter might have had an entirely different ending. Johnson's decision to wrestle coupled with some Penn State recruiting decisions that didn't work out exactly as planned, doomed Johnson's chance to be another Jack Ham story.

Looking ahead to the incoming freshman class of 1989 Coach Sandusky knew his defense would be faced in 1989, with home games against Virginia, Alabama and Notre Dame and an away game against Texas along with the usual schedule of Syracuse, Boston College, West Virginia, Maryland, Pitt, etc. He had to have eight big-time linebackers able to neutralize or outperform the caliber of athletes those teams would be putting on the field against the Lions. He had four seniors in their last year of eligibility and five players who would be back for at least one more year. In the wings there were four sophomores, none of whom played in 1988 (basically two of them never would). To replace the four that were graduating and expecting that at least three of the recruits would have to play in '89, Sandusky went for size. Three freshman were listed at 230 pounds or more - Greg Astle. 6'1", 230 lbs. from Winter Park, FL.; Rich McKenzie, 6'2", 230 lbs. from Fort Lauderdale, FL a consensus high school All-American, rated #1 linebacker in the nation by *Parade* magazine, Florida Player-of-the-Year, *USA Today* first team All-American and Eric Ravotti, 6'2" , 234 lbs. from Freeport , Pa.

honorable mention *USA Today* All-American squad, chosen for the Pennsylvania Big 33 All-Star game and a Big 33 teammate of Eric Johnson. There were three newcomers who weighed in slightly under 230 pounds – Ryan Grube, 6'4", 227 lbs. from Northhampton, PA ; Brian Monaghan, 6'2", 225 lbs. from Wexford, PA, *Parade* magazine All-American; Jason Oakman, 6'4", 222 lbs. from Spencerville, OH, first team All-State pick; and the lightest of all Reggie Givens, 5'11", 218 lbs. from Sussex, VA, Virginia Defensive Player-of-the-Year and *Scholastic Coach* magazine All-American.

As with Jack Ham, Eric Johnson's height and weight (objective figures) not his subjective football ability "weighed" against him. Unfortunately Johnson didn't have a Steve Smear to champion his cause and the fact that he was still wrestling when national letter-of–intent day arrived meant a school "signing" him was taking some risk that he might incur an injury in the following month.

In the fall of 1988 State had brought in four linebackers, Ivory Gethers from St. Johns Island, S.C., Ron Fields from NYC, Brett Wright from Pomfret, Md., and Tom Wade from Albuquerque, N.M., all would red-shirt.

As letter-of-intent day approached, it became apparent that Penn State was not going to offer Johnson a full scholarship, instead they were going to try to get him to walk on, something Johnson wasn't going to do, as much as he wanted to play for Penn State. He said earning a full scholarship was one of his goals and he didn't want that goal to go unfulfilled. Having gone public with his desire to play for Penn State, Johnson had put all of his eggs in one basket. He had no fall-back position, no other offer in his hip-pocket from Syracuse, West Virginia, Maryland, Rutgers or Temple, schools for whom he certainly could have played.

In a typical class act Jerry Sandusky went to Camp Hill to give the bad news to Johnson face-to-face; there would not be a scholarship offer, but they still encouraged him to walk on. Johnson told Coach Sandusky it was his goal to play football on a scholarship, but he had no offers. Sandusky then asked Johnson who he could call on his behalf, and Johnson said Richmond and William and Mary. Right in front of him Sandusky called both schools and on Sandusky's solid recommendation Richmond offered Johnson a full scholarship.

Later that night Johnson made one last call to Sandusky, at home, and Sandusky called Joe for the last time on his behalf. Fifteen minutes later Sandusky called back saying nothing had changed, and Johnson committed to Richmond the next morning. To the author, Johnson acknowledged the turn of events philosophically saying, "I have to think it just wasn't meant to be." He also said he would always have the utmost respect for Coach Sandusky and he was impressed that Sandusky would personally put in a call on his behalf.

As for the incoming 1989 Penn State scholarship linebacker recruits, Givens, McKenzie and Ravotti were thrown right into the breech. Givens, by far the smallest of the seven recruits (5"11" 218 lbs.), was in on 544 plays on defense and special teams, with 37 tackles. Ravotti participated in 163 plays mostly special teams with two tackles, while the consensus All-American, Florida Player of the Year, McKenzie had a year's eligibility go up in smoke when he was used for just 66 plays making four tackles. But injuries etc., made his use necessary. The rest of the 1989 class – Astle, Oakman, Monaghan and Grube all red-shirted as freshmen. Of the eleven 1988 and '89 linebacker recruits, four basically never played while Ryan Grube moved to tight end were he lettered. The remaining six had varying degrees of success with McKenzie, Givens and Ravotti probably having the most impact. Ivory Gethers, while lettering all four years after his freshman medical red-shirt year, never fully recovered from his 1988 ACL preseason injury. He logged 28 and 29 tackles in his last two years but the previous two years combined he had only 35, he never became a starter. Monaghan plugged along, totaling sixteen tackles in three years and then in his senior year he broke out as a ten game starter and he finished second on the team with 67 tackles in just his final year. Brett Wright proved to be an enigma. As a red-shirt sophomore he logged 27 tackles and started the first five games. However he lost the starting position to D'Onofrio in the sixth game and D'Onofrio held on to the starter spot until he was injured and lost for the season in the seventh game of the following season. Wright started four of the remaining five games but he did not play in the West Virginia game when he joined Powell and D'Ononfrio on the injured list. In 1992 Wright was a co-captain, nonetheless he didn't start in three games, including the last two of his senior year. He finished tied for 11th place with 27 tackles for the year, far behind underclassman linebackers Phil Yeboah-Kodie and Gelzheiser who had 63 and 44 tackles and Reggie Givens who had 59. Ravotti who registered only eighteen tackles his first two years did something rather amazing in 1991, starting five of the first six games at defensive tackle, and then starting the last two games of the year at outside linebacker, when Rich McKenzie went down with an injury. Ravotti chose to red-shirt after his junior year rather than share starting time with Rich McKenzie. He suffered a knee sprain in spring practice but did manage to start nine games and end up ninth with thirty tackles in the 1993 campaign.

Interestingly the player who put up the biggest numbers was Reggie

Givens the same size or smaller than Eric Johnson. Givens went from Virginia to Pennsylvania to play football while Johnson would go from Pennsylvania to Virginia to do his playing. In his career Givens had 35 starts to 26 for McKenzie, 21 for Ravotti, 17 for Wright and 10 for Monaghan. Givens also logged 184 tackles in his career well above McKenzie's 126 and Gethers, Wright, Monaghan and Ravotti who had 92, 92, 83 and 72 respectively.

Question: Besides their general size, what other fact was a 100% constant, relative to all of the 1988 and '89 linebacker recruits and Eric Johnson? Need a Hint? Here goes — South Carolina, Pittsburg, Pa., New York City, Maryland, New Mexico, Virginia, Florida, Northampton, Pa., and Ohio.

Answer: Every recruit lived and played his high school football farther from PSU than the 90 miles from Camp Hill to State College. See Toretti's recruiting rule #3, page 216.

In Eric Johnson, did Penn State miss another Jack Ham or a Shane Conlan? (Conlan was very lightly regarded in high school.) At the very least, did Penn State pass up a Trey Bauer, a Brian Gelzheiser, a Gary Gray, or possibly an Andre Collins or Michael Zordich?

How Johnson would have fared at a Division 1-A school like Penn State, no one can say with absolute certainty. What can be said with certainty is that Johnson's performance at the next level, Division 1-AA, set records and garnered awards which rank him at the top one percent of all those footballers who played in the Yankee Conference 1947-1996.

The following is his list of accomplishments:

1. Lettered four consecutive years,starting as a true freshman, 1989-1992
2. Played in every game, forty-four, 1989-1992
3. Started in his last forty-two games
4. Selected First team All Yankee Conference 1990-1992
5. Selected First team Collegiate All-State, State of Virginia 1990-1992
6. Selected First team Sports Network, Division 1-AA All American 1991-1992
7. Selected First team Walter Camp, Division 1-AA All American 1992
8. Selected First team Associated Press, Division 1-AA All American 1992
9. Elected University of Richmond Team Captain 1992
10. Chosen University of Richmond Most Valuable Player 1991,1992

11. Chosen University of Richmond Student/Athlete of the Year 1992
12. Led Yankee Conference in tackles 1990, '91, '92

In 1996 its final year in existence, the Yankee Conference's head coaches, athletic directors, sports information directors and members of the media chose a 50th Anniversary Team (1947-1996). Eric Johnson was one of the four linebackers chosen for this most prestigious team. Probably twelve hundred linebackers played in the Yankee Conference in those fifty years, putting Johnson in the top three-tenths of one percent of those linebackers.

"Eric Johnson, Walter Camp and Associated Press Division —I-AA All-American 1992 and member of Yankee Conference 1947-1996 Fifty-Year All-Star Team." (Picutre courtesy of University of Richmond Sports Information Department.)

CHAPTER 71

They Numbered Among Penn State's Best 1950–1999
And Other Trivia Questions for Non-Penn Staters

Penn State football uniform numbers, 1 through 99, will be worn by many football players over the years. In fact you will occasionally see two Penn State players on the home team sidelines wearing the same number, but certain numbers will most likely be linked with only one, or at most three or four players.

Since Penn State football players are required to attend class and achieve satisfactory grade point averages (GPAs) or they will never have the privilege of wearing a numbered Penn State football jersey, we will "turn the tables" in this chapter and put you the reader to the test and see if you can pass the examination that follows, matching uniform numbers with the names of the "best-known" Penn State players to wear some of those ninety-nine numbers. There were no numbers lower than 10 or higher than 95 during the Paterno era through the 1972 season. (From 1973 through 1984 numbers ranged from 10 to 99 and in 1985 single digit jersey numbers first appeared.)

Here is the test: (Only players whose Penn State careers started and ended between 1950 and 1999 are valid answers.)

Question 1. The eight jersey numbers which bring to mind one player and probably one player only, are numbers 11, 22, 33, 39, 54, 60, 68 and 86. Give yourself two points for each one you correctly identify. Deduct one point for a non-answer and subtract three points for a wrong answer.

Question 2. Identify one or more players who wore, the following numbers (there can be more than one correct answer.) A correct answer is worth three points with a maximum of six points for each number.

19	67
24	78
31	79
34	81
43	82
53	94

Question 3. Identify the quarterbacks who wore the following numbers, two points for a correct answer, a maximum of two points per number.

9	22
12	25
14	33

Question 4. Penn State has had many outstanding running backs, in addition to Heisman Trophy winner John Cappelletti. Name four of them who wore #32. Three points for each correct answer.

| 1. | 3. |
| 2. | 4. |

Question 5. Numerous running backs and wide receivers had outstanding years and/or careers wearing the following numbers, identify as many as you can. Two points for each correct answer.

#10	#42
#23	#44
#25	#48

Question 6. Two place kickers wore the #13. Name them. Three points for each correct answer.

1.

2.

Name the place-kickers (not punters) who wore the following numbers. Three points for each correct answer.

#10
#14
#20
#31
#99

Grade

A	More than 120 points
B	More than 89 points
C	More than 59 points
D	More than 44 points (Sit out two games)
E	44 or less points (Ineligible for the rest of the season)

Interesting patterns emerge when we examine the uniform numbers 1-99. Since single digit numbers weren't used prior to the 1985 season, our list shows less than twenty (in the author's sujective opinion) "outstanding" players who wore numbers 1 through 9. Strangely the four numbers 49 through 52 show only five outstanding players one an All-American; while eleven outstanding players including four All-Americans wore numbers, #53 or #54.

The author found that numbers 4, 7, 8, 36, 40, 41, 45, 46, 47, 49, 50,

51, 52, 59, 61, 86, 87, 88, 96 and 98 weren't very popular among the marquee players. Only eighteen "outstanding" players wore those twenty numbers, compared to sixty-six players who wore the fourteen numbers 10, 11, 12, 32, 53, 54, 68, 69, 75, 78, 79, 81, 95 and 99.

Selected College Football Trivia Questions

1. Did The University of Pennsylvania ever appear in a post season bowl games?
   What Bowl?   When?   Score and Opponent?
2. When was the first indoor football game played?
   a) 1887
   b) 1914
   c) 1932
   d) 1939
   e) 1949
   f) 1955
3. What football team has a mascot named Ralphie?
4. What university was first chartered as the Union Academy and nine years later took the name Trinity College?
5. Which Division I university has a naval rank as its nickname?
6. Who was University of Pennsylvania head football coach in 1920,21 & 22?
   a) Ludlow Wray
   b) George Woodruff
   c) John Heisman
   d) Harvey Harmon
7. What university team that has just one school color originally had as its two colors, rose pink and pea green?
8. What university has as its colors, maroon and burnt orange?
9. How many Ivy League teams have a color (or colors) in their nickname?
10. The Associated Press began selecting a football national champion in 1936. Which six teams have been number one most often?
11. Which four States have had the most number one teams?
12. The last lineman to win the Heisman Trophy was? What year?
13. When football scoring rules were first standardized how many points were the following scores worth? Touchdown? Field Goal (Drop kick)?
14. The value of a touchdown was increased from 5 points to 6 points when?

15. Which of the following states have never had a national champion?
    a) South Carolina
    b) Washington
    c) Oregon
    d) Utah
    e) Colorado
    f) New York
    g) Illinois
    h) Maryland
16. Which of the following were nicknames for the Nebraska football teams before they became the Cornhuskers ?
    a) Old Gold Knights
    b) Antelopes
    c) Bug Eaters
17. Which university has as its nickname a meteorological term and a bird as its mascot?

CHAPTER 72

Just Call Me "Joe"

We've turned back the pages of time and examined Penn State when it was just a college, and looked at its football program, in the early twentieth century. We have, in much greater detail, given you an insider's look at Joe Paterno and the Penn State football program during his first ten years as head coach. A number of chapters have been devoted to revealing his great traits and attributes.

The author has never known Joe to tell a dirty story which certainly has served him well over the years. Paterno also has another hard and fast rule; he will not get into an evaluation of any player Penn State has recruited until he has appeared in a varsity game – not just practice. The author made the mistake of asking Paterno what he was going to do to keep all of his five tailbacks (Cordell Mitchell, Omar Easy, Eric McCoo, Larry Johnson and Kenny Watson) happy in the then up-coming 1999 season. Paterno replied "Larry who?" Only then did I realize that while Johnson had performed *for the varsity*, the performance was in a spring practice game not a regular season game. Therefore Paterno wouldn't comment. Interestingly one of the halfbacks just mentioned Cordell Mitchell was half of a Mitchell, halfback and Harris (Aaron), fullback backfield; thirty years after Paterno's original Lydell Mitchell, halfback and Franco Harris, fullback combination.

As the years go by, Penn State detractors, and some supporters, who don't know what they are talking about suggest periodically that Penn State should fire Joe Paterno and the whole coaching staff "because they've been there too long." There are many reasons for Penn State's success on the gridiron and one of them is the longevity of the coaching staff. Two of the most valuable assets are the cohesiveness of the coaching staff and something that goes hand-in-hand with that, the summer football camp held at Penn State. Coaching staffs that continually turn over, have problems communicating. When Jerry Sandusky left State and Al Golden came in as the new linebacker coach in 2000, certain terminology had to be clarified, as Tom Bradley and Golden used different terms for the same thing. Pro quarterbacks who switch teams often have to learn an entirely new system of play-calling. Something as fundamental as the "gaps" in the offensive line are numbered differently in different systems. Having the same staff saves teaching the newcomer a new system. Having the same coaches means maintaining the same relationships and rapport with high school coaches for recruiting purposes from year to year and with those coaches who accompany their players to a Penn State football camp. Coaches, like other persons, enjoy dealing with the same persons they have grown to know and trust over the years. Football camps enable the staff running the camp the opportunity to identify prospects early on. Penn State definitely was in the vanguard when it came to getting "early" verbal commitments, a tactic virtually everyone else has been forced to copy. And while there are many reasons why a high school football player selects a certain school, invariably the most influential factor is the school that contacted the player first. It's hardest to say "No" to the coach with whom you've have the longest relationship.

What are Paterno's greatest attributes as a coach? Firstly his organizational skills, followed by his "drive" and his oneness of purpose Also his ability to "push" his players and his communication and motivational skills when speaking to small and large groups of people. Also his ability as a game day coach, when he doesn't get too conservative. His aversion to the quarterback sneak and his conservative calls cost State the 1979 Sugar Bowl. When Mike Guman was repulsed on fourth down on a favorite Penn State play Paterno fell back on Earle Edward's statement in Chapter 6, "We went with our best play." But one of his coaches said, "Joe, you forgot how many times you've used that play."

On the sidelines on game day Paterno loves to be with his players, close to the action, close to the officials, immersed in the game environment to sense how things are going, the mood of his team etc., in order to properly judge when it's a good time to take a gamble and when it is better to be conservative and keep working for better field position. In fact LaVar Arrington was quoted as saying, "Joe is not just coaching those games; he's playing them. He's out there with us, living the games, that's what makes him tick." If you noticed, Arrington referred to his head coach as "Joe." This did not in anyway show a lack of respect for his mentor. As Paterno was just a few years older than the players he was coaching when he arrived at Penn State, he had the players call him Joe rather than coach and that hasn't changed to this day. Other coaches, Penn Staters, people on the street even his son, assistant coach Jay Paterno all call him Joe. However Steve Spurrier coach of the Florida 'Gators when he found himself on the same dais with Paterno a few years ago, hit a home run with Paterno when he suggested that in deference to "Joe" he would like to call him "Coach Joe" as younger coaches did years ago with Coach Paul "Bear" Bryant calling him "Coach Bear."

There are two phrases that when I first heard them from Paterno's lips, I thought were just politically-correct statements. Things he and his fellow head coaches said, just to try to impress the right people and to "keep the troops in line." The first referred to academics and the second referred to practice.

I know a lot of recruits (who go to schools where less than 35% of the football players graduate – at Penn State 76% graduate) let talk of academics and "staying eligible" go in one ear and out the other. They know things will be done to keep them eligible until their playing days are finished. Rather than having a smug-smile on their faces these players should be highly upset realizing that from their toil the university, the head coach etc. reap great rewards. Additionally their play funds all the other intercollegiate sports at their university. And then when they are of no more value to their school they are cast aside and they have no diploma, no degree and no chance at a white collar job after all the risks they took and injuries they suffered. If they are counting on an NFL career they should know that the average career of an NFL player is four years and that's not enough time to put aside a retirement nest egg to live on from age 28 to death, unless you die very early. Many All-American high school footballers don't make the grade in college and many that do suffer injuries which end their professional careers before they ever start. Even outstanding players like Curtis Enis, Blair Thomas, and D.J. Dozier who rose through the college ranks to become first round NFL picks, had short "Pro" careers. So what are the odds facing the average "hot shot" high school football player.

Of the Penn State players who lettered starting in 1990 (approximately 200) only 40 were on NFL rosters as of June 2000 and seven of those were free agents. Those are not very comforting odds. Therefore in one of Joe's first talks with incoming freshman he makes it clear that what he and his assistant coaches told the players' parents, high school coaches and teachers wasn't just window dressing. If a player doesn't keep up academically he will not play for Paterno no matter how well he is performing on the football field. Paterno will stand in front of the group and say words to this effect "No matter what you think; here, academics come first, then football." He will then take his thumb and index finger and holding them just a millimeter apart he will say, "They (academics and football) are this close together but make no mistake, academics are number one and football is number two. Many players have found out the hard way that Paterno wasn't kidding. Penn State football players who don't get their degree are very much in the minority. (Another Big Ten school, we won't name, graduates about as many football players as Penn State doesn't.)

Paterno probably wasn't the first to make this statement about practice, but I first heard him say it, "You play like you practice." When I heard this I thought "Of course you'd say that," what coach would say, "We practice during the week but just to keep in shape. On Saturday I turn my superior athletes loose and they just overwhelm the poor guys on the other team." If that were true, the following statement by an ex-coach would be a huge lie. He said, "Football is the greatest team sport ever devised." This can be proven very easily. You can take five good basketball players or nine good baseball players from several different teams, let them warm-up together and talk on the bench, during time-outs and between innings and they can play a good team that's been together for some time and they will have an even chance of winning. Take twenty-two All-Star football players who haven't played together before, have them play a team of very good players who have been playing together for a season and the All-Star team will almost surely lose.

So practice is important and that's where Joe's organizational skills shine. Practice at PSU is rush-rush. Two minutes on this drill, four minutes on that one. When one of the assistant coaches Fran Ganter, for example, pleads his case to Paterno for five more minutes of the total practice time Joe's reply, rather than "All right," will most likely be, "See if Jerry (Sandusky) will give you five of his minutes." At some time during practice there will be situational drills e.g. – two minutes remaining on the game clock, One time-out-left. Ball on our 30 yard line. Field Goal needed to win. Or first and goal on the four yard line, touchdown and two point conversion needed to win. One time out left.

Other times the secondary will be practicing defenses and "calls" based on time remaining, down and distance. Meanwhile the linebackers, quarterbacks and receivers will be "doing their thing." Time is always of the essence to the extent that practice is more hectic than a game and of course Paterno is always right there pointing out errors, yelling in his inimitable way. (Many players become very good at mimicking his voice and words.) One player said about practice under Paterno, "It's like playing for your Dad and he's always in a bad mood."

How long will Paterno continue to coach? The answer most likely will be as long as he has his health (mental and physical) his energy and as long as *he* thinks he is doing the job up to *his* standards. Understandably PSU officials will be most reluctant to tell him he *must* retire; for P.R. reasons and because of his value to the university beyond the football program. Additionally in the back of the administration's mind has to be what happened to the football programs at Alabama after

Bear Bryant retired, Army after Earl "Red" Blaik retired, Texas after Darrell Royal, Oklahoma after "Bud" Wilkinson and Barry Switzer, USC after John McKay and Notre Dame's gradual decline after Ara Parseghian and its precipitous fall after Lou Holtz. Could this happen in Happy Valley or might the passing of the baton not affect the program's success as was the case at Nebraska when Bob "Sweet Old Bob" Devaney retired and Tom Osborne took over.

What will happen at Penn State will probably depend upon who the new head coach will be. While some folks will be campaigning for "new blood", Penn State might suffer some defections from the staff which could effect recruiting if the new head coach doesn't come from within and if Tom Bradley, should he not be the head coach, is not given a substantial inducement to stay.

Occasionally the author hears speculation that Joe Paterno is hanging on long enough to hand the reins to his son, Jay. Even with Paterno's clout we're talking about the bellwether sport at PSU which means tens of millions of dollars to the university every year and I doubt the Board of Trustees would permit a new head coach to be named without a thorough and considered candidate search.

In any event, Paterno has taken us along with him on a marvelous adventure, he has given us entertainment and thrills and he has educated us in ways (on and off the football field) too numerous to mention. We at Penn State and the sporting public in general owe him a debt beyond repayment. So, for as long as it lasts, as my father might have said to his benefactor in Chapter 23 … "Thanks for the ride", Joe.

CHAPTER 73

Answers to Chapter 71 Questions (Pages 313-316)

Question 1   #11 LaVar Arrington   #54 Bruce Clark
              #22 John Cappelletti   #60 Matt Millen
              #33 Jack Ham*   #68 Mike Reid
                   Richie Lucas*   #86 Courtney Brown
              #39 Curtis Enis

*We will allow either Ham or Lucas as a correct answer.

Question 2   #19 Tony Sacca, Gregg Garrity, Tom Donovan,
                   Jimmy Scott
              #24 O.J. McDuffie, Charlie Pittman, Mike Guman,
                   Pete Liske
              #31 Shane Conlan, Andre Collins
              #34 Franco Harris, Bob White
              #43 Brandon Short, Mike Zordich
              #53 Bill Lenkaitis, Glenn Ressler, Randy Crowder
              #67 Greg Buttle, Dave Robinson
              #78 Mike Munchak, Andy Stynchula, Ron Heller
              #79 Mike Hartenstine, Bill Contz, Dave Szott
              #81 John Skorupan, Kyle Brady, Jack Curry, Bob Bassett
              #82 Ted Kwalick, Mickey Shuler, Kenny Jackson,
                   Jerry Sandusky
              #94 Chet Parlavecchio

Question 3   # 9 Mike McQueary
              #12 Tom Shuman, Kerry Collins, Tom Bill
              #14 Todd Blackledge, Chuck Fusina, John Shaffer
              #22 Milt Plum, Chuck Burkhart
              #25 Galen Hall, Tom Sherman
              #33 Richie Lucas

Question 4   #32 Matt Suhey   #32 Tom Donchez
              #32 Blair Thomas   #32 Ki-Jana Carter

Question 5   #10 Bobby Engram
              #23 Lydell Mitchell, Bobby Campbell
              #25 Curt Warner, Chuck Herd
              #42 Lenny Moore, D.J. Dozier
              #44 Jimmy Cefalo, Jon Williams, Tim Manoa

	#48	Booker Moore, Rich Mauti
Question 6	#13	Nick Gancitano
	#13	Eric Etze
	#10	Matt Bahr, Ray Tarasi, Brian Franco, Massimo Manca
	#14	Travis Forney
	#20	Brett Conway
	#31	Herb Menhardt
	#99	Chris Bahr

Answers to Selected College Football Trivia Questions

#1 The University of Pennsylvania lost to Oregon in the January 1, 1917 Rose Bowl Game, 14-0.

#2 Penn beat Rutgers 13-0 in Madison Square Garden in 1887.

#3 The University of Colorado

#4 Duke University

#5 The Vanderbilt University Commodores

#6 John Heisman

#7 Syracuse University (Orange is its only official color.)

#8 Virginia Tech

#9 Five Dartmouth (Big Green), Harvard (Crimson),Cornell (Big Red), Penn (The Red and Blue), Brown (Brown Bears or Bruins).

#10 Most national champions (tie) – Notre Dame and Oklahoma – seven; Alabama – six; Minnesota, Nebraska and Miami – four.

#11 States with most national champions

Tie	Indiana – seven	Notre Dame – seven
	Oklahoma – seven	Oklahoma U. – seven
	Alabama - seven	Alabama – six, Auburn – one
	Florida – seven	Miami – four, Florida State – two, Florida – one

#12 Leon Hart in 1949

#13 Touchdown was worth 4 points; a field goal (drop kick) was worth 5 points.

#14 In 1912.

#15 c, and g. The national champions from a, b, d, e, f and h were respectively – Clemson, Washington, BYU, Colorado, Army and Syracuse and Maryland.

#16 All (a, b, and c).

#17 Iowa State Cyclones. The Cardinal is its mascot and logo.

EPILOGUE

On Saturday, October 27, 2001 Joe Paterno became the winningest head coach in Division I-A football history, passing the legendary Paul "Bear" Bryant, as his Penn State Nittany Lions beat Ohio State, 29-27. Bryant has amassed 323 wins while coaching at Maryland, Kentucky, Texas A&M and Alabama. Paterno's 324 wins (and counting) at one university, is 67 more in that category than his nearest fellow coach, LaVell Edwards, who recently retired after a stellar career at BYU. However, measuring Paterno's success by the number of games his teams won, misses the point by a mile. He coaches young men in the game of football, but more importantly he prepares them for life after football, and here he has had a thousand wins. (The number of players who lettered during his tenure at Penn State and went on the contribute *off* the gridiron.) Many went on to play in the NFL but many more went on to become successes in the business world and as educators, coaches of other young men, physicians, dentists, accountants, lawyers etc.

The question the author is asked more often than any other, by persons who think he might know something they don't know, is, "When will Joe retire?"

Knowing Joe as I do, I think he will coach as long as his health allows him to, and as long as his pride tells him he is still performing up to his standards. He has no compelling reason to retire and play golf, since he doesn't golf. (Although, as he said one time to the author after trying my putter on the putting green, "I think I'd be good as this game." Joe has never lacked self confidence.)

As long as he can still lead the team running out of the tunnel into Beaver Stadium (maybe someday on to Paterno Field) and can still run "gassers' on the practice field, I see him coaching for at least three more years. When a 70 year-old man interacts almost daily with 20 year-old young men, his experience and their youth must surely rub off on each other. Bearing in mind the question that one of the greatest baseball pitchers of all time, Satchel Paige, postulated, "How old would you be if you didn't know how old you are?" any guess at Joe's retirement date is "a shot in the dark" or more aptly put in football parlance more of a "Hail Mary pass."

Regardless, the man fulfilled his father's wish that he "be somebody and the effect he has had and the lives he has touched, altered and even molded can't be counted.

Thank goodness Penn State, and we at Penn State have had him for his entire career, however long that may be.

INDEX

* denotes Penn State players

Nye, Dirk*, 245

O

O'Brien, Pat, portraying Knute
Rockne, 264
Odell, Tom*:
1975 season, 323–324, 327–330, 332
with young fan (photo), 333
Officiating, challenges of, 321–322
Ohio State University:
gunning for number one in 1969,
77–78
versus Penn State (1963), 235
versus Penn State (1964), 241–246
versus Penn State (1975), 325, 326–
327
Ohio University:
versus Penn State (1967), 27
versus Penn State (1969), 73
versus Penn State (1973), 289
versus Penn State (1974), 311
O'Hora, "Betts," 221, 230–231, 232
O'Hora, James R., 58–59
O'Hora, Jim*:
on Beaver Stadium, 92
bid to coach at USC, 230–231
and Buttle's locker-room knockout,
317–319
1968 coaching season, 57–58, 61
early coaching career, 196–197, 205–
207
longevity as coach, 256, 258
at Mahanoy Township (photo), 184
as Paterno's mentor, 221–223
as Penn State defensive coach, 5, 7,
16, 180
PSU coaching staff, 1953 (photo),
232
PSU coaching staff, 1960 (photo),
244
and PSU versus OSU (1964), 242–
243

as recruiter, 49–50, 225–227
with Reid and Smear (photo), 48
as student (1930s), 179–183
World War II service, 213
Oklahoma, University of:
versus Penn State (1972 Sugar
Bowl), 275–276
Oklahoma, versus Michigan (1975
Orange Bowl), 330
O'Neil, Ed*:
as All-American linebacker, 45, 51
versus Greg Buttle, 302–303
joke on Paterno, 287–288
1971 season, 270
1973 season, 283–284, 284
Onkotz, Dennis*:
as All-American linebacker, 45, 51
conversations with, 351–352
Eric Johnson compared to, 356
as Hall of Famer (photos), 42, 353
high school years, 38-40
1967 N.C. State game, 5–26
1967 Ohio University game, 27
1970 Orange Bowl, 82–84
playing positions, 41–42
1967 season, 58
1968 season, 61, 64–65
1969 season, 73–74, 75, 77
Tim Mongomery compared to, 31
Orange Bowl:
Oklahoma versus Michigan State
(1975), 330
Penn State versus Kansas (1969),
66–67
Penn State versus LSU (1973), 289–
295
Penn State versus Missouri (1970),
77–83
trophies displayed in Rec Hall, 345
Oregon, University of:
Bezdek at, 111
versus Penn State (1963), 235